# ROBERT BROWNING

## A SELECTION OF POEMS

(1835–1864)

# ROBERT BROWNING

## A SELECTION OF POEMS

# (1835–1864)

Edited by

## W. T. YOUNG, M.A.

Cambridge:
at the University Press

1929

# CAMBRIDGE
## UNIVERSITY PRESS

University Printing House, Cambridge CB2 8BS, United Kingdom

Published in the United States of America by Cambridge University Press, New York

Cambridge University Press is part of the University of Cambridge.

It furthers the University's mission by disseminating knowledge in the pursuit of education, learning and research at the highest international levels of excellence.

www.cambridge.org
Information on this title: www.cambridge.org/9781107663411

© Cambridge University Press 1911

First edition 1911
First published 1911
Reprinted 1915, 1920, 1923, 1924, 1929
First paperback edition 2014

*A catalogue record for this publication is available from the British Library*

ISBN 978-1-107-66341-1 Paperback

# PREFACE

THIS selection comprises some forty poems of Browning which may be taken to exemplify his characteristic thought, feeling, poetic method and style. They all come, with the single exception of the epilogue to Book I of *The Ring and the Book*, between the years 1835 and 1864. The Introduction to the book is by deliberate intention not an essay on Browning; nor does it give much biographical detail, since this can only be illuminating in the hands of a teacher. It is designed, first, to suggest what the poet owes and gives to his age, both in the general drift and tendency, and in the more specific aspect of literature; secondly to define and correlate some of the main features of Browning's art and doctrine; and thirdly to indicate lines along which the student may profitably pursue his researches. There is no exhaustive treatment of any one theme—merely outlines, which the student may follow, or may qualify as his further reading prompts him. The Notes—which are the outcome of several years of teaching—aim at the solution of difficulties of allusion for the most part; occasionally there is interpretation and even paraphrase. These are intended to help in a first reading; no one is likely to accept them in place of the poems after such initial use. Notes on the many painters named by Browning give indication where pictures by them may be seen in London.

It may be permissible to call attention to the notes on *A Grammarian's Funeral*, which disclose a source of the poem not hitherto noticed, and may be thought to throw some light on the question whether the Teutonic or the Italian renaissance was in the poet's mind.

The text of the *Dramatic Lyrics, Romances* and *Men and Women* is drawn from the three volume edition of 1863, from which later complete editions show but few marked variations. The text of *Dramatis Personae* is from the edition of 1864.

I am indebted to Professor Elton for his careful perusal of the Introduction and Notes in proof, though he must not be held sponsor for any opinions expressed there. I am also under obligation to my colleague, Mr J. Dover Wilson, for a similar kindness in regard to the Notes.

W. T. Y.

*October*, 1911.

# CONTENTS

*Browning redistributed his poems for the later editions under the headings Dramatic Lyrics, Dramatic Romances, Men and Women, and Dramatis Personae. This order has been followed in the arrangement of the poems in this selection. The volumes in which they originally appeared however are indicated in the notes to each poem.*

# INTRODUCTION

## I

### BROWNING AND HIS AGE

BROWNING'S busy intellectual curiosity and vivid
interest in men were allied with a singular aloofness
from the movements and revolutions of his time. He
was born in 1812, so that in the year of the Reform
Bill he was 20 years of age, but scarcely a note in his
writings indicates that this forceful irruption of de-
mocracy—or any of the later extensions of the franchise
—exercised a formative influence over his mind. His
poetry is equally free from speculation upon the effects
of Irish policy, the Corn Laws, the Factory Acts,
Chartism, the Crimean War, the Indian Mutiny, and
the process of commercial expansion between 1830 and
1840. These developments left a deep impression on
Tennyson's mind and coloured his prognostication of
man's destiny; "the ringing grooves of change" have
their terminus, as it were, at "the Parliament of Man,
the Federation of the world." While Tennyson's recep-
tive mind was impregnated with much of the disquiet
and incertitude of his time, through which he slowly
won his way to a faith in some orderly consummation,
Browning's mind was impervious to doubt, and his
confidence in the value of life was constitutionally
unshakable, "it means intensely and means good."

His creed carried him buoyantly over waves which threatened to engulf the cultured spirit of Tennyson. England plays an insignificant part in his work; a reference or two, in *Home-Thoughts from Abroad* and *Home-Thoughts from the Sea* and *Nationality in Drinks*, are not enough to constitute him a patriotic poet. True he spent a great part of his life in Italy. But he did not take up his residence there until his thirty-fourth year. We must conclude therefore that his patriotism was to say the least reticent, rather than exulting and defiant as Tennyson's was. Even in Italy his interest in the momentous national struggle enacted before his eyes was never so intense as that of his wife, whose *Casa Guidi Windows* gave evidence of the keenest sympathy with Cavour and the rest of the Tuscan patriots, though he loved Italy for its art and its beauty. Political movements were to Browning simply backgrounds upon which the individual was the more sharply silhouetted, and abstract ideals had little meaning for his poetry until they were focused in a concrete human personality. This in fact was one of the two ways in which the poet did lie open to the influence of his epoch. He would analyse the mingled hypocrisy, self-deception and sincerity of such a product of his time as Blougram, with unflagging, often unpoetic, zest; but he was in the main indifferent to the abstract issues of tractarianism, rationalism, and materialism—

> "Greek endings with the little passing-bell
> That signify some faith's about to die."

*The Patriot* is an imagined incident for which his immediate observation of the Italian struggle provided

the basis. But neither this nor *The Italian in England*
suggests anything of the range and scope which exalt
Meredith's *Sandra Belloni* and *Vittoria* into veritable
epics. These poems portray loyalty in three splendid
instances, but they are only incidentally concerned
with the fortunes of Austria and Italy. *The Ring and
the Book* has its scenes in Rome and Arezzo, but it is
a story of 1698, not of the nineteenth century. And
though the broader aspects of religion interested him
more than any other generalisation, yet what lingers
in the memory from the reading of *Christmas Eve* is
not the theology of the Zion Chapel Meeting House, but
the oddly assorted and indelibly delineated congregation
which assembles within it:

> "the fat weary woman
> Panting and bewildered, down-clapping
> Her umbrella with a mighty report
> Grounded it by me, wry and flapping,
> A wreck of whalebones";

and

> "the many-tattered
> Little old-faced, peaking sister-turned-mother
> Of the sickly babe."

An aspect of life did not become the more significant
or arresting to him because it touched a large concourse
of humanity. He preferred the microcosm of an individual character where all the elements of life are
blended, to the numerous assembly where aspirations
are rife which exaggerate and distend some separate
feature to the detriment of proportion in the whole.

There was a second fashion in which Browning was
indebted to his time. Wherever contemporary thought

attained some new height and shed illumination over
some dark province of the mind, the poet gave heed.
In philosophy and in science such conceptions emerged.
He stoutly professed his ignorance of the German
philosophers, and of their English evangelists, Coleridge
and Carlyle. Nevertheless his theory of life would
topple to disaster if it were deprived of its foundations
of Idealism which enabled him to interpret the universe
in terms of mind, to rout the scepticism and despair
which are the concomitants of a materialistic philosophy,
to admit evil and misery as the necessary counterparts
in thought of good and happiness.

In science the aspect of the evolutionary doctrine
which co-ordinated and classified and so elucidated
the disordered multitude of facts touched him far less
than that which asserted the continuity and progress
of all existence. When he said that the essential
principles of Darwinism had been familiar to him for
years, he made it clear that he was rather indifferent
to the application of this conception to the physical
universe, for that in its full implication was entirely
novel. He scoffed at the pretensions of science to
explain the moral emotions on natural grounds (*Bishop
Blougram's Apology*, lines 824—834). In fact therefore
although the idea of development pervades all his
poems which are not purely lyrical, yet its main inci-
dence was for him in the spiritual world. There it
sanctions and encourages man in his endeavour to
fulfil the dictates of his best ideals. So powerful an
ingredient of his thought is it that even the oriental
fatalistic emblem of the Potter and the Clay glows
with the energy of the strife towards perfection. In

this sense we are justified in regarding *Rabbi Ben Ezra* as a paean of spiritual evolution.

It was not through any disability to apprehend the characteristics of an age that he stood apart from the currents of his own. On the contrary one of his most remarkable powers was that of suggesting the temper and fashions of a whole period of history. Of the Middle Ages to some extent, and of the Italian Renaissance without qualification, he is one of our most trustworthy interpreters; witness for instance the representation of the hideously disproportioned zeal of the church in quelling heresy, in *The Heretic's Tragedy*, the equipage and conduct of the ordeal by joust in *Count Gismond*, and the gentle piety and venomous spite, vividly contrasted products of the monastic system, in *The Spanish Cloister*. The earlier and more exalted spirit of the Renaissance is typified in *A Grammarian's Funeral*; its later and more sophisticated outcome in *The Bishop orders his Tomb*. So too the poems of Florence, *Andrea* and *Fra Lippo* chief among them, are an epitome of the city's artistic life at the zenith of its fame.

## II

### BROWNING AND ROMANTICISM

The first phase of the romantic conquest closed, broadly speaking, with the death of Shelley in 1822. *Pauline* was published in 1833 and *Paracelsus* in 1835, sufficiently long after the period of triumph to witness such a disintegration of some of its energies and the re-direction of others as invariably follows upon the dominance of any one mood or form in literature. Still being a poet of the nineteenth century, his only choice lay between being more or less of a romanticist. The traditions established by his predecessors appear to be these: a love of natural scenes, a vindication of the simpler emotions in song, an interest in remote times and places, an acute sensitiveness to beauty, a bent towards the wonderful and mysterious (verging dangerously at times upon the merely indefinite and vague, at other times upon the merely surprising and creepy), an introspective lyricism tinged with a pervading melancholy, and a certain endlessness and formlessness in structure and expression.

How did Browning stand in regard to these traditions?

He was a nature poet, for since Wordsworth the muse of poetry and the spirit of nature are indissolubly wedded. He sketched with equal mastery broad landscape effects and arresting snatches of momentary vision. But he did not, as Taine says of the others, "always walk, look at nature, and think of human destiny." Since however his view of the plan and function of nature was so decidedly singular it has been reserved for separate illustration. In his records of human emotion he was not only concerned with its dignity, its simplicity, its moral purport, but much more with its causes and sources. He was more prone to analyse than to find graceful and rhythmical utterance for it. Again he ranged over centuries and continents for his subjects, and found them in the Italy of the Renaissance and to-day, the French camp, the

Spanish Cloister, Palestine and Russia, just as the
pre-Christian era afforded him a Cleon, the Middle
Ages a Paracelsus, and the nineteenth century a
Blougram. In this he was of the romanticists, "one
crowd with many a crest"; but he wore his crest with a
difference. For first, he filled these scenes with accurate
and obtrusive detail, not the laborious erudition with
which Southey weighted the footnotes to *Madoc*, but
woven cunningly as in *Karshish* into the fabric of the
poem; this is one of the grounds on which Browning
may be called a realist. And secondly, though he was
a free citizen of all these kingdoms, states and western
islands, they were not simply picturesque scenes, but
varying abodes of the personality of men, supremely
interesting because they brought into focus some aspect
of the mind which no other combination of circum-
stances ever set in so clear a light. Two epochs have
chiefly been the haunts of the English romanticists,
Greece and the Middle Ages. When romanticism
attained its renaissance in the middle of the century,
and the pre-Raphaelites, with the aid of the sister art
of painting, directed all its energies to the Middle
Ages, Rossetti to its esoteric and mystical, Morris to its
democratic and industrial, and Newman to its devotional
elements, Browning parted from them, retaining only
a love for the grotesque, the blending of the comic and
the terrible, of which he has such masterpieces as
*Caliban*, *The Spanish Cloister* and *Holy-Cross Day*.
He turned to Greece with an industrious devotion;
more still to no historical region at all, but to a kind
of intellectual realism, making poetry out of his every-
day thinking and study of men. It is sometimes

denied that he has the keen sensitiveness to beauty of a Keats or a Tennyson. But the criticism cannot be upheld in face of lines uttered in a fine careless rapture such as these:

> "the sprinkled isles,
> Lily on lily, that o'erlace the sea,
> And laugh their pride when the light wave lisps 'Greece'";

or these from *Paracelsus*:

> "Day by day
> New pollen on the lily-petal grows,
> And still more labyrinthine buds the rose."

Here colour, form and cadence are supremely adequate to the most glorious as to the most delicate imaginative scene. Nevertheless a restless mental curiosity did too often tease him from the expression of such visions, and in some later work he lost the secret of the poet's alchemy, which transmutes thought to beauty, recovering it triumphantly however in the harvest of his Indian summer in *Asolando*. He had not much aptitude for the insolubly mysterious. He rarely handled the mystery of enchantment, though he did it with astonishing skill in *Childe Roland* and *The Flight of the Duchess*. In general he thought things sufficiently wonderful without their being either unprecedented or miraculous. The mystery of infinity was a challenge and an irritant to him; his intellect quickly took up a scent and followed hard upon the trail, till the heart of the mystery was plucked.

> "I go to prove my soul!
> I see my way as birds their trackless way—
> I shall arrive!"

The sources of knowledge and power were to be discovered and known in one way or another:

"The rest may reason and welcome; 'tis we musicians know,"

he says in *Abt Vogler*. Death and the hidden future roused defiance in him rather than awe:

"I would hate that death bandaged my eyes, and forbore,
    And bade me creep past."

The one impenetrable mystery to him was the fathomless depth of love. It was here that Browning underwent his "renaissance of wonder," coming upon

"the novel
Silent silver lights and darks undreamed of,
Where I hush and bless myself with silence."

In lyric he was capable of the graceful impersonal allusiveness of the Elizabethans, of the subtle blending of perfume and memory in the manner of Keats, and most rarely of the introspective Shelleyan kind. But his dramatic instinct led him much more frequently to probe the thought and feeling of lovers in situations unique, momentary and intense—the unsuccessful, or the faithless, or the gloriously triumphant. Except in *One Word More*, parts of *By the Fireside* and in the apostrophe "O! lyric love," he did not give expression to personal sentiment; in other words, his lyrics are dramatic and by the same token not necessarily either melancholy or introspective. They are prone however like the verses of Donne and Chapman, his poetical kinsmen, to obey a precept afterwards enunciated by Meredith, another of the same clan, "Be wary of the disrelish of brain-stuff!" The last of the characteristics of romanticism named above was an impatience of the stringent boundaries of form and construction. Browning is often charged with formlessness and verbosity; and certainly it was an age of formlessness. The longer poems of the time have generally a beginning, an indistinguishable middle and no end. The genius for unity, composition and structure which presided over the birth of *Tom Jones*, *The Decline and Fall* and *The Dunciad* in the eighteenth century, had no share in the making of *The Excursion*, *Christabel*, *Don Juan*, *Hyperion*, or *Hellas* in the nineteenth. But Browning was not formless. There is a marvellous sense of proportion in the importance assigned to various features in his dramatic monologues; every element plays a significant but not over-emphasized part: hence the unity of atmosphere and effect. The intricacy of his studies was not due to an inability to capture and present a single impression; it was because his vision was so clear and comprehensive that he viewed his subject on numerous planes. Whilst our tendency is to conventionalize and classify, he sought to make his readers see and understand each of his characters in their habit as they lived and thought and purposed. His sense of form was so strong that he allowed himself to be insufficiently reticent of detail. Yet whatever may be thought of the excessive luxuriance of *The Ring and the Book* it would be difficult to point to a work in English exhibiting such sustained constructive capacity. As for his verbosity, economy not prodigality of diction was his fault; a recent critic, Professor Walker, states the case: " he gives expression to many thoughts when a few would suffice; the total effect might be produced in less space than he takes."

If therefore we describe him as a romanticist, it must be with many reservations. Shelley and to a less degree Keats were the only poetical personalities who left any impress upon him. He was too independent and original to be imitative. He scarcely falls under any recognised rubric. On every count we have examined in this section he has "the trick of singularity." His overplus of intellect in poetical composition, his dramatic instinct, his analytical tendency, his decided sense of form and outline made him an intellectual realist in an age dominated by romanticism.

## III
### CHOICE OF SUBJECT

"My stress lay on incidents in the development of the soul" the poet wrote in the letter to Milsand which precedes *Sordello*; and that remained his supreme interest from first to last. But the soul has numerous points of contact with the outer world, and of these his temperament leaned specially towards Nature, the Arts, Love, Belief and Personality; succeeding sections deal with these last two.

### i. *Nature*

In descriptions of nature he revels in brilliant clear colours such as glow in "fierce and flashing splendour" in the sun and atmosphere of Italy; his distaste for the "gaudy melon-flower" was the result of a moment of transient recoil. He disregards in the main the suggestions of depth and mystery given by subtle intertwinings of light and shade, but displays a characteristic liking for sudden and startling contrasts. He rivets attention upon single prominent features or patches in the whole scheme; or upon sharp serrated edges, violent irregularities of outline, and rough broken contour; as for instance in *Paracelsus*:

> "Over the waters in the vaporous west
> The sun goes down as in a sphere of gold,
> Behind the outstretched city, which between,
> With all that length of domes and minarets,
> Athwart the splendour, black and crooked run
> Like a Turk verse along a scimitar."

Akin to this is his liking for spikes and spears and wedges. One of many similar decisive cleaving strokes is described in *By the Fireside*:

> "How sharp the silver spear-heads charge
> When Alp meets Heaven in snow."

In general two things are true of his landscapes. Firstly they are real, they belong to the actual scene of some incident, and they have elements which impress the idea of actuality. Secondly man finds the nature he is fitted for, appropriate backgrounds for thought and emotion; for instance Caliban sprawls "in the pit's much mire,"

> "in the cool slush,
> And feels about his spine small eft-things course,
> Run in and out each arm, and make him laugh."

For the Grammarian:

> "Here—here's his place, where meteors shoot, clouds form,
> Lightnings are loosened,
> Stars come and go! let joy break with the storm—
> Peace let the dew send—
> Lofty designs must close in like effects:
> Loftily lying,
> Leave him—still loftier than the world suspects
> Living and dying."

Like Shelley he is fond of wind and sky. He strikes out a rare image for the air which bows the feathery grasses of the Campagna,

"An everlasting wash of air."

The opening lyric of *Pippa Passes* is one of many descriptions of the dawn, a phenomenon which fascinated him, like all sudden transformation, budding or flaming forth and vigorous beginning. The single syllable of the first line seems to fling wide the shutters and flood the world with rose and gold.

He has a theory of the relations of man and nature. Nature emanates from God; so also does man who is the crown of nature, giving significance to what was chaos.

"Never a senseless gust now man is born."

No common spirit breathes through them both however; they are two entities, though for a moment their forces may coalesce, as in *By the Fireside*:

"A moment after and hands unseen
  Were hanging the night around us fast.
But we knew that a bar was broken between
  Life and life; we were mixed at last
In spite of the mortal screen.

The forests had done it; there they stood—
  We caught for a second the powers at play;
They had mingled us so, for once and for good,
  Their work was done—we might go or stay,
They relapsed to their ancient mood."

The union is but momentary, they become disparate for the long periods of normal existence. It is true that in the poet's observation human emotion may

*b* 2

irradiate nature and nature may stir feeling in man and give wider significance to his exploits as in the two short poems *Meeting at Night* and *Parting at Morning*:

### MEETING AT NIGHT.

"The grey sea and the long black land;
And the yellow half-moon large and low;
And the startled little waves that leap
In fiery ringlets from their sleep,
As I gain the cove with pushing prow,
And quench its speed i' the slushy sand.

Then a mile of warm sea-scented beach;
Three fields to cross till a farm appears;
A tap at the pane, the quick sharp scratch
And blue spurt of a lighted match,
And a voice less loud, through its joys and fears,
Than the two hearts beating each to each!"

### PARTING AT MORNING.

"Round the cape of a sudden came the sea,
And the sun looked over the mountain's rim;
And straight was a path of gold for him,
And the need of a world of men for me."

Nature here is nothing more than a part of man's environment; he may find it good to look upon:

"Oh! good gigantic smile o' the brown old earth,
This autumn morning! How he sets his bones
To bask i' the sun, and thrusts out knees and feet
For the ripple to run over in its mirth";

but there is no vital sympathy, no message to be felt through community of spirit; neither is nature a refuge for broken spirits, as often in Shelley. On the contrary

it has a mocking sinister disdain at times, as of some
heartless spectator. An extreme example is to be
found in *Childe Roland*:

> "day
> Came back again for that ! before it left,
> The dying sunset kindled through a cleft:
> The hills, like giants at a hunting, lay,
> Chin upon a hand, to see the game at bay—
> Now stab and end the creature--to the heft !"

## ii. *The Arts*

> "But Art,—wherein man nowise speaks to men,
> Only to mankind,—Art may tell a truth
> Obliquely, do the thing shall breed the thought,
> Nor wrong the thought, missing the mediate word.
> So may you paint your picture, twice show truth,
> Beyond mere imagery on the wall,—
> So, note by note, bring music from your mind,
> Deeper than ever the Andante dived,—
> So write a book shall mean, beyond the facts,
> Suffice the eye and save the soul beside."

Poetry, painting and music were the arts which
specially attracted the study of Browning, and he
found certain qualities common to them all. First he
derived pleasure from every exercise of creative power,
whether it were Caliban's grotesque structure of an
idle summer day, or his own plaster casts in Florence
(smashed to atoms as soon as finished), or the swiftly
emerging conception in Fra Lippo's mind:

> "the breathless fellow at the altar-foot,
> Fresh from his murder, safe and sitting there
> With the little children round him in a row
> Of admiration, half for his beard and half

> For that white anger of his victim's son
> Shaking a fist at him with one fierce arm,
> Signing himself with the other because of Christ
> (Whose sad face on the cross sees only this
> After the passion of a thousand years)
> Till some poor girl, her apron o'er her head
> Which the intense eyes looked through, came at eve
> On tip-toe, said a word, dropped in a loaf,
> Her pair of ear-rings and a bunch of flowers
> The brute took growling, prayed, and then was gone."

In all his creations there was a marked instinct for the solid, something sensibly shaped by the grip and craft of the hand, like the clay on the potter's wheel; even the transitory glories of Abt Vogler's music took the palpable form of architecture.

Secondly, he maintained a consistent attitude towards both technique and connoisseurship. With an unusual knowledge of the technicalities of each of these arts he had at the same time a poor estimation of mere craftsmanship. The faultless drawing of Andrea del Sarto, the intricate subtleties of the fugues of the master of Saxe-Gotha, simply betray their impotence when called upon to exercise the crucial function of the artist. "Out of me, out of me," cries the faultless painter, remembering the passionate exaltation, defiant of precepts and rules, of Rafael and Michael Angelo.

> "But where's music, the dickens!"

exclaims the organist bewildered by the mathematical muddle of Master Hugues' composition; whereas in assured calm, Abt Vogler frames out of three sounds, "not a fourth sound, but a star."

Dilettantism carried even less weight with him than

technique. The Bishop of St Praxed's and the Duke of Ferrara are soundly equipped with critical taste and knowledge. But they toil not, neither do they spin; they contribute nothing; they are content with the mere pride of possession.

Thirdly, creation, technique, and the taste of the virtuoso, were all of them of less significance to him than the soul of the artist. This was partly because the artist is already a spirit isolated from the common herd. Browning had little feeling for the indistinguishable multitude. It was partly also because the artist is in many ways the symbolic figure of humanity for him. What he says in *Paracelsus* of men at large is much more obviously the case with the artist:

> "Truth is within ourselves; it takes no rise
> From outward things, whate'er you may believe :
> There is an inmost centre in us all,
> Where truth abides in fulness; and around
> Wall upon wall, the gross flesh hems it in,
> This perfect clear perception—which is truth ;
> A baffling and perverting carnal mesh
> Blinds it, and makes all error: and '*to know*'
> Rather consists in opening out a way
> Whence the imprisoned splendour may escape,
> Than in effecting entry for a light
> Supposed to be without !"

Again, the artist's life is exactly what Browning held to be the history of mankind; a struggle for expression, a strife to attain an ideal. Paracelsus aspires and attains. It is in each case a struggle waged against many obstacles, against a refractory medium, and with sometimes not more than a dim perception of what is to be the outcome. It is furthermore a conflict in which—this is a cardinal point in Browning—man must trust his own inner judgment, as the artist can only portray his own inner conception. To both of them there come at times those visitings from infinity, moments of contact with the transcendent and the eternal, which secure by their flash of illumination some further step of progress; for both, this light is dulled by the immediacy of the material world, "Heaven's gift takes earth's abatement." In both the hope is fostered that the broken arc will become the perfect round, and thus both "Have a bliss to die with dim-descried."

There are not many poets in Browning's varied portrait gallery. Shelley has his splendid tribute in *Pauline* and in *Memorabilia*, and Keats in *Popularity*. The figure of Aprile in *Paracelsus* is too vague and shadowy; it seems to indicate that the passion of love and the desire of beauty, however benevolent and however intense, are powerless unless allied with the passion for knowledge of which Paracelsus himself is the exemplar. Sordello too is rather an ineffectual soul only lighting upon the secret of adjusting his infinite vision to the narrow limits of time and space at the moment of death. *How it strikes a Contemporary* gives us an unimaginative contemporary's conclusions about the observant and sensitive poet of Valladolid, popularly misunderstood (most of Browning's poets were), and superstitiously shunned. *Transcendentalism* is a remonstrance against a poet whose tough and difficult thought is clad in a very scanty garb of melody; it slyly glances at the public attitude towards himself. In *One Word More* he shifts from the dramatic to the lyrical key to pay a delicate homage to his wife. But there are here no studies, except perhaps Balaustion, of the executive talent at work in poetry such as that of Fra Lippo in painting and Abt Vogler in music. In truth Browning's views on his own art were set out most clearly not in any verse, but in the *Introductory Essay* which he wrote to precede the (supposed) letters of Shelley, published in 1852. In this he developed the distinction between the objective and the subjective poet, attributing to the former the task of reproducing "things external, whether the phenomena of the scenic universe, or the manifested action of the human heart and brain"; whilst of the latter he says: "Not with the combination of humanity in action but with the primal elements of humanity he has to do; he digs where he stands,— preferring to seek them in his own soul as the nearest reflex of that absolute Mind, according to the intuitions of which he desires to perceive and speak." Thus the lyric poet is exalted above the dramatic and rightly so if "truth is within ourselves," in the sense that Browning intended to convey. Shelley's "noblest and predominating characteristic" is "his simultaneous perception of Power and Love in the absolute, and of Beauty and Good in the concrete, while he throws, from his poet's station between both, swifter, subtler, and more numerous films for the connexion of each with each than have been thrown by any modern artificer of whom I have knowledge."..."I would rather consider Shelley's poetry as a sublime fragmentary essay towards a presentment of the correspondency of the universe to Deity, of the natural to the spiritual, and of the actual to the ideal...." It is a splendid apology for poetry, and granted certain saving clauses, as true of Browning's genius as of Shelley's.

Of painting he wrote in *Pictor Ignotus, Old Pictures in Florence, Fra Lippo Lippi* and *Andrea del Sarto* and some other poems; but it is in those named that he entered most into the artist's point of view, showing how the artist works and still more how he feels. It is noticeable that he did not interpret the greatest masters, but obscure workers like Pictor Ignotus, or such as have risen only to the second rank, as Andrea, or have salient qualities of temperament, like Fra Lippo and Andrea again. Browning had a most human tolerance and leniency for what misses supreme attainment. It is essential to his creed. Pictor Ignotus and Andrea are studies of failure in painting; each of them is aware of a loftier ideal, but the causes of failure to realise it differ in the two cases. The unknown painter is timid and technically unaccomplished and sinks acquiescingly into oblivion. Del Sarto is the faultless painter and has had visitings of ambition to vie with Leonardo and Michael Angelo; but he has a soul too shrivelled and impotent to inspire his icily perfect drawing. *Old Pictures in Florence* gives evidence of the poet's minute acquaintance with the galleries, his quick eye for idiosyncrasy in technique and inspiration, his energetic justification of these pioneers of the more vital art of Italy when the art of Greece had attained perfection in its own still kind; and lastly his championship of the effort which fails, in harness, as against the petty mastery which succeeds without strife in a puny or

imitative task. Fra Lippo in his hearty acceptance of
the physical universe, his "homage to the perishable
clay," has more kinship with another aspect of the
poet's disposition, namely the pagan impartiality of his
appreciation for

> "The beauty and the wonder and the power,
> The shapes of things, their colours, lights and shades,
> Changes, surprises—";

he puts in a lucid statement also an alternative purpose
of art:

> "For, don't you mark, we're made so that we love
> First when we see them painted, things we have passed
> Perhaps a hundred times nor cared to see;
> And so they are better painted—better to us,
> Which is the same thing. Art was given for that—
> God uses us to help each other so,
> Lending our minds out."

The poet did not often take the picture for its own
sake, he did not often—an exception is the poem *A
Face*—transcribe the picture directly into words, as
Rossetti does for instance in *Fiammetta*; nor for all his
knowledge of the craft would he be satisfied with the
judgment of a painting from the point of view of pure
dexterity with pigment and canvas; in one way or
another his mind would pursue the implication and
association of the work. This is only a little less true
of the case of sculpture.

Of the early poems on music *Saul* gives expression
to the frank joyousness of youth in songs of the fields,
of bodily swiftness and strength, of martial prowess,
of the celebration of valour and the praise of dead
heroes. *A Toccata of Galuppi's* spins out a thin melody

which floats faintly over an ocean of ingenuity in composition, reflecting the momentary brilliance and final moral slightness or insignificance of eighteenth century Venice. When the intricate form of the fugue has been analysed in *Master Hugues of Saxe-Gotha*, the synthesis of the dissected parts proves to have no breath of vitality, no magical rhythm to set echoing chords in the soul, even in the generous, if a little hot-tempered, judgment of the organist. In these poems as well as in *Abt Vogler* the art itself comes to the fore, the executant fades into the background, and with him the interest in a definite personality. It is a mere accident that the marvellous chord should be struck out by Abt Vogler; but it is no accident that Andrea's pictures are silver-grey or that Fra Lippo's are something bold and sensuous and realistic; and this dethronement of the artist's personality is consonant with Browning's claim for music that it infinitely surpasses the plastic arts and even poetry. It is, in fact, no longer an art but a revelation, " the finger of God, a flash of the will that can." By poetry and painting we see facets of the truth, gain fragmentary clues to the eternal mind, through recognised formulas, "in obedience to laws." Music is the language of God's converse with the soul.

In some of the *Parleyings* of 1887 he discusses these matters more argumentatively ; music in *Charles Avison*, and painting in *Gerard de Lairesse*, and most of what he thought on the subjects of imagination and the arts finds brilliant expression in the more impersonal parts of *Fifine at the Fair*.

### iii. Love

It is another evidence of the poet's curiously dramatic instinct that whilst his own love ran so unhesitating and propitious a course, he should have explored so often the eddies and backwaters and torrents in the current of love. It is not sufficient for him to pen "descriptions of the fairest wights," or to find exquisite diction and imagery to figure forth a mood, such as the song for Mariana, "Take, O, take those lips away"; nor does he like Donne pry into the weird secrets of the past,

> "I long to talk with some old lover's ghost,
> Who died before the god of love was born."

He treats of actual passion and he stays at whatever moment in its course promises to distil its richest significance. He seems almost the first to realise that these moments are not necessarily those of the rapture of possession and enjoyment, or the fierce bitterness of rejection, but may be any one of the scores of episodes in the long chronicle. Hence the novelty of the situations in his love poetry. And again he stands apart because romance and passion rarely came singly to him; his questing, examining intellect led him to segregate all the strands of the mood, to trace it back to its origins and to peer forward to its outcome. If he portrays failure as in *Cristina* or *The Lost Mistress* or *The Last Ride Together*, it is not an occasion either for some tempestuous outburst of grief or for the airy persiflage of Suckling; but rather for the manliness of temper which gathers strength out of defeat, weaves the experience into the fabric of character and imbues

its resignation with new thought and resolve for other
ventures. The tragedies of love are for Browning's
women rather than for his men. The inconstancy he
pictures is that dreaded by a wife after her husband's
death, as in *Any Wife to any Husband*, or of one who
is constantly endeavouring to seize the hem of the garment of fidelity, but in vain as in *Two in the Campagna*.
No poet falls so rarely into the sentimentalism which
Meredith describes "fiddling harmonics on the strings
of sensualism." He is not always the poet of love
faltering or baffled. He can pipe as melodiously as
any Elizabethan a song in praise of beauty:

> "Nay but you who do not love her,
>     Is she not pure gold, my mistress?
> Holds earth aught—speak truth—above her?
>     Aught like this tress, see, and this tress,
>     And this last fairest tress of all,
>     So fair, see, ere I let it fall?
>
> Because you spend your lives in praising;
>     To praise, you search the wide world over:
> Then why not witness, calmly gazing,
>     If earth holds aught—speak truth—above her?
>     Above this tress, and this, I touch
>     But cannot praise, I love so much!"

He can find words too for the splendid glow of
youthful passion as in the opening of *In a Gondola*.

> "I send my heart up to thee, all my heart,
>     In this my singing.
> For the stars help me, and the sea bears part;
>     The very night is clinging
> Closer to Venice' streets, to leave one space
> Above me, whence thy face
> May light my joyous heart to thee, its dwelling-place."

But the triumphs of love are sung in poems of wifehood and motherhood. The heroine of *The Inn Album* says:

"Womanliness means only motherhood :
All love begins and ends there,—roams enough,
But, having run the circle, rests at home."

Pompilia, in *The Ring and the Book*, drawn as Swinburne says "with piercing and overpowering tenderness," is the masterpiece in Browning's gallery of woman characters. In such poems his own marriage enriched both imagination and emotion. The story of his marriage in September, 1846, is an oft-told tale; the marvellous prelude to it is the theme of the *Correspondence of E. B. B. and R. B.*, one of the supreme love stories in literature. The vigorous foot which he put through the obtuse and noxious tyranny of Elizabeth Barrett's father, the clear-sighted impulse and decisive action which swept her from an imprisoned and anaemic inactivity to the open air and sky of Italy, and his audacious faith in her capacity for the manifold concerns of home and motherhood, were a thousand times justified in the unclouded felicity of a union in which intellect, passion and parenthood were equally powerful strands.

## IV

### BROWNING'S ESTIMATE OF LIFE

In his survey of life he treats certain elements as axiomatic. He never questions the existence of a supreme authority, or God, controlling the manifold energies of the world. He is not however of the

pantheistic school of Wordsworth; for though he can
see evidence of the hand and intention of God in the
most unpromising quarters, yet his individualising
instinct, more keenly alive to the separations and
divisions than to the continuities of existence, conceived of God as a distinct personality from the life of
nature and man. He is not on the other hand a Deist,
positing a Deity infinitely remote and unmindful of the
lot of the created universe, or tyrannous, as in Shelley,
or actively ironic as in Thomas Hardy. Sympathetic
communion is established between the Creator and the
created by the attributes of power, knowledge, and
love. Since God is his name for our highest conception,
his interpretation of the universe is in terms of the
highest attribute of God. The poet reaches this
spiritual solution of the problem of existence by more
than one path. First, his own warmth and glow of
feeling leads him to choose the emotional quality of
love, or as he puts it, to appeal from the head to the
heart. Secondly, every idealist elects to interpret the
whole of the material available for judgment in terms
of the best in it; and Browning has many times averred
that "love is best." Thirdly when he compares these
three qualities, he finds that power alone is not enough.
It might create a world, it might direct with an iron
rigidity the mechanical forces which it set in operation,
but it is not a principle which will solve for man the
perplexities of his environment, enable him to distil
the rarest essence out of the years, or give him any
hope to arm his heart against misfortune and despair.
Knowledge, at first (as in *Paracelsus*) a glorious gift,
afterwards lost its glamour in his eyes; so far from

conceding that knowledge could serve as a channel to the Divine Mind, he came to scorn it and ridicule it and belittle its capacity to deal even with the primary impressions of sense; such is the drift of those polemical poems, like *La Saisiaz*, of his later years. But love, which kindles and exalts both power and knowledge, he deems to be the quality by which man touches the infinite, the quality common to God and man. What Coleridge apprehended once in a single enchanted stanza, is an all-pervading truth to Browning:

> "All thoughts, all passions, all delights,
> Whatever stirs this mortal frame,
> All are but ministers of Love,
> And feed his sacred flame."

One of the supreme moments in all Browning is that in which the brutal criminal Guido, condemned to execution, makes his fearful appeal for mercy to Christ, Maria, God, mere names to him, and then in a single moment of inspiration, to the love of his wife Pompilia, upon whom he has wrought the most foul and dastardly wrong:

> "I am the Granduke's,—no, I am the Pope's!
> Abate,—Cardinal,—Christ,—Maria,—God,...
> Pompilia, will you let them murder me?"

Love then is the philosophic principle which harmonizes and unifies all being; at the same time the creative cause,

> "God! Thou art Love! I build my faith on that";

and the sustaining and perfecting power,

> "So the All-Great were the All-Loving too."

It is also the moral ideal; the end towards which man strives to advance,

> "O, world as God has made it! all is beauty:
> And knowing this, is love, and love is duty."

But no theory can have any worth as an optimistic reading of life which does not reconcile its beneficent principle with the prevalence of evil, pain and misery. To understand how the poet effects this reconciliation it is necessary to look a little closer into his conception of the meaning and end of man's history; for he does not take refuge in the philosophic abstraction that evil is the necessary counterpart of good in thought; he accepts evil as a thing real enough to be an instrument in the hands of love.

The most familiar category of thought to us is that of evolution. Browning is a passionate adherent of the theory; but he is not contented with a merely physical outcome of the process. His conviction is that the ideal is being constantly enlarged; the end towards which we struggle reveals itself as a thing richer and richer as we go on. The loftiest prophecy, the noblest belief, is the truest for those who conceive it; and further what is loftiest and noblest in one generation will be surpassed by something still loftier and therefore still truer in the next; so that life is progress in two senses; first in the steady enrichment of man's ideal as he approaches closer to the absolute— that is God, and God is love—and secondly in the sense that the achievements of men are successively nobler from age to age. Ideal and achievement are two parallel infinite series.

Life then is a persistent struggle towards an ideal never completely attained, never even to be completely attained. The whole worth of life, the whole purpose of the love which gave it birth, lies not in perfection ("What's come to perfection perishes"), but in the effort to become perfect; not in accomplishment, but in the strife to accomplish. If then we are always striving to become perfect, we are always imperfect, and the consciousness of imperfection and evil is the price we pay for the realisation of something greater and better than ourselves, and at the same time it is the opportunity offered to us to advance. We cannot have victory without the foe. Evil is therefore a condition of man's moral life, and of his moral progress.

" And what is our failure here but a triumph's evidence
For the fulness of the days ? Have we withered or agonized ?
Why else was the pause prolonged but that singing might
    issue thence ?
Why rushed the discords in but that harmony should be
    prized ? "

This is the way in which Browning absorbs evil into a theory of life of which love is the fundamental principle. He does not pronounce with the facile optimism of Pope and Bolingbroke that " whatever is, is right," but rather that whatever is, is wrong, for the excellent purpose that we may put it right, and in the effort acquire new moral power :

    " Then, welcome each rebuff
        That turns earth's smoothness rough,
    Each sting that bids nor sit nor stand but go !
        Be our joys three-parts pain !
        Strive, and hold cheap the strain ;
    Learn nor account the pang ; dare, never grudge the throe !"

Life is a probation in which strife, moral valour, and the guidance of the highest conception we have yet attained are the best equipment. But it is not a probation to fit us for some perfect state in which we are to rest doffing our armour in some easeful Elysium, or for some Buddhistic absorption into the eternal stillness of contemplation. The struggle never ceases; evil is not to be submerged beneath the tide of universal forbearance and love as in Shelley's *Prometheus*; nor does it recoil destructively upon itself as Milton conceived in *Comus*:

> "And mix no more with goodness, when at last,
> Gathered like scum, and settled to itself,
> It shall be in eternal restless change
> Self-fed and self-consumed."

Evil is as permanent as good; and therefore man is literally "ever a fighter," facing "adventures brave and new," for whom the signal is in Browning's last poetic utterance:

> "Strive and thrive! cry 'Speed,—fight on, fare ever
> There as here.'"

The other firmly grounded belief which supports the structure of his theory is the immortality of the soul; no novel doctrine, except in the enlarged and deepened application which he gives to it. Like Malvolio, he thinks nobly of the soul; and if this doctrine is pressed home to its logical issues, it carries in implication all the paradoxical audacities of the poet's creed. For first, man lives in two worlds, the finite and the infinite; he is conscious of the spiritual world by the enthusiasms, longings and aspirations in the soul, where they exist like imprisoned splendours. Next if there are two worlds for the soul, there are two standards of judgment for conduct. The man who succeeds as the world counts, has failed utterly by the criterion of infinity; the ideal which is attainable in the finite world cannot possibly have had any trace of the infinite in it. Similarly he who, believing that " Man has Forever," leaves " Now, for dogs and apes," is sure to be incomprehensible to the world, to fail by its standards; and this is the kind of failure that Browning so constantly exalts:

> "This high man, with a great thing to pursue,
>     Dies ere he knows it.
>   That low man goes on adding one to one,
>     His hundred's soon hit:
>   This high man, aiming at a million,
>     Misses an unit."

Failure of this kind is, as Professor Henry Jones has it, "the last word but one." It is expressed in other words in *Andrea del Sarto*;

> "Ah, but a man's reach should exceed his grasp,
>   Or what's a heaven for?"

We come here upon the confirmation of the doctrine that imperfection and failure are man's glory; the ideals which the soul illumines are beacons in the far distance; their unattainability is both the prophecy and the instigation of progress.

It follows likewise that judgment is passed, not on the thing accomplished,

> "Not on the vulgar mass
> Called 'work' must sentence pass,
> Things done, that took the eye and had the price";

but upon the impulse, the intention, the nobility of soul which prompts the attempt, and which may only emerge into clear consciousness, "when eternity affirms the conception of an hour."

> "All I could never be,
> All, men ignored in me,
> This, I was worth to God, whose wheel the pitcher shaped."

What is attempted in such a spirit cannot be completed in the limited sphere of the temporal; on the earth there are the "broken arcs; in the heaven, a perfect round."

In the light of this conception death becomes not the herald of extinction, but

> "A groom
> That brings a taper to the outward room";

where the soul may pursue its designs unfettered and unhindered; this is the faith which inspires *The Epilogue to Asolando* and *Prospice*:

> "For sudden the worst turns the best to the brave,
>     The black minute's at end,
> And the element's rage, the fiend voices that rave,
>     Shall dwindle, shall blend,
> Shall change, shall become first a peace out of pain,
>     Then a light, then thy breast,
> O thou soul of my soul! I shall clasp thee again,
>     And with God be the rest!"

# V

## FORM AND STYLE

Browning discovered through assiduous trial that his genius, though dramatic, was not fitted for the production of stage plays. Even the best of his seven or eight dramas, *The Blot on the Scutcheon* (1843), betrays his limitations. That part of the dramatist's equipment which consists in self-detachment and the projection and portrayal of many individual characters he possessed in full measure; but he was less able to present character in action on the painted scene. His wont was to stop short at the stage of impulse, intention and thought before they fructify in action. How insignificant action appeared to him is shown in his use of one single plot for twelve complete poems in *The Ring and the Book*. His is not the drama of the outer world of events, but of the inner world of the soul, where nothing is of importance until it is transmuted into a form influencing mind and character. Of this world Mrs Browning wrote in *Aurora Leigh* that it

> " may outgrow
> The simulation of the painted scene,
> Boards, actors, prompters, gaslight, and costume,
> And take for a nobler stage the soul itself,
> In shifting fancies and celestial lights,
> With all its grand orchestral silences,
> To keep the pauses of the rhythmic sounds."

As he peered more and more intently into the half-hidden crevices and shadowy secrecies of the mind, he wrought out for himself a novel form in which to depict his novel reading of man, namely the dramatic monologue. This is a kind of comprehensive soliloquy, absorbing into its substance by the speaker's keenly observant glance the surrounding scenery and audience; bringing all that is pertinent to the chosen moment by the channels of memory, argument, curiosity and association; adding through the deep-graven lines which habit has incised upon character much which the soul would fain conceal, or is even unconscious of the necessity for concealing; and enriching the current of self-revealing speech with the product of any other emotion which may have been powerful enough to share in the fashioning of this critical moment. A swift glance may light upon a new figure and in a few deft strokes he stands out vividly from the rest of the group, as in *Fra Lippo*;

> " I'd like his face—
> His, elbowing his comrade in the door,
> With the pike and lantern,—"

Or memory busies itself in *The Bishop orders his Tomb* about the lifelong envy between the Bishop and his predecessor Gandolf; or again medical prepossession and habit fill *Karshish* with observations of local herbs and diseases. The scenery and accessories of these dramas are not forwarded by the carpenter, they are vital and organic parts of the poems. Our conception of these Men and Women and of all that determines their state at the psychological moment develops with far greater swiftness than the drama can command, in response to these touches following in rapid succession, sketched in with trenchant precision, and falling with inevitable artistry into harmony and perspective.

Generally in these poems some event crystallizes all the elements of personality about itself so that a soul's history is told in an episode of an hour. The pressure of circumstance forces into high relief the real underlying temperament obscured by some disguising veneer in normal times; the elements and energies of life are tightly knotted in microcosmic completeness. Such situations—Browning's is "pre-eminently the poetry of situations," says Pater—afford him obvious pleasure in unravelling the almost inextricable tangle of motive, good, bad, and purblind; of confession, sophistry and self-deception; of every kind of complication and aberration of thought. The typical apologies and self-justifications of his subjects give him the fullest opportunity of exhibiting his talent as debater and leading counsel, one of whose arts is to induce his victim to speak freely in self-defence; it is the occasion on which people are apt to reveal most. The poet acquired such sure mastery of his method that he could use it to any degree of complexity. Truth could be reflected, refracted, distorted till it seemed to lose all semblance of itself. In *Bishop Blougram's Apology* the mists that hide truth gather and disperse, bank themselves into an opaque curtain and again thin out into isolated units of cloud with bewildering rapidity of change. The *Epistle* of Karshish records a view the writer is half inclined and half ashamed to confess about a dead person reputed to have had a miraculous influence over a deluded Israelite; only in the postscript is his judicial rejection tempered and overcome by his emotional sympathy. Browning had Milton's unwavering faith in truth.

"I cannot praise a fugitive and cloistered virtue unexercised, and unbreathed, that never sallies out and sees her adversary, but slinks out of the race, where that immortal garland is to be run for, not without dust and heat."

The variations from this kind of monologue are not very considerable. The dramatic romance and idyll no doubt are fuller of figures and have more suggestion of story, passing from incident to incident in chronological order. The student would gain an understanding of the methods if he asked himself how Browning would have told the story of *Macbeth* and how much of the Shakespearean play could go unchanged into the later poet's form.

In some of the *Dramatis Personae* he turns from his probings in the depths of personality to assert in ringing confident tones the doctrines of the noble life. These poems fall below the standard of dramatic intimacy and realism of the earlier works. *Rabbi Ben Ezra* for instance purports to be a poem of age, but it breathes throughout the adventurous spirit of youth. From this time forward speculation, argument and exhortation usurp the place of character in his affections. It is worth noting that the dramatic monologues are written mostly in blank verse, free and vigorous in rhythm, racy and actual, bristling with colloquialisms, engaged in the subtle play of debate as in *Blougram*, or bounding and sweeping along as in *Fra Lippo*, or meandering and digressing as in *The Bishop of St Praxed's*, but in any case almost unconscious of any sense of resistance in words. The poems of moral fervour and exhortation are not in blank verse, but in diverse forms of lyrical stanza, in each case admirably suited in the result (and this is the only possible criterion) to the content of the poem, witness *Abt Vogler* and *A Grammarian's Funeral*, two out of many possible instances.

When Browning was introduced to the Chinese ambassador as a fellow-poet he asked him in what kind of poetical composition he was most adept. The ambassador after a moment's consideration replied "the enigmatical." Browning acknowledged the kinship of their gifts. Enigmatical better describes the poet's style than the more customary epithet obscure. That there is no obscurity of thought is finally demonstrated by Swinburne's classic digression in the essay on George Chapman.

"He (Browning) is something too much the reverse of obscure; he is too brilliant and subtle for the ready reader of a ready writer to follow with any certainty the track of an intelligence which moves with such incessant rapidity, or even to realise with what spider-like swiftness and sagacity his building spirit leaps and lightens to and fro and backward and forward as it lives along the animated line of its labour, springs from thread to thread and darts from centre to circumference of the glittering and quivering web of living thought, woven from the inexhaustible stores of his perception and kindled from the inexhaustible fire of his imagination. He never thinks but at full speed."

The difficulties one encounters, in fact, are very largely those of diction; of these, three things may be said. First, he sought his subjects in many remote regions, and his allusions are drawn from many little-known sources, so that one must read, for instance,

*Sordello* in close proximity to a particularly minute encyclopaedia. Secondly, he went about to secure compression (after being chided for the volubility of *Pauline*) by an excessive use of ellipsis of relatives, connectives and the like, the result resembling the explosive stenography of Alfred Jingle, which adds at times an uncongenial element of syntactical conundrum to his work. Thirdly, the obscurity even from these causes has been much exaggerated and lies to some extent at the door of the indolent reader; "I never pretended to offer a substitute for a cigar or a game at dominoes to an idle man," says the poet. And it may be proved by trial that the reading of half a dozen of Browning's poems is the best possible training for the reading of any other half-dozen; in plain words the difficulty is that of accustoming oneself to a new style; in this case familiarity breeds competence.

Though it would be a grave error to suppose that he entirely eschewed grace, sweetness and melodic variety, to challenge attention by oddities and novelties, yet his diction and rhythm have the quality of aggressive pungent singularity oftener than that of exquisite beauty. It is worth noting that he apprenticed himself to poetry by a careful study of Johnson's Dictionary. As for his rhythm, possibly, like Donne, another Ishmaelite, he was a purposeful iconoclast. Browning sometimes breaks in harshly and unmusically upon the sweet rhythmical cadence, the easy modulations, the perpetual tunefulness of much lyric verse from Spenser to Swinburne, as Wagner did with his suspensions and discords upon those of Italian opera. Like Donne,

though with less obvious disdain, he mocks and aston-
ishes rather than gratifies contemporary taste, having
a special fondness for the shock of the actual in the
midst of the imaginative picture, and for prosaic rhythms
among those of poetry. His grotesque rhymes are
perhaps part of the same defiance of convention. Sometimes they are barbaric excrescences; they are almost
intolerable in *A Grammarian's Funeral*; sometimes
they are the product of mere exuberance of skill like
the mediaeval gargoyle; here a wild infectious gaiety
carries them off. The classic instances are in *The Pied
Piper of Hamelin.*

# VI

## CONCLUSION

"Shakespeare is not our poet but the world's,
  Therefore on him no speech! and brief for thee,
  Browning! Since Chaucer was alive and hale
  No man has walked along our roads with step
  So active, so enquiring eye, or tongue
  So varied in discourse. But warmer climes
  Give brighter plumage, stronger wing: the breeze
  Of Alpine heights thou playest with, borne on
  Beyond Sorrento and Amalfi, where
  The Siren waits thee, singing song for song."

These lines of Landor's record succinctly enough
most of Browning's temperamental qualities. His
simple, direct, vigorous nature was homogeneous
throughout. In observation he was keenly alert, in
interest wide without prejudice, in sympathy large-
minded. If in him intellect was apt to follow sinuous

and indirect paths, emotion rang true and went straight
to its mark. Force and strength appealed to him
as it did to Carlyle. In nature he observed, for instance,
how

"Spring's arrowy summons goes right to the aim,
And some mountain, the last to withstand her, that held...
...on a broad bust of stone
A year's snow bound about for a breastplate,—leaves grasp of
     the sheet;
Fold on fold all at once it crowds thunderously down to his feet,
And there fronts you, stark, black, but alive yet, your mountain
     of old";

in bodily action he noted

"the strong right-hand clenched stronger
As it would pluck a lion by the jaw";

and described

"the cool silver shock
Of the plunge in a pool's living water";

and he spoke of art in *Fifine at the Fair* in these
phrases;

"Art,—which I may style the love of loving, rage
Of knowing, seeing, feeling the absolute truth of things
For truth's sake, whole and sole, not any good truth brings
The knower, seer, feeler, beside,—instinctive Art
Must fumble for the whole, once fixing on a part
However poor, surpass the fragment, and aspire
To reconstruct thereby the ultimate entire."

He was neither polished, precious nor decadent,
nor anything, in fact, but forthright and resolute, even
in his subtlety. There was a kind of humorous fitness
in the printing of the first complete edition of his poems
in America as a supplement to a railway guide. He

restores confidence in the conception of progress by his sense of the actual; we are with him bodily in the fray, whilst Shelley with a more delicate sense of beauty may sometimes seem to be a remote disembodied voice chanting unearthly melodies above the din and impact of battle. It was this grappling with facts and crushing out of them a heightened feeling for the worth of life which gave value to Browning's optimism. Like Meredith he reached the conclusion

> "Our questions are a mortal brood,
> Our work is everlasting."

Meredith attained it by a stern faith in the silent austerity of earth. Browning's argument—sketched in a previous section—was not so severe a discipline; and personal conviction was a larger factor than in the other poet, for he found corroboration in the very immensity of his hope. Yet neither his doctrine nor his native assurance would have confirmed his belief, had he not supported it by the whole weight of experience gathered in the most diverse quarters; on this ground he contended that man was developing his finer and sloughing his baser qualities from generation to generation. The impulse to strenuousness, effort and resolution which this idea brought is far from being exhausted and is likely for long to make Browning a rare remedial and tonic companion. Robustness and manliness were his dominant notes, lethargy—"the unlit lamp and the ungirt loin"—the unpardonable sin; every sign of energy, initiative and persistence contained a major portion of good, even though by conventional standards it might be labelled irregular, grotesque or immoral; whilst every indication of lassitude, weak resignation or immobility, though it might possess the negative virtue of abstention, was nevertheless a defrauding of the potential power of the universe.

He was richly endowed artistically, being sculptor, painter, musician as well as poet and humorist; he had balanced sanity and charity of judgment; breadth of interest and sympathy like the universal tolerance and beneficence of the sun; a healthy exhilarating ardour in the cause of humanity, for whom he conceived a magnificent philosophical and moral goal; yet it is possible that the thing of largest ethical import which he uttered was one of the simplest;

"How good is man's life, the mere living! how fit to employ
All the heart and the soul and the senses, for ever in joy!"

He died in harness, for his last volume, *Asolando*, was published on the day of his death, December 12, 1889.

### BOOKS ON BROWNING.

*Dictionary of National Biography.* Mrs Sutherland Orr, *Handbook to Browning's Works*; and *Life and Letters.* Berdoe, *Browning Cyclopaedia.* Arthur Symons, *An Introduction to the Study of Browning.* W. Sharp, *Robert Browning* (Great Writers). Stopford Brooke, *The Poetry of Robert Browning.* Professor Dowden, *Robert Browning.* Professor Herford, *Robert Browning.* G. K. Chesterton, *Browning* (English Men of Letters). Professor Henry Jones, *Browning as a Philosophical and Religious Teacher.* A. C. Pigou, *Browning as a Religious Teacher.* Hall Griffin, *Life of Browning.*

# POEMS BY BROWNING

## I. From PARACELSUS

Heap cassia, sandal-buds, and stripes
  Of labdanum, and aloe-balls,
Smeared with dull nard an Indian wipes
  From out her hair: such balsam falls
  Down sea-side mountain pedestals,      5
From tree-tops where tired winds are fain,
Spent with the vast and howling main,
To treasure half their island-gain.

And strew faint sweetness from some old
  Egyptian's fine worm-eaten shroud      10
Which breaks to dust when once unrolled;
  Or shredded perfume, like a cloud
  From closet long to quiet vowed,
With mothed and dropping arras hung,
Mouldering her lute and books among      15
As when a queen, long dead, was young.

## II. From PIPPA PASSES

The year's at the spring,
And day's at the morn;
Morning's at seven;
The hill-side's dew-pearled;
The lark's on the wing;                    5
The snail's on the thorn;
God's in His heaven—
All's right with the world!

## III. CAVALIER TUNES

### MARCHING ALONG

#### I

Kentish Sir Byng stood for his King,
Bidding the crop-headed Parliament swing:
And, pressing a troop unable to stoop
And see the rogues flourish and honest folk droop,
Marched them along, fifty-score strong,        5
Great-hearted gentlemen, singing this song.

#### II

God for King Charles! Pym and such carles
To the Devil that prompts 'em their treasonous parles!
Cavaliers, up! Lips from the cup,
Hands from the pasty, nor bite take nor sup    10
Till you're

  (*Chorus*) *marching along, fifty-score strong,*
          *Great-hearted gentlemen, singing this song.*

### III

Hampden to Hell, and his obsequies' knell
Serve Hazelrig, Fiennes, and young Harry as well!
England, good cheer! Rupert is near!    15
Kentish and loyalists, keep we not here
  (*Chorus*)  *Marching along, fifty-score strong,*
            *Great-hearted gentlemen, singing this song?*

### IV

Then, God for King Charles! Pym and his snarls
To the Devil that pricks on such pestilent carles!  20
Hold by the right, you double your might;
So, onward to Nottingham, fresh for the fight,
  (*Chorus*)  *March we along, fifty-score strong,*
            *Great-hearted gentlemen, singing this song!*


## GIVE A ROUSE

### I

King Charles, and who'll do him right now?
King Charles, and who's ripe for fight now?
Give a rouse: here's, in Hell's despite now,
King Charles!

### II

Who gave me the goods that went since?    5
Who raised me the house that sank once?
Who helped me to gold I spent since?
Who found me in wine you drank once?
  (*Chorus*)  *King Charles, and who'll do him right now?*
            *King Charles, and who's ripe for fight now?*
            *Give a rouse: here's, in Hell's despite now,*
            *King Charles!*

### III

To whom used my boy George quaff else,
By the old fool's side that begot him?
For whom did he cheer and laugh else,                    15
While Noll's damned troopers shot him?
 (*Chorus*) *King Charles, and who'll do him right now?*
     *King Charles, and who's ripe for fight now?*
     *Give a rouse: here's, in Hell's despite now,*
     *King Charles!*                    20


## BOOT AND SADDLE

### I

Boot, saddle, to horse, and away!
Rescue my Castle, before the hot day
Brightens to blue from its silvery grey,
 (*Chorus*) *Boot, saddle, to horse, and away!*

### II

Ride past the suburbs, asleep as you'd say;                    5
Many's the friend there, will listen and pray
"God's luck to gallants that strike up the lay,
 (*Chorus*) *"Boot, saddle, to horse, and away!"*

### III

Forty miles off, like a roebuck at bay,
Flouts Castle Brancepeth the Roundheads' array:    10
Who laughs, "Good fellows ere this, by my fay,
 (*Chorus*) *"Boot, saddle, to horse, and away?"*

IV

Who? My wife Gertrude; that, honest and gay,
Laughs when you talk of surrendering, "Nay!
"I've better counsellors; what counsel they?    15
    (*Chorus*)   "*Boot, saddle, to horse, and away !*"


## IV. THE LOST LEADER

I

Just for a handful of silver he left us,
    Just for a riband to stick in his coat—
Found the one gift of which fortune bereft us,
    Lost all the others she lets us devote;
They, with the gold to give, doled him out silver,    5
    So much was theirs who so little allowed:
How all our copper had gone for his service!
    Rags—were they purple, his heart had been proud!
We that had loved him so, followed him, honoured him,
    Lived in his mild and magnificent eye,    10
Learned his great language, caught his clear accents,
    Made him our pattern to live and to die!
Shakespeare was of us, Milton was for us,
    Burns, Shelley, were with us,—they watch from their
        graves!
He alone breaks from the van and the freemen,    15
    He alone sinks to the rear and the slaves!

## II

We shall march prospering,—not thro' his presence;
  Songs may inspirit us,—not from his lyre;
Deeds will be done,—while he boasts his quiescence,
  Still bidding crouch whom the rest bade aspire:   20
Blot out his name, then, record one lost soul more,
  One task more declined, one more footpath untrod,
One more triumph for devils, and sorrow for angels,
  One wrong more to man, one more insult to God!
Life's night begins: let him never come back to us!  25
  There would be doubt, hesitation and pain,
Forced praise on our part—the glimmer of twilight,
  Never glad confident morning again!
Best fight on well, for we taught him,—strike gallantly,
  Menace our heart ere we master his own;   30
Then let him receive the new knowledge and wait us,
  Pardoned in Heaven, the first by the throne!


## V. "HOW THEY BROUGHT THE GOOD NEWS FROM GHENT TO AIX"

### [16—]

#### I

I sprang to the stirrup, and Joris, and he;
I galloped, Dirck galloped, we galloped all three;
"Good speed!" cried the watch, as the gate-bolts
    undrew;
"Speed!" echoed the wall to us galloping through;
Behind shut the postern, the lights sank to rest,  5
And into the midnight we galloped abreast.

## II

Not a word to each other; we kept the great pace
Neck by neck, stride by stride, never changing our place;
I turned in my saddle and made its girths tight,
Then shortened each stirrup, and set the pique right, 10
Rebuckled the cheek-strap, chained slacker the bit,
Nor galloped less steadily Roland a whit.

## III

'Twas moonset at starting; but while we drew near
Lokeren, the cocks crew and twilight dawned clear;
At Boom, a great yellow star came out to see;    15
At Düffeld, 'twas morning as plain as could be;
And from Mecheln church-steeple we heard the half-
    chime,
So Joris broke silence with, "Yet there is time!"

## IV

At Aerschot, up leaped of a sudden the sun,
And against him the cattle stood black every one, 20
To stare thro' the mist at us galloping past,
And I saw my stout galloper Roland at last,
With resolute shoulders, each butting away
The haze, as some bluff river headland its spray.

## V

And his low head and crest, just one sharp ear bent
    back                                        25
For my voice, and the other pricked out on his track;
And one eye's black intelligence,—ever that glance
O'er its white edge at me, his own master, askance!
And the thick heavy spume-flakes which aye and anon
His fierce lips shook upwards in galloping on.    30

### VI

By Hasselt, Dirck groaned; and cried Joris, "Stay
　　spur!
"Your Roos galloped bravely, the fault's not in her,
"We'll remember at Aix"—for one heard the quick
　　wheeze
Of her chest, saw the stretched neck and staggering
　　knees,
And sunk tail, and horrible heave of the flank,　　35
As down on her haunches she shuddered and sank.

### VII

So we were left galloping, Joris and I,
Past Looz and past Tongres, no cloud in the sky;
The broad sun above laughed a pitiless laugh,
'Neath our feet broke the brittle bright stubble like
　　chaff;　　　　　　　　　　　　　　　　40
Till over by Dalhem a dome-spire sprang white,
And "Gallop," gasped Joris, "for Aix is in sight!"

### VIII

"How they'll greet us!"—and all in a moment his roan
Rolled neck and croup over, lay dead as a stone;
And there was my Roland to bear the whole weight　45
Of the news which alone could save Aix from her fate,
With his nostrils like pits full of blood to the brim,
And with circles of red for his eye-sockets' rim.

### IX

Then I cast loose my buffcoat, each holster let fall,
Shook off both my jack-boots, let go belt and all,　50

Stood up in the stirrup, leaned, patted his ear,
Called my Roland his pet-name, my horse without
　　peer;
Clapped my hands, laughed and sang, any noise, bad
　　or good,
Till at length into Aix Roland galloped and stood.

### X

And all I remember is, friends flocking round      55
As I sate with his head 'twixt my knees on the ground;
And no voice but was praising this Roland of mine,
As I poured down his throat our last measure of wine,
Which (the burgesses voted by common consent)
Was no more than his due who brought good news
　　from Ghent.                                       60

## VI.  GARDEN FANCIES

### THE FLOWER'S NAME

#### I

Here's the garden she walked across,
　　Arm in my arm, such a short while since:
Hark, now I push its wicket, the moss
　　Hinders the hinges and makes them wince!
She must have reached this shrub ere she turned,  5
　　As back with that murmur the wicket swung;
For she laid the poor snail, my chance foot spurned,
　　To feed and forget it the leaves among.

## II

Down this side of the gravel-walk
  She went while her robe's edge brushed the box:  10
And here she paused in her gracious talk
  To point me a moth on the milk-white phlox.
Roses, ranged in valiant row,
  I will never think that she passed you by!
She loves you noble roses, I know;  15
  But yonder, see, where the rock-plants lie!


## III

This flower she stopped at, finger on lip,
  Stooped over, in doubt, as settling its claim;
Till she gave me, with pride to make no slip,
  Its soft meandering Spanish name:  20
What a name! was it love, or praise?
  Speech half-asleep, or song half-awake?
I must learn Spanish, one of these days,
  Only for that slow sweet name's sake.


## IV

Roses, if I live and do well,  25
  I may bring her, one of these days,
To fix you fast with as fine a spell,
  Fit you each with his Spanish phrase;
But do not detain me now; for she lingers
  There, like sunshine over the ground,  30
And ever I see her soft white fingers
  Searching after the bud she found.

### V

Flower, you Spaniard, look that you grow not,
  Stay as you are and be loved for ever!
Bud, if I kiss you 'tis that you blow not,        35
  Mind, the shut pink mouth opens never!
For while thus it pouts, her fingers wrestle,
  Twinkling the audacious leaves between,
Till round they turn and down they nestle—
  Is not the dear mark still to be seen?        40

### VI

Where I find her not, beauties vanish;
  Whither I follow her, beauties flee;
Is there no method to tell her in Spanish
  June's twice June since she breathed it with me?
Come, bud, show me the least of her traces,        45
  Treasure my lady's lightest foot-fall
—Ah, you may flout and turn up your faces—
  Roses, you are not so fair after all!

### SIBRANDUS SCHAFNABURGENSIS

### I

Plague take all your pedants, say I!
  He who wrote what I hold in my hand,
Centuries back was so good as to die,
  Leaving this rubbish to cumber the land;
This, that was a book in its time,        5
  Printed on paper and bound in leather,
Last month in the white of a matin-prime
  Just when the birds sang all together.

## II

Into the garden I brought it to read,
    And under the arbute and laurustine        10
Read it, so help me grace in my need,
    From title-page to closing line.
Chapter on chapter did I count,
    As a curious traveller counts Stonehenge;
Added up the mortal amount;                    15
    And then proceeded to my revenge.

## III

Yonder's a plum-tree with a crevice
    An owl would build in, were he but sage;
For a lap of moss, like a fine pont-levis
    In a castle of the middle age,             20
Joins to a lip of gum, pure amber;
    When he'd be private, there might he spend
Hours alone in his lady's chamber:
    Into this crevice I dropped our friend.

## IV

Splash, went he, as under he ducked,          25
    —I knew at the bottom rain drippings stagnate;
Next a handful of blossoms I plucked
    To bury him with, my bookshelf's magnate;
Then I went in-doors, brought out a loaf,
    Half a cheese, and a bottle of Chablis;    30
Lay on the grass and forgot the oaf
    Over a jolly chapter of Rabelais.

V

Now, this morning, betwixt the moss
  And gum that locked our friend in limbo,
A spider had spun his web across,                35
  And sate in the midst with arms a-kimbo:
So, I took pity, for learning's sake,
  And, *de profundis, accentibus lætis,*
*Cantate!* quoth I, as I got a rake,
  And up I fished his delectable treatise.        40


VI

Here you have it, dry in the sun,
  With all the binding all of a blister,
And great blue spots where the ink has run,
  And reddish streaks that wink and glister
O'er the page so beautifully yellow:            45
  Oh, well have the droppings played their tricks!
Did he guess how toadstools grow, this fellow?
  Here's one stuck in his chapter six!


VII

How did he like it when the live creatures
  Tickled and toused and browsed him all over,   50
And worm, slug, eft, with serious features,
  Came in, each one, for his right of trover;
When the water-beetle with great blind deaf face
  Made of her eggs the stately deposit,
And the newt borrowed just so much of the preface 55
  As tiled in the top of his black wife's closet?

### VIII

All that life, and fun, and romping,
  All that frisking and twisting and coupling,
While slowly our poor friend's leaves were swamping
  And clasps were cracking, and covers suppling! 60
As if you had carried sour John Knox
  To the play-house at Paris, Vienna, or Munich,
Fastened him into a front-row box,
  And danced off the ballet with trousers and tunic.

### IX

Come, old martyr! What, torment enough is it?     65
  Back to my room shall you take your sweet self!
Good bye, mother-beetle; husband-eft, *sufficit!*
  See the snug niche I have made on my shelf.
A.'s book shall prop you up, B.'s shall cover you,
  Here's C. to be grave with, or D. to be gay,     70
And with E. on each side, and F. right over you,
  Dry-rot at ease till the Judgment-day!

## VII. SOLILOQUY OF THE SPANISH CLOISTER

### I

Gr-r-r—there go, my heart's abhorrence!
  Water your damned flower-pots, do!·
If hate killed men, Brother Lawrence,
  God's blood, would not mine kill you!
What? your myrtle-bush wants trimming?     5
  Oh, that rose has prior claims—
Needs its leaden vase filled brimming?
  Hell dry you up with its flames!

## II

At the meal we sit together:
  *Salve tibi!* I must hear                  10
Wise talk of the kind of weather,
  Sort of season, time of year:
*Not a plenteous cork-crop: scarcely*
  *Dare we hope oak-galls, I doubt:*
*What's the Latin name for "parsley"?*      15
  What's the Greek name for Swine's Snout?

## III

Whew! We'll have our platter burnished,
  Laid with care on our own shelf!
With a fire-new spoon we're furnished,
  And a goblet for ourself,                 20
Rinsed like something sacrificial
  Ere 'tis fit to touch our chaps—
Marked with L. for our initial!
  (He-he! There his lily snaps!)

## IV

*Saint*, forsooth! While brown Dolores      25
  Squats outside the Convent bank,
With Sanchicha, telling stories,
  Steeping tresses in the tank,
Blue-black, lustrous, thick like horsehairs,
  —Can't I see his dead eye glow,           30
Bright as 'twere a Barbary corsair's?
  (That is, if he'd let it show!)

### V

When he finishes refection,
  Knife and fork he never lays
Cross-wise, to my recollection,                    35
  As do I, in Jesu's praise.
I, the Trinity illustrate,
  Drinking watered orange-pulp—
In three sips the Arian frustrate;
  While he drains his at one gulp!                 40

### VI

Oh, those melons! If he's able
  We're to have a feast; so nice!
One goes to the Abbot's table,
  All of us get each a slice.
How go on your flowers? None double?              45
  Not one fruit-sort can you spy?
Strange!—And I, too, at such trouble,
  Keep them close-nipped on the sly!

### VII

There's a great text in Galatians,
  Once you trip on it, entails                     50
Twenty-nine distinct damnations,
  One sure, if another fails.
If I trip him just a-dying,
  Sure of Heaven as sure can be,
Spin him round and send him flying                55
  Off to Hell, a Manichee?

### VIII

Or, my scrofulous French novel,
  On grey paper with blunt type!
Simply glance at it, you grovel
  Hand and foot in Belial's gripe:                    60
If I double down its pages
  At the woeful sixteenth print,
When he gathers his greengages,
  Ope a sieve and slip it in't?

### IX

Or, there's Satan!—one might venture            65
  Pledge one's soul to him, yet leave
Such a flaw in the indenture
  As he'd miss till, past retrieve,
Blasted lay that rose-acacia
  We're so proud of! *Hy, Zy, Hine* ...          70
'St, there's Vespers! *Plena gratiâ*
  *Ave, Virgo!* Gr-r-r—you swine!

## VIII. THE LOST MISTRESS

### I

All's over, then: does truth sound bitter
  As one at first believes?
Hark, 'tis the sparrows' good-night twitter
  About your cottage eaves!

### II

And the leaf-buds on the vine are woolly,          5
  I noticed that, to-day;
One day more bursts them open fully
  —You know the red turns grey.

### III

To-morrow we meet the same then, dearest?
    May I take your hand in mine?      10
Mere friends are we,—well, friends the merest
    Keep much that I'll resign:

### IV

For each glance of that eye so bright and black,
    Though I keep with heart's endeavour,—
Your voice, when you wish the snowdrops back,    15
    Though it stay in my soul for ever!—

### V

Yet I will but say what mere friends say,
    Or only a thought stronger;
I will hold your hand but as long as all may,
    Or so very little longer!      20

## IX. EVELYN HOPE

### I

Beautiful Evelyn Hope is dead!
    Sit and watch by her side an hour.
That is her book-shelf, this her bed;
    She plucked that piece of geranium-flower,
Beginning to die too, in the glass;      5
    Little has yet been changed, I think—
The shutters are shut, no light may pass
    Save two long rays thro' the hinge's chink.

## II

Sixteen years old when she died!
　Perhaps she had scarcely heard my name;　　10
It was not her time to love: beside,
　Her life had many a hope and aim,
Duties enough and little cares,
　And now was quiet, now astir,
Till God's hand beckoned unawares,—　　　15
　And the sweet white brow is all of her.

## III

Is it too late then, Evelyn Hope?
　What, your soul was pure and true,
The good stars met in your horoscope,
　Made you of spirit, fire and dew—　　　20
And, just because I was thrice as old,
　And our paths in the world diverged so wide,
Each was nought to each, must I be told?
　We were fellow mortals, nought beside?

## IV

No, indeed! for God above　　　　　　　25
　Is great to grant, as mighty to make,
And creates the love to reward the love:
　I claim you still, for my own love's sake!
Delayed it may be for more lives yet,
　Through worlds I shall traverse, not a few:　　30
Much is to learn and much to forget
　Ere the time be come for taking you.

V

But the time will come,—at last it will,
  When, Evelyn Hope, what meant, I shall say,
In the lower earth, in the years long still,         35
  That body and soul so pure and gay?
Why your hair was amber, I shall divine,
  And your mouth of your own geranium's red—
And what you would do with me, in fine,
  In the new life come in the old one's stead.     40

VI

I have lived, I shall say, so much since then,
  Given up myself so many times,
Gained me the gains of various men,
  Ransacked the ages, spoiled the climes;
Yet one thing, one, in my soul's full scope,         45
  Either I missed or itself missed me—
And I want and find you, Evelyn Hope!
  What is the issue? let us see!

VII

I loved you, Evelyn, all the while;
  My heart seemed full as it could hold—         50
There was place and to spare for the frank young
      smile
  And the red young mouth and the hair's young gold.
So, hush,—I will give you this leaf to keep—
  See, I shut it inside the sweet cold hand.
There, that is our secret! go to sleep;         55
  You will wake, and remember, and understand.

## X. HOME-THOUGHTS, FROM ABROAD

### I

Oh, to be in England
Now that April's there,
And whoever wakes in England
Sees, some morning, unaware,
That the lowest boughs and the brush-wood sheaf    5
Round the elm-tree bole are in tiny leaf,
While the chaffinch sings on the orchard bough
In England—now!

### II

And after April, when May follows,
And the whitethroat builds, and all the swallows!    10
Hark, where my blossomed pear-tree in the hedge
Leans to the field and scatters on the clover
Blossoms and dewdrops—at the bent spray's edge—
That's the wise thrush; he sings each song twice over,
Lest you should think he never could recapture    15
The first fine careless rapture!
And though the fields look rough with hoary dew,
All will be gay when noontide wakes anew
The buttercups, the little children's dower,
—Far brighter than this gaudy melon-flower!    20

## XI. HOME-THOUGHTS, FROM THE SEA

Nobly, nobly Cape Saint Vincent to the North-West
    died away;
Sunset ran, one glorious blood-red, reeking into Cadiz
    Bay;
Bluish mid the burning water, full in face Trafalgar lay;
In the dimmest North-East distance, dawned Gibraltar
    grand and gray;
"Here and here did England help me: how can I help
    England?"—say,        5
Whoso turns as I, this evening, turn to God to praise
    and pray,
While Jove's planet rises yonder, silent over Africa.


## XII. SAUL

### I

Said Abner, "At last thou art come! Ere I tell, ere
    thou speak,
Kiss my cheek, wish me well!" Then I wished it,
    and did kiss his cheek.
And he, "Since the King, O my friend, for thy
    countenance sent,
Neither drunken nor eaten have we; nor until from
    his tent
Thou return with the joyful assurance the King liveth
    yet,        5
Shall our lip with the honey be bright, with the
    water be wet.

For out of the black mid-tent's silence, a space of
three days,
Not a sound hath escaped to thy servants, of prayer
or of praise,
To betoken that Saul and the Spirit have ended their
strife,
And that, faint in his triumph, the monarch sinks back
upon life. 10

## II

Yet now my heart leaps, O beloved! God's child, with
his dew
On thy gracious gold hair, and those lilies still living
and blue
Just broken to twine round thy harp-strings, as if no
wild heat
Were now raging to torture the desert!"

## III

Then I, as was meet,
Knelt down to the God of my fathers, and rose on
my feet, 15
And ran o'er the sand burnt to powder. The tent
was unlooped;
I pulled up the spear that obstructed, and under I
stooped;
Hands and knees on the slippery grass-patch, all
withered and gone,
That extends to the second enclosure, I groped my
way on
Till I felt where the foldskirts fly open. Then once
more I prayed, 20
And opened the foldskirts and entered, and was not
afraid,

But spoke, "Here is David, thy servant!"    And no
　　voice replied.
At the first I saw nought but the blackness; but soon
　　I descried
A something more black than the blackness—the vast
　　the upright
Main prop which sustains the pavilion: and slow into
　　sight                                                    25
Grew a figure against it, gigantic and blackest of all:
Then a sunbeam, that burst thro' the tent-roof, showed
　　Saul.

### IV

He stood as erect as that tent-prop; both arms stretched
　　out wide
On the great cross-support in the centre, that goes to
　　each side:
He relaxed not a muscle, but hung there, as, caught
　　in his pangs                                            30
And waiting his change the king-serpent all heavily
　　hangs,
Far away from his kind, in the pine, till deliverance come
With the spring-time,—so agonized Saul, drear and
　　stark, blind and dumb.

### V

Then I tuned my harp,—took off the lilies we twine
　　round its chords
Lest they snap 'neath the stress of the noontide—
　　those sunbeams like swords!                             35
And I first played the tune all our sheep know, as,
　　one after one,
So docile they come to the pen-door, till folding be done.

They are white and untorn by the bushes, for lo, they
    have fed
Where the long grasses stifle the water within the
    stream's bed;
And now one after one seeks its lodging, as star follows
    star                         40
Into eve and the blue far above us,—so blue and so far!

### VI

—Then the tune, for which quails on the cornland
    will each leave his mate
To fly after the player; then, what makes the crickets
    elate,
Till for boldness they fight one another: and then,
    what has weight
To set the quick jerboa a-musing outside his sand
    house—                           45
There are none such as he for a wonder, half bird and
    half mouse!
God made all the creatures and gave them our love
    and our fear,
To give sign, we and they are His children, one family
    here.

### VII

Then I played the help-tune of our reapers, their
    wine-song, when hand
Grasps at hand, eye lights eye in good friendship, and
    great hearts expand             50
And grow one in the sense of this world's life.—And
    then, the last song
When the dead man is praised on his journey—"Bear,
    bear him along

With his few faults shut up like dead flowerets! are
    balm-seeds not here
To console us? The land has none left, such as he
    on the bier.
Oh, would we might keep thee, my brother!"—And
    then, the glad chaunt       55
Of the marriage,—first go the young maidens, next,
    she whom we vaunt
As the beauty, the pride of our dwelling.—And then,
    the great march
Wherein man runs to man to assist him and buttress
    an arch
Nought can break; who shall harm them, our friends?
    —Then, the chorus intoned
As the Levites go up to the altar in glory enthroned.
But I stopped here—for here in the darkness, Saul
    groaned.      61

### VIII

And I paused, held my breath in such silence, and
    listened apart;
And the tent shook, for mighty Saul shuddered—and
    sparkles 'gan dart
From the jewels that woke in his turban at once
    with a start—
All its lordly male-sapphires, and rubies courageous
    at heart.      65
So the head—but the body still moved not, still hung
    there erect.
And I bent once again to my playing, pursued it
    unchecked,
As I sang,—

### IX

"Oh, our manhood's prime vigour!
  no spirit feels waste,

Not a muscle is stopped in its playing, nor sinew
  unbraced.

Oh, the wild joys of living! the leaping from rock
  up to rock—                    70

The strong rending of boughs from the fir-tree,—the
  cool silver shock

Of the plunge in a pool's living water,—the hunt of
  the bear,

And the sultriness showing the lion is couched in his lair.

And the meal—the rich dates yellowed over with gold
  dust divine,

And the locust's-flesh steeped in the pitcher! the full
  draught of wine,              75

And the sleep in the dried river-channel where bul-
  rushes tell

That the water was wont to go warbling so softly
  and well.

How good is man's life, the mere living! how fit to
  employ

All the heart and the soul and the senses, for ever
  in joy!

Hast thou loved the white locks of thy father, whose
  sword thou didst guard          80

When he trusted thee forth with the armies, for
  glorious reward?

Didst thou see the thin hands of thy mother, held
  up as men sung

The low song of the nearly-departed, and heard her
  faint tongue

Joining in while it could to the witness, 'Let one more
    attest,

I have lived, seen God's hand thro' a lifetime, and all
    was for best!'              85

Then they sung thro' their tears in strong triumph,
    not much—but the rest.

And thy brothers, the help and the contest, the working
    whence grew

Such result as, from seething grape-bundles, the spirit
    strained true!

And the friends of thy boyhood—that boyhood of
    wonder and hope,

Present promise, and wealth of the future beyond the
    eye's scope,—         90

Till lo, thou art grown to a monarch; a people is thine;

And all gifts, which the world offers singly, on one
    head combine!

On one head, all the beauty and strength, love and
    rage, (like the throe

That, a-work in the rock, helps its labour and lets
    the gold go)

High ambition and deeds which surpass it, fame crown-
    ing it,—all         95

Brought to blaze on the head of one creature—King
    Saul!"

## X

And lo, with that leap of my spirit,—heart, hand, harp
    and voice,

Each lifting Saul's name out of sorrow, each bidding
    rejoice

Saul's fame in the light it was made for—as when, dare I say,

The Lord's army, in rapture of service, strains through its array, 100

And upsoareth the cherubim-chariot—" Saul !" cried I, and stopped,

And waited the thing that should follow. Then Saul, who hung propt

By the tent's cross-support in the centre, was struck by his name.

Have ye seen when Spring's arrowy summons goes right to the aim,

And some mountain, the last to withstand her, that held (he alone, 105

While the vale laughed in freedom and flowers) on a broad bust of stone

A year's snow bound about for a breastplate,—leaves grasp of the sheet ?

Fold on fold all at once it crowds thunderously down to his feet,

And there fronts you, stark, black, but alive yet, your mountain of old,

With his rents, the successive bequeathings of ages untold— 110

Yea, each harm got in fighting your battles, each furrow and scar

Of his head thrust 'twixt you and the tempest—all hail, there they are !

Now again to be softened with verdure, again hold the nest

Of the dove, tempt the goat and its young to the green on its crest

For their food in the ardours of summer! One long
    shudder thrilled          115
All the tent till the very air tingled, then sank and
    was stilled
At the King's self left standing before me, released
    and aware.
What was gone, what remained? all to traverse 'twixt
    hope and despair;
Death was past, life not come: so he waited. Awhile
    his right hand
Held the brow, helped the eyes left too vacant forth-
    with to remand        120
To their place what new objects should enter: 'twas
    Saul as before.
I looked up and dared gaze at those eyes, nor was
    hurt any more
Than by slow pallid sunsets in autumn, ye watch
    from the shore,
At their sad level gaze o'er the ocean—a sun's slow
    decline
Over hills which, resolved in stern silence, o'erlap and
    entwine        125
Base with base to knit strength more intense: so, arm
    folded in arm
O'er the chest whose slow heavings subsided.

### XI

                What spell or what charm,
(For, awhile there was trouble within me) what next
    should I urge
To sustain him where song had restored him?—Song
    filled to the verge

His cup with the wine of this life, pressing all that
    it yields 130
Of mere fruitage, the strength and the beauty! Beyond,
    on what fields,
Glean a vintage more potent and perfect to brighten
    the eye
And bring blood to the lip, and commend them the
    cup they put by?
He saith, "It is good;" still he drinks not; he lets
    me praise life.
Gives assent, yet would die for his own part.

## XII

             Then fancies grew rife 135
Which had come long ago on the pastures, when round
    me the sheep
Fed in silence—above, the one eagle wheeled slow as
    in sleep,
And I lay in my hollow, and mused on the world
    that might lie
'Neath his ken, though I saw but the strip 'twixt the
    hill and the sky:
And I laughed—"Since my days are ordained to be
    passed with my flocks, 140
Let me people at least, with my fancies, the plains
    and the rocks,
Dream the life I am never to mix with, and image the
    show
Of mankind as they live in those fashions I hardly
    shall know!

Schemes of life, its best rules and right uses, the courage
    that gains,
And the prudence that keeps what men strive for."
    And now these old trains         145
Of vague thought came again; I grew surer; so once
    more the string
Of my harp made response to my spirit, as thus—

### XIII

                        "Yea, my king,"
I began—"thou dost well in rejecting mere comforts
    that spring
From the mere mortal life held in common by man
    and by brute:
In our flesh grows the branch of this life, in our soul
    it bears fruit.         150
Thou hast marked the slow rise of the tree,—how its
    stem trembled first
Till it passed the kid's lip, the stag's antler; then
    safely outburst
The fan-branches all round; and thou mindest when
    these too, in turn
Broke a-bloom and the palm-tree seemed perfect; yet
    more was to learn,
Ev'n the good that comes in with the palm-fruit.
    Our dates shall we slight,         155
When their juice brings a cure for all sorrow? or
    care for the plight
Of the palm's self whose slow growth produced them?
    Not so! stem and branch
Shall decay, nor be known in their place, while the
    palm-wine shall staunch

Every wound of man's spirit in winter. I pour thee
    such wine.
Leave the flesh to the fate it was fit for! the spirit
    be thine!                              160
By the spirit, when age shall o'ercome thee, thou still
    shalt enjoy
More indeed, than at first when inconscious, the life
    of a boy.
Crush that life, and behold its wine running! each
    deed thou hast done
Dies, revives, goes to work in the world; until e'en
    as the sun
Looking down on the earth, though clouds spoil him,
    though tempests efface,                  165
Can find nothing his own deed produced not, must
    everywhere trace
The results of his past summer-prime,—so, each ray
    of thy will,
Every flash of thy passion and prowess, long over, shall
    thrill
Thy whole people the countless, with ardour, till they
    too give forth
A like cheer to their sons, who in turn, fill the South
    and the North                         170
With the radiance thy deed was the germ of. Carouse
    in the Past!
But the license of age has its limit; thou diest at
    last:
As the lion when age dims his eyeball, the rose at
    her height,
So with man—so his power and his beauty for ever
    take flight.

No! again a long draught of my soul-wine! look forth
o'er the years—                                                    175
Thou hast done now with eyes for the actual; begin
with the seer's!
Is Saul dead? in the depth of the vale make his
tomb—bid arise
A grey mountain of marble heaped four-square, till,
built to the skies,
Let it mark where the great First King slumbers:
whose fame would ye know?
Up above see the rock's naked face, where the record
shall go                                                          180
In great characters cut by the scribe,—Such was Saul,
so he did;
With the sages directing the work, by the populace
chid,—
For not half, they'll affirm, is comprised there! Which
fault to amend,
In the grove with his kind grows the cedar, whereon
they shall spend
(See, in tablets 'tis level before them) their praise,
and record                                                        185
With the gold of the graver, Saul's story,—the statesman's great word
Side by side with the poet's sweet comment. The
river's a-wave
With smooth paper-reeds grazing each other when
prophet-winds rave:
So the pen gives unborn generations their due and
their part
In thy being! Then, first of the mighty, thank God
that thou art."                                                  190

## XIV

And behold while I sang ... But O Thou who didst
  grant me that day,
And before it not seldom hast granted, Thy help to
  essay
Carry on and complete an adventure,—my Shield and
  my Sword
In that act where my soul was Thy servant, Thy word
  was my word,—
Still be with me, who then at the summit of human
  endeavour                                           195
And scaling the highest, man's thought could, gazed
  hopeless as ever
On the new stretch of Heaven above me—till, mighty
  to save,
Just one lift of Thy hand cleared that distance—God's
  throne from man's grave!
Let me tell out my tale to its ending—my voice to
  my heart
Which can scarce dare believe in what marvels last
  night I took part,                                  200
As this morning I gather the fragments, alone with
  my sheep,
And still fear lest the terrible glory evanish like
  sleep!
For I wake in the grey dewy covert, while Hebron
  upheaves
The dawn struggling with night on his shoulder, and
  Kidron retrieves
Slow the damage of yesterday's sunshine.

## XV

I say then,—my song    205
While I sang thus, assuring the monarch, and ever
   more strong
Made a proffer of good to console him—he slowly
   resumed
His old motions and habitudes kingly. The right hand
   replumed
His black locks to their wonted composure, adjusted
   the swathes
Of his turban, and see—the huge sweat that his
   countenance bathes,    210
He wipes off with the robe; and he girds now his loins
   as of yore,
And feels slow for the armlets of price, with the clasp
   set before.
He is Saul, ye remember in glory,—ere error had
   bent
The broad brow from the daily communion; and still,
   though much spent
Be the life and the bearing that front you, the same,
   God did choose,    215
To receive what a man may waste, desecrate, never
   quite lose.
So sank he along by the tent-prop, till, stayed by
   the pile
Of his armour and war-cloak and garments, he leaned
   there awhile,
And so sat out my singing,—one arm round the tent-
   prop, to raise
His bent head, and the other hung slack—till I touched
   on the praise    220

I foresaw from all men in all times, to the man patient
    there ;
And thus ended, the harp falling forward. Then first
    I was 'ware
That he sat, as I say, with my head just above his
    vast knees
Which were thrust out on each side around me, like
    oak-roots which please
To encircle a lamb when it slumbers. I looked up to
    know           225
If the best I could do had brought solace: he spoke
    not, but slow
Lifted up the hand slack at his side, till he laid it
    with care
Soft and grave, but in mild settled will, on my brow:
    thro' my hair
The large fingers were pushed, and he bent back my
    head, with kind power—
All my face back, intent to peruse it, as men do a
    flower.          230
Thus held he me there with his great eyes that
    scrutinized mine—
And oh, all my heart how it loved him! but where
    was the sign?
I yearned—"Could I help thee, my father, inventing
    a bliss,
I would add to that life of the Past, both the Future
    and this ;
I would give thee new life altogether, as good, ages
    hence,          235
As this moment,—had love but the warrant, love's
    heart to dispense!"

## XVI

Then the truth came upon me. No harp more—no
song more! out-broke—

## XVII

"I have gone the whole round of Creation: I saw and
I spoke!
I, a work of God's hand for that purpose, received in
my brain
And pronounced on the rest of his handwork—returned
him again                                                    240
His creation's approval or censure: I spoke as I saw.
I report, as a man may of God's work—all's love, yet
all's law!
Now I lay down the judgeship He lent me. Each
faculty tasked
To perceive Him, has gained an abyss, where a dew-
drop was asked.
Have I knowledge? confounded it shrivels at Wisdom
laid bare.                                                    245
Have I forethought? how purblind, how blank, to
the Infinite Care!
Do I task any faculty highest, to image success?
I but open my eyes,—and perfection, no more and no
less,
In the kind I imagined, full-fronts me, and God is
seen God
In the star, in the stone, in the flesh, in the soul and
the clod.                                                     250
And thus looking within and around me, I ever renew
(With that stoop of the soul which in bending upraises
it too)

The submission of Man's nothing-perfect to God's All-
    Complete,
As by each new obeisance in spirit, I climb to His
    feet!
Yet with all this abounding experience, this Deity
    known,           255
I shall dare to discover some province, some gift of
    my own.
There's a faculty pleasant to exercise, hard to hood-
    wink,
I am fain to keep still in abeyance, (I laugh as I think)
Lest, insisting to claim and parade in it, wot ye, I worst
E'en the Giver in one gift.—Behold! I could love if
    I durst!           260
But I sink the pretension as fearing a man may o'ertake
God's own speed in the one way of love: I abstain,
    for love's sake!
—What, my soul? see thus far and no farther? when
    doors great and small,
Nine-and-ninety flew ope at our touch, should the
    hundredth appal?
In the least things, have faith, yet distrust in the
    greatest of all?           265
Do I find love so full in my nature, God's ultimate gift,
That I doubt His own love can compete with it? here,
    the parts shift?
Here, the creature surpass the Creator, the end, what
    Began?—
Would I fain in my impotent yearning do all for
    this man,
And dare doubt He alone shall not help him, who yet
    alone can?           270

Would it ever have entered my mind, the bare will,
    much less power,
To bestow on this Saul what I sang of, the marvellous
    dower
Of the life he was gifted and filled with? to make
    such a soul,
Such a body, and then such an earth for insphering
    the whole?
And doth it not enter my mind (as my warm tears
    attest)      275
These good things being given, to go on, and give
    one more, the best?
Ay, to save and redeem and restore him, maintain
    at the height
This perfection,—succeed with life's dayspring, death's
    minute of night?
Interpose at the difficult minute, snatch Saul, the
    mistake,
Saul, the failure, the ruin he seems now,—and bid
    him awake      280
From the dream, the probation, the prelude, to find
    himself set
Clear and safe in new light and new life,—a new
    harmony yet
To be run, and continued, and ended—who knows?—
    or endure!
The man taught enough by life's dream, of the rest
    to make sure;
By the pain-throb, triumphantly winning intensified
    bliss,      285
And the next world's reward and repose, by the
    struggles in this.

### XVIII

"I believe it! 'tis Thou, God, that givest, 'tis I who
    receive:
In the first is the last, in Thy will is my power to
    believe.
All's one gift: Thou canst grant it moreover, as prompt
    to my prayer
As I breathe out this breath, as I open these arms
    to the air.    290
From Thy will, stream the worlds, life and nature,
    thy dread Sabaoth:
*I* will?—the mere atoms despise me! and why am
    I not loth
To look that, even that in the face too? why is it I dare
Think but lightly of such impuissance? what stops
    my despair?
This:—'tis not what man Does which exalts him, but
    what man Would do!    295
See the King—I would help him but cannot, the wishes
    fall through.
Could I wrestle to raise him from sorrow, grow poor
    to enrich,
To fill up his life, starve my own out, I would—
    knowing which,
I know that my service is perfect. Oh, speak through
    me now!
Would I suffer for him that I love? So wouldst Thou
    —so wilt Thou!    300
So shall crown Thee the topmost, ineffablest, uttermost
    crown—
And Thy love fill infinitude wholly, nor leave up nor
    down

One spot for the creature to stand in! It is by no breath,
Turn of eye, wave of hand, that salvation joins issue
    with death!
As Thy Love is discovered almighty, almighty be
    proved                                   305
Thy power, that exists with and for it, of being
    Beloved!
He who did most, shall bear most; the strongest shall
    stand the most weak.
'Tis the weakness in strength that I cry for! my flesh,
    that I seek
In the Godhead! I seek and I find it. O Saul, it
    shall be
A Face like my face that receives thee: a Man like
    to me,                                     310
Thou shalt love and be loved by, for ever: a Hand
    like this hand
Shall throw open the gates of new life to thee! See
    the Christ stand!"

### XIX

I know not too well how I found my way home in
    the night.
There were witnesses, cohorts about me, to left and
    to right,
Angels, powers, the unuttered, unseen, the alive, the
    aware—                                 315
I repressed, I got through them as hardly, as strugglingly
    there,
As a runner beset by the populace famished for news—
Life or death. The whole earth was awakened, hell
    loosed with her crews;

And the stars of night beat with emotion, and tingled
  and shot
Out in fire the strong pain of pent knowledge: but I
  fainted not,                                                    320
For the Hand still impelled me at once and supported,
  suppressed
All the tumult, and quenched it with quiet, and holy
  behest,
Till the rapture was shut in itself, and the earth
  sank to rest.
Anon at the dawn, all that trouble had withered from
  earth—
Not so much, but I saw it die out in the day's tender birth;
In the gathered intensity brought to the grey of the hills;
In the shuddering forests' new awe; in the sudden
  wind-thrills;
In the startled wild beasts that bore off, each with
  eye sidling still
Though averted with wonder and dread; in the birds
  stiff and chill
That rose heavily, as I approached them, made stupid
  with awe!                                                      330
E'en the serpent that slid away silent,—he felt the
  new Law.
The same stared in the white humid faces upturned
  by the flowers;
The same worked in the heart of the cedar, and moved
  the vine-bowers:
And the little brooks witnessing murmured, persistent
  and low,
With their obstinate, all but hushed voices—"E'en so,
  it is so!"                                                     335

## XIII.  BY THE FIRE-SIDE

### I

How well I know what I mean to do
  When the long dark Autumn evenings come,
And where, my soul, is thy pleasant hue?
  With the music of all thy voices, dumb
In life's November too!            5

### II

I shall be found by the fire, suppose,
  O'er a great wise book as beseemeth age,
While the shutters flap as the cross-wind blows,
  And I turn the page, and I turn the page,
Not verse now, only prose!        10

### III

Till the young ones whisper, finger on lip,
  "There he is at it, deep in Greek—
Now then, or never, out we slip
  To cut from the hazels by the creek
A mainmast for our ship."        15

### IV

I shall be at it indeed, my friends!
  Greek puts already on either side
Such a branch-work forth as soon extends
  To a vista opening far and wide,
And I pass out where it ends.        20

### V

The outside-frame like your hazel-trees—
  But the inside-archway narrows fast,
And a rarer sort succeeds to these,
  And we slope to Italy at last
And youth, by green degrees.        25

## VI

I follow wherever I am led,
  Knowing so well the leader's hand:
Oh, woman-country, wooed not wed,
  Loved all the more by earth's male-lands,
Laid to their hearts instead!                30

## VII

Look at the ruined chapel again
  Half-way up in the Alpine gorge.
Is that a tower, I point you plain,
  Or is it a mill or an iron forge
Breaks solitude in vain?                35

## VIII

A turn, and we stand in the heart of things;
  The woods are round us, heaped and dim;
From slab to slab how it slips and springs—
  The thread of water single and slim,
Through the ravage some torrent brings!                40

## IX

Does it feed the little lake below?
  That speck of white just on its marge
Is Pella; see, in the evening glow,
  How sharp the silver spear-heads charge
When Alp meets Heaven in snow.                45

## X

On our other side is the straight-up rock;
  And a path is kept 'twixt the gorge and it
By boulder-stones where lichens mock
  The marks on a moth, and small ferns fit
Their teeth to the polished block.                50

### XI

Oh, the sense of the yellow mountain flowers,
  And the thorny balls, each three in one,
The chestnuts throw on our path in showers!
  —For the drop of the woodland fruit's begun
These early November hours,                    55

### XII

That crimson the creeper's leaf across
  Like a splash of blood, intense, abrupt,
O'er a shield else gold from rim to boss,
  And lay it for show on the fairy-cupped
Elf-needled mat of moss,                       60

### XIII

By the rose-flesh mushrooms, undivulged
  Last evening—nay, in to-day's first dew
Yon sudden coral nipple bulged
  Where a freaked, fawn-coloured, flaky crew
Of toad-stools peep indulged.                  65

### XIV

And yonder, at foot of the fronting ridge
  That takes the turn to a range beyond,
Is the chapel reached by the one-arched bridge
  Where the water is stopped in a stagnant pond
Danced over by the midge.                      70

### XV

The chapel and bridge are of stone alike,
  Blackish-grey and mostly wet;
Cut hemp-stalks steep in the narrow dyke.
  See here again, how the lichens fret
And the roots of the ivy strike!               75

### XVI

Poor little place, where its one priest comes
  On a festa-day, if he comes at all,
To the dozen folk from their scattered homes,
  Gathered within that precinct small
By the dozen ways one roams—                    80

### XVII

To drop from the charcoal-burners' huts,
  Or climb from the hemp-dressers' low shed,
Leave the grange where the woodman stores his nuts,
  Or the wattled cote where the fowlers spread
Their gear on the rock's bare juts.              85

### XVIII

It has some pretension too, this front,
  With its bit of fresco half-moon-wise
Set over the porch, Art's early wont:
  'Tis John in the Desert, I surmise,
But has borne the weather's brunt—               90

### XIX

Not from the fault of the builder, though,
  For a pent-house properly projects
Where three carved beams make a certain show,
  Dating—good thought of our architect's—
'Five, six, nine, he lets you know.              95

### XX

And all day long a bird sings there,
  And a stray sheep drinks at the pond at times;
The place is silent and aware;
  It has had its scenes, its joys and crimes,
But that is its own affair.                      100

### XXI

My perfect wife, my Leonor,
  Oh, heart my own, oh, eyes, mine too,
Whom else could I dare look backward for,
  With whom beside should I dare pursue
The path grey heads abhor?                    105

### XXII

For it leads to a crag's sheer edge with them;
  Youth, flowery all the way, there stops—
Not they; age threatens and they contemn,
  Till they reach the gulf wherein youth drops,
One inch from our life's safe hem!            110

### XXIII

With me, youth led...I will speak now,
  No longer watch you as you sit
Reading by fire-light, that great brow
  And the spirit-small hand propping it
Mutely, my heart knows how—                   115

### XXIV

When, if I think but deep enough,
  You are wont to answer, prompt as rhyme;
And you, too, find without a rebuff
  The response your soul seeks many a time
Piercing its fine flesh-stuff.                 120

### XXV

My own, confirm me! If I tread
  This path back, is it not in pride
To think how little I dreamed it led
  To an age so blest that by its side
Youth seems the waste instead?                 125

### XXVI

My own, see where the years conduct!
  At first, 'twas something our two souls
Should mix as mists do; each is sucked
  Into each now: on, the new stream rolls,
Whatever rocks obstruct.                    130

### XXVII

Think, when our one soul understands
  The great Word which makes all things new—
When earth breaks up and Heaven expands—
  How will the change strike me and you
In the House not made with hands?           135

### XXVIII

Oh, I must feel your brain prompt mine,
  Your heart anticipate my heart,
You must be just before, in fine,
  See and make me see, for your part,
New depths of the Divine!                   140

### XXIX

But who could have expected this,
  When we two drew together first
Just for the obvious human bliss,
  To satisfy life's daily thirst
With a thing men seldom miss?               145

### XXX

Come back with me to the first of all,
  Let us lean and love it over again—
Let us now forget and now recall,
  Break the rosary in a pearly rain,
And gather what we let fall!                150

Y. B.                                    4

### XXXI

What did I say?—that a small bird sings
  All day long, save when a brown pair
Of hawks from the wood float with wide wings
  Strained to a bell: 'gainst the noon-day glare
You count the streaks and rings.      155

### XXXII

But at afternoon or almost eve
  'Tis better; then the silence grows
To that degree, you half believe
  It must get rid of what it knows,
Its bosom does so heave.      160

### XXXIII

Hither we walked, then, side by side,
  Arm in arm and cheek to cheek,
And still I questioned or replied,
  While my heart, convulsed to really speak,
Lay choking in its pride.      165

### XXXIV

Silent the crumbling bridge we cross,
  And pity and praise the chapel sweet,
And care about the fresco's loss,
  And wish for our souls a like retreat,
And wonder at the moss.      170

### XXXV

Stoop and kneel on the settle under—
  Look through the window's grated square:
Nothing to see! for fear of plunder,
  The cross is down and the altar bare,
As if thieves don't fear thunder.      175

### XXXVI

We stoop and look in through the grate,
  See the little porch and rustic door,
Read duly the dead builder's date,
  Then cross the bridge we crossed before,
Take the path again—but wait!　　　　　180

### XXXVII

Oh moment, one and infinite!
  The water slips o'er stock and stone;
The West is tender, hardly bright:
  How grey at once is the evening grown—
One star, the chrysolite!　　　　　185

### XXXVIII

We two stood there with never a third,
  But each by each, as each knew well:
The sights we saw and the sounds we heard,
  The lights and the shades made up a spell
Till the trouble grew and stirred.　　　　　190

### XXXIX

Oh, the little more, and how much it is!
  And the little less, and what worlds away!
How a sound shall quicken content to bliss,
  Or a breath suspend the blood's best play,
And life be a proof of this!　　　　　195

### XL

Had she willed it, still had stood the screen
  So slight, so sure, 'twixt my love and her:
I could fix her face with a guard between,
  And find her soul as when friends confer,
Friends—lovers that might have been.　　　　　200

### XLI

For my heart had a touch of the woodland time,
   Wanting to sleep now over its best.
Shake the whole tree in the summer-prime,
   But bring to the last leaf no such test:
"Hold the last fast!" runs the rhyme.     205

### XLII

For a chance to make your little much,
   To gain a lover and lose a friend,
Venture the tree and a myriad such,
   When nothing you mar but the year can mend!
But a last leaf—fear to touch!     210

### XLIII

Yet should it unfasten itself and fall
   Eddying down till it find your face
At some slight wind—(best chance of all)
   Be your heart henceforth its dwelling-place
You trembled to forestal!     215

### XLIV

Worth how well, those dark grey eyes,
   —That hair so dark and dear, how worth
That a man should strive and agonise,
   And taste a very hell on earth
For the hope of such a prize!     220

### XLV

Oh, you might have turned and tried a man,
   Set him a space to weary and wear,
And prove which suited more your plan,
   His best of hope or his worst despair,
Yet end as he began.     225

### XLVI

But you spared me this, like the heart you are,
  And filled my empty heart at a word.
If you join two lives, there is oft a scar,
  They are one and one, with a shadowy third;
One near one is too far. 230

### XLVII

A moment after, and hands unseen
  Were hanging the night around us fast.
But we knew that a bar was broken between
  Life and life; we were mixed at last
In spite of the mortal screen. 235

### XLVIII

The forests had done it; there they stood;
  We caught for a second the powers at play:
They had mingled us so, for once and for good,
  Their work was done—we might go or stay,
They relapsed to their ancient mood. 240

### XLIX

How the world is made for each of us!
  How all we perceive and know in it
Tends to some moment's product thus,
  When a soul declares itself—to wit,
By its fruit—the thing it does! 245

### L

Be Hate that fruit or Love that fruit,
  It forwards the General Deed of Man,
And each of the Many helps to recruit
  The life of the race by a general plan;
Each living his own, to boot. 250

### LI

I am named and known by that hour's feat;
 There took my station and degree:
So grew my own small life complete
 As nature obtained her best of me—
One born to love you, Sweet!                    255

### LII

And to watch you sink by the fire-side now
 Back again, as you mutely sit
Musing by fire-light, that great brow
 And the spirit-small hand propping it
Yonder, my heart knows how!                    260

### LIII

So, the earth has gained by one man more,
 And the gain of earth must be Heaven's gain too,
And the whole is well worth thinking o'er
 When the autumn comes: which I mean to do
One day, as I said before.                    265


## XIV. THE GUARDIAN-ANGEL:

### A PICTURE AT FANO

#### I

Dear and great Angel, wouldst thou only leave
 That child, when thou hast done with him, for me!
Let me sit all the day here, that when eve
 Shall find performed thy special ministry
And time come for departure, thou, suspending    5
Thy flight, mayst see another child for tending,
 Another still, to quiet and retrieve.

II

Then I shall feel thee step one step, no more,
  From where thou standest now, to where I gaze,
—And suddenly my head is covered o'er          10
  With those wings, white above the child who prays
Now on that tomb—and I shall feel thee guarding
Me, out of all the world; for me, discarding
  Yon Heaven thy home, that waits and opes its door!

III

I would not look up thither past thy head          15
  Because the door opes, like that child, I know,
For I should have thy gracious face instead,
  Thou bird of God! And wilt thou bend me low
Like him, and lay, like his, my hands together,
And lift them up to pray, and gently tether          20
  Me, as thy lamb there, with thy garment's spread?

IV

If this was ever granted, I would rest
  My head beneath thine, while thy healing hands
Close-covered both my eyes beside thy breast,
  Pressing the brain, which too much thought expands,
Back to its proper size again, and smoothing          26
Distortion down till every nerve had soothing,
  And all lay quiet, happy and supprest.

V

How soon all worldly wrong would be repaired!
  I think how I should view the earth and skies          30
And sea, when once again my brow was bared
  After thy healing, with such different eyes.

O, world, as God has made it! all is beauty:
And knowing this, is love, and love is duty.
  What further may be sought for or declared?    35

### VI

Guercino drew this angel I saw teach
  (Alfred, dear friend!)—that little child to pray,
Holding the little hands up, each to each
  Pressed gently,—with his own head turned away
Over the earth where so much lay before him    40
Of work to do, though Heaven was opening o'er him,
  And he was left at Fano by the beach.

### VII

We were at Fano, and three times we went
  To sit and see him in his chapel there,
And drink his beauty to our soul's content    45
  —My angel with me too: and since I care
For dear Guercino's fame, (to which in power
And glory comes this picture for a dower,
  Fraught with a pathos so magnificent)

### VIII

And since he did not work so earnestly    50
  At all times, and has else endured some wrong,—
I took one thought his picture struck from me,
  And spread it out, translating it to song.
My Love is here. Where are you, dear old friend?
How rolls the Wairoa at your world's far end?    55
  This is Ancona, yonder is the sea.

## XV. INCIDENT OF THE FRENCH CAMP

### I

You know, we French stormed Ratisbon:
  A mile or so away
On a little mound, Napoleon
  Stood on our storming-day;
With neck out-thrust, you fancy how,     5
  Legs wide, arms locked behind,
As if to balance the prone brow
  Oppressive with its mind.

### II

Just as perhaps he mused "My plans
  "That soar, to earth may fall,     10
"Let once my army-leader Lannes
  "Waver at yonder wall,"—
Out 'twixt the battery-smokes there flew
  A rider, bound on bound
Full-galloping; nor bridle drew     15
  Until he reached the mound.

### III

Then off there flung in smiling joy,
  And held himself erect
By just his horse's mane, a boy:
  You hardly could suspect—     20
(So tight he kept his lips compressed,
  Scarce any blood came through)
You looked twice ere you saw his breast
  Was all but shot in two.

## IV

"Well," cried he, "Emperor, by God's grace　　25
"We've got you Ratisbon!
"The Marshal's in the market-place,
"And you'll be there anon
"To see your flag-bird flap his vans
"Where I, to heart's desire,　　　　　　30
"Perched him!" The Chief's eye flashed; his plans
Soared up again like fire.

## V

The Chief's eye flashed; but presently
Softened itself, as sheathes
A film the mother eagle's eye　　　　　35
When her bruised eaglet breathes:
"You're wounded!" "Nay," his soldier's pride
Touched to the quick, he said:
"I'm killed, Sire!" And, his Chief beside,
Smiling the boy fell dead.　　　　　　40

## XVI. MY LAST DUCHESS

### FERRARA.

That's my last Duchess painted on the wall,
Looking as if she were alive; I call
That piece a wonder, now: Frà Pandolf's hands
Worked busily a day, and there she stands.
Will't please you sit and look at her? I said　　5
"Frà Pandolf" by design, for never read
Strangers like you that pictured countenance,
The depth and passion of its earnest glance,

But to myself they turned (since none puts by
The curtain I have drawn for you, but I)     10
And seemed as they would ask me, if they durst,
How such a glance came there; so, not the
    first
Are you to turn and ask thus. Sir, 'twas not
Her husband's presence only, called that spot
Of joy into the Duchess' cheek: perhaps     15
Frà Pandolf chanced to say "Her mantle laps
"Over my Lady's wrist too much," or "Paint
"Must never hope to reproduce the faint
"Half-flush that dies along her throat;" such stuff
Was courtesy, she thought, and cause enough     20
For calling up that spot of joy. She had
A heart ... how shall I say? ... too soon made glad,
Too easily impressed; she liked whate'er
She looked on, and her looks went everywhere.
Sir, 'twas all one! My favour at her breast,     25
The dropping of the daylight in the West,
The bough of cherries some officious fool
Broke in the orchard for her, the white mule
She rode with round the terrace—all and each
Would draw from her alike the approving speech, 30
Or blush, at least. She thanked men,—good; but
    thanked
Somehow ... I know not how ... as if she ranked
My gift of a nine-hundred-years-old name
With anybody's gift. Who'd stoop to blame
This sort of trifling? Even had you skill     35
In speech—(which I have not)—to make your will
Quite clear to such an one, and say "Just this
"Or that in you disgusts me; here you miss,

"Or there exceed the mark"—and if she let
Herself be lessoned so, nor plainly set          40
Her wits to yours, forsooth, and made excuse,
—E'en then would be some stooping, and I chuse
Never to stoop. Oh, Sir, she smiled, no doubt,
Whene'er I passed her; but who passed without
Much the same smile? This grew; I gave commands;
Then all smiles stopped together. There she stands 46
As if alive. Will't please you rise? We'll meet
The company below, then. I repeat,
The Count your Master's known munificence
Is ample warrant that no just pretence          50
Of mine for dowry will be disallowed;
Though his fair daughter's self, as I avowed
At starting, is my object. Nay, we'll go
Together down, Sir! Notice Neptune, though,
Taming a sea-horse, thought a rarity,          55
Which Claus of Innsbruck cast in bronze for me.

## XVII. THE LAST RIDE TOGETHER

### I

I said—Then, Dearest, since 'tis so,
Since now at length my fate I know,
Since nothing all my love avails,
Since all, my life seemed meant for, fails,
  Since this was written and needs must be— 5
My whole heart rises up to bless
Your name in pride and thankfulness!
Take back the hope you gave,—I claim
Only a memory of the same,
—And this beside, if you will not blame,      10
  Your leave for one more last ride with me.

## II

My mistress bent that brow of hers;
Those deep dark eyes where pride demurs
When pity would be softening through,
Fixed me a breathing-while or two        15
    With life or death in the balance: right!
The blood replenished me again;
My last thought was at least not vain:
I and my mistress, side by side
Shall be together, breathe and ride,        20
So one day more am I deified—
    Who knows but the world may end to-night.

## III

Hush! if you saw some western cloud
All billowy-bosomed, over-bowed
By many benedictions—sun's        25
And moon's and evening star's at once—
    And so, you, looking and loving best,
Conscious grew, your passion drew
Cloud, sunset, moonrise, star-shine too,
Down on you, near and yet more near,        30
Till flesh must fade for heaven was here!—
Thus leant she and lingered—joy and fear!
    Thus lay she a moment on my breast.

## IV

Then we began to ride. My soul
Smoothed itself out—a long-cramped scroll        35
Freshening and fluttering in the wind.
Past hopes already lay behind.
    What need to strive with a life awry?

Had I said that, had I done this,
So might I gain, so might I miss.                    40
Might she have loved me? just as well
She might have hated,—who can tell?
Where had I been now if the worst befell?
   And here we are riding, she and I.

V

Fail I alone, in words and deeds?                  45
Why, all men strive and who succeeds?
We rode; it seemed my spirit flew,
Saw other regions, cities new,
   As the world rushed by on either side.
I thought,—All labour, yet no less                 50
Bear up beneath their unsuccess.
Look at the end of work, contrast
The petty Done, the Undone vast,
This Present of theirs with the hopeful Past!
   I hoped she would love me: here we ride.  55

VI

What hand and brain went ever paired?
What heart alike conceived and dared?
What act proved all its thought had been?
What will but felt the fleshly screen?
   We ride and I see her bosom heave.            60
There's many a crown for who can reach.
Ten lines, a statesman's life in each!
The flag stuck on a heap of bones,
A soldier's doing! what atones?
They scratch his name on the Abbey-stones.         65
   My riding is better, by their leave.

### VII

What does it all mean, poet? well,
Your brains beat into rhythm—you tell
What we felt only; you expressed
You hold things beautiful the best,                    70
  And pace them in rhyme so, side by side.
'Tis something, nay 'tis much—but then,
Have you yourself what's best for men?
Are you—poor, sick, old ere your time—
Nearer one whit your own sublime                       75
Than we who never have turned a rhyme?
  Sing, riding's a joy! For me, I ride.

### VIII

And you, great sculptor—so you gave
A score of years to Art, her slave,
And that's your Venus—whence we turn                   80
To yonder girl that fords the burn!
  You acquiesce, and shall I repine?
What, man of music, you, grown grey
With notes and nothing else to say,
Is this your sole praise from a friend,                85
"Greatly his opera's strains intend,
"But in music we know how fashions end!"
  I gave my youth—but we ride, in fine.

### IX

Who knows what's fit for us? Had fate
Proposed bliss here should sublimate                    90
My being; had I signed the bond—
Still one must lead some life beyond,
  —Have a bliss to die with, dim-descried.

This foot once planted on the goal,
This glory-garland round my soul,     95
Could I descry such? Try and test!
I sink back shuddering from the quest—
Earth being so good, would Heaven seem best?
  Now, Heaven and she are beyond this ride.

### X

And yet—she has not spoke so long!     100
What if Heaven be that, fair and strong
At life's best, with our eyes upturned
Whither life's flower is first discerned,
  We, fixed so, ever should so abide?
What if we still ride on, we two,     105
With life for ever old yet new,
Changed not in kind but in degree,
The instant made eternity,—
And Heaven just prove that I and she
  Ride, ride together, for ever ride?     110

## XVIII. THE PIED PIPER OF HAMELIN;
### A CHILD'S STORY
*(written for, and inscribed to, W. M. the younger.)*

### I

Hamelin Town's in Brunswick,
  By famous Hanover city;
    The river Weser, deep and wide,
    Washes its wall on the southern side;
    A pleasanter spot you never spied;     5
  But, when begins my ditty,
    Almost five hundred years ago,
    To see townsfolk suffer so
      From vermin, was a pity.

## II

Rats!                                                              10
They fought the dogs, and killed the cats,
  And bit the babies in the cradles,
  And ate the cheeses out of the vats,
    And licked the soup from the cooks' own ladles,
  Split open the kegs of salted sprats,              15
  Made nests inside men's Sunday hats,
  And even spoiled the women's chats,
      By drowning their speaking
      With shrieking and squeaking
In fifty different sharps and flats.                 20

## III

At last the people in a body
  To the Town Hall came flocking:
"'Tis clear," cried they, "our Mayor's a noddy;
  "And as for our Corporation—shocking
"To think we buy gowns lined with ermine      25
"For dolts that can't or won't determine
"What's best to rid us of our vermin!
"You hope, because you're old and obese,
"To find in the furry civic robe ease?
"Rouse up, Sirs! Give your brains a racking    30
"To find the remedy we're lacking,
"Or, sure as fate, we'll send you packing!"
At this the Mayor and Corporation
Quaked with a mighty consternation.

## IV

An hour they sate in council,                        35
  At length the Mayor broke silence:
"For a guilder I'd my ermine gown sell;

"I wish I were a mile hence!
"It's easy to bid one rack one's brain—
"I'm sure my poor head aches again                40
"I've scratched it so, and all in vain.
"Oh for a trap, a trap, a trap!"
Just as he said this, what should hap
At the chamber door but a gentle tap?
"Bless us," cried the Mayor, "what's that?"     45
(With the Corporation as he sat,
Looking little though wondrous fat;
Nor brighter was his eye, nor moister
Than a too-long-opened oyster,
Save when at noon his paunch grew mutinous    50
For a plate of turtle green and glutinous)
"Only a scraping of shoes on the mat?
"Anything like the sound of a rat
"Makes my heart go pit-a-pat!"


**V**

"Come in!"—the Mayor cried, looking bigger:  55
And in did come the strangest figure!
His queer long coat from heel to head
Was half of yellow and half of red;
And he himself was tall and thin,
With sharp blue eyes, each like a pin,          60
And light loose hair, yet swarthy skin,
No tuft on cheek nor beard on chin,
But lips where smiles went out and in—
There was no guessing his kith and kin!
And nobody could enough admire                  65
The tall man and his quaint attire:
Quoth one: "It's as my great-grandsire,

"Starting up at the Trump of Doom's tone,
"Had walked this way from his painted tomb-
    stone!"

### VI

He advanced to the council-table:                                70
And, "Please your honours," said he, "I'm able,
"By means of a secret charm, to draw
"All creatures living beneath the sun,
"That creep or swim or fly or run,
"After me so as you never saw!                                   75
"And I chiefly use my charm
"On creatures that do people harm,
"The mole and toad and newt and viper;
"And people call me the Pied Piper."
(And here they noticed round his neck                            80
A scarf of red and yellow stripe,
To match with his coat of the self-same cheque;
And at the scarf's end hung a pipe;
And his fingers, they noticed, were ever straying
As if impatient to be playing                                    85
Upon this pipe, as low it dangled
Over his vesture so old-fangled.)
"Yet," said he, "poor piper as I am,
"In Tartary I freed the Cham,
"Last June, from his huge swarms of gnats;                       90
"I eased in Asia the Nizam
"Of a monstrous brood of vampire-bats:
"And, as for what your brain bewilders,
"If I can rid your town of rats
"Will you give me a thousand guilders?"                          95
"One? fifty thousand!"—was the exclamation
Of the astonished Mayor and Corporation.

## VII

Into the street the Piper stept,
  Smiling first a little smile,
As if he knew what magic slept         100
  In his quiet pipe the while;
Then, like a musical adept,
To blow the pipe his lips he wrinkled,
And green and blue his sharp eyes twinkled
Like a candle-flame where salt is sprinkled;         105
And ere three shrill notes the pipe uttered,
You heard as if an army muttered;
And the muttering grew to a grumbling;
And the grumbling grew to a mighty rumbling;
And out of the houses the rats came tumbling.         110
Great rats, small rats, lean rats, brawny rats,
Brown rats, black rats, grey rats, tawny rats,
Grave old plodders, gay young friskers,
  Fathers, mothers, uncles, cousins,
Cocking tails and pricking whiskers,         115
  Families by tens and dozens,
Brothers, sisters, husbands, wives—
Followed the Piper for their lives.
From street to street he piped advancing,
And step for step they followed dancing,         120
Until they came to the river Weser
Wherein all plunged and perished!
—Save one who, stout as Julius Cæsar,
Swam across and lived to carry
(As he, the manuscript he cherished)         125
To Rat-land home his commentary:

Which was, "At the first shrill notes of the pipe,
"I heard a sound as of scraping tripe,
"And putting apples, wondrous ripe,
"Into a cider-press's gripe:      130
"And a moving away of pickle-tub-boards,
"And a leaving ajar of conserve-cupboards,
"And a drawing the corks of train-oil-flasks,
"And a breaking the hoops of butter-casks;
"And it seemed as if a voice      135
"(Sweeter far than by harp or by psaltery
"Is breathed) called out, Oh rats, rejoice!
"The world is grown to one vast drysaltery!
"So munch on, crunch on, take your nuncheon,
"Breakfast, supper, dinner, luncheon!      140
"And just as a bulky sugar-puncheon,
"All ready staved, like a great sun shone
"Glorious scarce an inch before me,
"Just as methought it said, Come, bore me!
"—I found the Weser rolling o'er me."      145

### VIII

You should have heard the Hamelin people
Ringing the bells till they rocked the steeple;
"Go," cried the Mayor, "and get long poles!
"Poke out the nests and block up the holes!
"Consult with carpenters and builders,      150
"And leave in our town not even a trace
"Of the rats!"—when suddenly, up the face
Of the Piper perked in the market-place,
With a, "First, if you please, my thousand guilders!"

## IX

A thousand guilders! The Mayor looked blue;     155
So did the Corporation too.
For council dinners made rare havock
With Claret, Moselle, Vin-de-Grave, Hock;
And half the money would replenish
Their cellar's biggest butt with Rhenish.     160
To pay this sum to a wandering fellow
With a gipsy coat of red and yellow!
"Beside," quoth the Mayor with a knowing wink,
"Our business was done at the river's brink;
"We saw with our eyes the vermin sink,     165
"And what's dead can't come to life, I think.
"So, friend, we're not the folks to shrink
"From the duty of giving you something for drink,
"And a matter of money to put in your poke;
"But as for the guilders, what we spoke     170
"Of them, as you very well know, was in joke.
"Beside, our losses have made us thrifty.
"A thousand guilders! Come, take fifty!"

## X

The Piper's face fell, and he cried,
"No trifling! I can't wait, beside!     175
"I've promised to visit by dinner time
"Bagdat, and accept the prime
"Of the Head-Cook's pottage, all he's rich in,
"For having left, in the Caliph's kitchen,
"Of a nest of scorpions no survivor—     180
"With him I proved no bargain-driver,
"With you, don't think I'll bate a stiver!
"And folks who put me in a passion
"May find me pipe to another fashion."

## XI

"How?" cried the Mayor, "d'ye think I'll brook     185
"Being worse treated than a Cook?
"Insulted by a lazy ribald
"With idle pipe and vesture piebald?
"You threaten us, fellow? Do your worst,
"Blow your pipe there till you burst!"     190

## XII

Once more he stept into the street;
  And to his lips again
Laid his long pipe of smooth straight cane;
  And ere he blew three notes (such sweet
Soft notes as yet musician's cunning     195
  Never gave the enraptured air)
There was a rustling, that seemed like a bustling
Of merry crowds justling at pitching and hustling,
Small feet were pattering, wooden shoes clattering,
Little hands clapping and little tongues chattering,   200
And, like fowls in a farm-yard when barley is scattering,
Out came the children running.
All the little boys and girls,
With rosy cheeks and flaxen curls,
And sparkling eyes and teeth like pearls,     205
Tripping and skipping, ran merrily after
The wonderful music with shouting and laughter.

## XIII

The Mayor was dumb, and the Council stood
As if they were changed into blocks of wood,
Unable to move a step, or cry     210
To the children merrily skipping by—
And could only follow with the eye

That joyous crowd at the Piper's back.
But how the Mayor was on the rack,
And the wretched Council's bosoms beat,      215
As the Piper turned from the High Street
To where the Weser rolled its waters
Right in the way of their sons and daughters!
However he turned from South to West,
And to Koppelberg Hill his steps addressed,      220
And after him the children pressed;
Great was the joy in every breast.
"He never can cross that mighty top!
"He's forced to let the piping drop,
"And we shall see our children stop!"      225
When, lo, as they reached the mountain's side,
A wondrous portal opened wide,
As if a cavern was suddenly hollowed;
And the Piper advanced and the children followed,
And when all were in to the very last,      230
The door in the mountain side shut fast.
Did I say, all? No! One was lame,
And could not dance the whole of the way;
And in after years, if you would blame
His sadness, he was used to say,—      235
"It's dull in our town since my playmates left!
"I can't forget that I'm bereft
"Of all the pleasant sights they see,
"Which the Piper also promised me.
"For he led us, he said, to a joyous land,      240
"Joining the town and just at hand,
"Where waters gushed and fruit-trees grew,
"And flowers put forth a fairer hue,
"And everything was strange and new;

"The sparrows were brighter than peacocks here,    245
"And their dogs outran our fallow deer,
"And honey-bees had lost their stings,
"And horses were born with eagles' wings:
"And just as I became assured
"My lame foot would be speedily cured,             250
"The music stopped and I stood still,
"And found myself outside the Hill,
"Left alone against my will,
"To go now limping as before,
"And never hear of that country more!"             255

### XIV

Alas, alas for Hamelin!
   There came into many a burgher's pate
   A text which says, that Heaven's Gate
   Opes to the Rich at as easy rate
As the needle's eye takes a camel in!              260
The Mayor sent East, West, North and South
To offer the Piper, by word of mouth,
   Wherever it was men's lot to find him,
Silver and gold to his heart's content,
If he'd only return the way he went,               265
   And bring the children behind him.
But when they saw 'twas a lost endeavour,
And Piper and dancers were gone for ever,
They made a decree that lawyers never
   Should think their records dated duly           270
If, after the day of the month and year,
These words did not as well appear,
"And so long after what happened here
   "On the Twenty-second of Júly,

"Thirteen hundred and seventy-six:"                    275
And the better in memory to fix
The place of the children's last retreat,
They called it, the Pied Piper's Street—
Where any one playing on pipe or tabor
Was sure for the future to lose his labour.             280
Nor suffered they hostelry or tavern
   To shock with mirth a street so solemn;
But opposite the place of the cavern
   They wrote the story on a column,
And on the great Church-Window painted                 285
The same, to make the world acquainted
How their children were stolen away;
And there it stands to this very day.
And I must not omit to say
That in Transylvania there's a tribe                    290
Of alien people that ascribe
The outlandish ways and dress
On which their neighbours lay such stress,
To their fathers and mothers having risen
Out of some subterraneous prison                       295
Into which they were trepanned
Long time ago in a mighty band
Out of Hamelin town in Brunswick land,
But how or why, they don't understand.


## XV

So, Willy, let me and you be wipers                    300
Of scores out with all men—especially pipers:
And, whether they pipe us free, from rats or fróm mice,
If we've promised them aught, let us keep our promise.

## XIX. A GRAMMARIAN'S FUNERAL

[*Time*—Shortly after the revival of learning in Europe.]

Let us begin and carry up this corpse,
  Singing together.
Leave we the common crofts, the vulgar thorpes,
  Each in its tether
Sleeping safe on the bosom of the plain,            5
  Cared-for till cock-crow:
Look out if yonder's not the day again
  Rimming the rock-row!
That's the appropriate country; there, man's thought,
  Rarer, intenser,                                  10
Self-gathered for an outbreak, as it ought,
  Chafes in the censer!
Leave we the unlettered plain its herd and crop;
  Seek we sepulture
On a tall mountain, citied to the top,              15
  Crowded with culture!
All the peaks soar, but one the rest excels;
  Clouds overcome it;
No, yonder sparkle is the citadel's
  Circling its summit!                              20
Thither our path lies; wind we up the heights:
  Wait ye the warning?
Our low life was the level's and the night's;
  He's for the morning!
Step to a tune, square chests, erect the head,      25
  'Ware the beholders!
This is our master, famous, calm, and dead,
  Borne on our shoulders.

Sleep, crop and herd! sleep, darkling thorpe and croft,
    Safe from the weather!          30
He, whom we convey to his grave aloft,
    Singing together,
He was a man born with thy face and throat,
    Lyric Apollo!
Long he lived nameless: how should spring take note   35
    Winter would follow?
Till lo, the little touch, and youth was gone!
    Cramped and diminished,
Moaned he, "New measures, other feet anon!
    "My dance is finished"?          40
No, that's the world's way! (keep the mountain-side,
    Make for the city,)
He knew the signal, and stepped on with pride
    Over men's pity;
Left play for work, and grappled with the world    45
    Bent on escaping:
"What's in the scroll," quoth he, "thou keepest furled?
    "Show me their shaping,
"Theirs, who most studied man, the bard and sage,—
    "Give!"—So he gowned him,        50
Straight got by heart that book to its last page:
    Learned, we found him!
Yea, but we found him bald too—eyes like lead,
    Accents uncertain:
"Time to taste life," another would have said,     55
    "Up with the curtain!"—
This man said rather, "Actual life comes next?
    "Patience a moment!
"Grant I have mastered learning's crabbed text,
    "Still, there's the comment.         60

"Let me know all! Prate not of most or least,
  "Painful or easy:
"Even to the crumbs I'd fain eat up the feast,
  "Ay, nor feel queasy!"
Oh, such a life as he resolved to live,          65
  When he had learned it,
When he had gathered all books had to give!
  Sooner, he spurned it.
Image the whole, then execute the parts—
  Fancy the fabric                               70
Quite, ere you build, ere steel strike fire from
    quartz,
  Ere mortar dab brick!


(Here's the town-gate reached: there's the market-
    place
  Gaping before us.)
Yea, this in him was the peculiar grace          75
  (Hearten our chorus)
That before living he'd learn how to live—
  No end to learning:
Earn the means first—God surely will contrive
  Use for our earning.                           80
Others mistrust and say—"But time escapes!
  "Live now or never!"
He said, "What's time? leave Now for dogs and
    apes!
  "Man has Forever."
Back to his book then: deeper drooped his head: 85
  *Calculus* racked him:
Leaden before, his eyes grew dross of lead:
  *Tussis* attacked him.

"Now, Master, take a little rest!"—not he!
    (Caution redoubled!                                   90
Step two a-breast, the way winds narrowly)
    Not a whit troubled,
Back to his studies, fresher than at first,
    Fierce as a dragon
He (soul-hydroptic with a sacred thirst)        95
    Sucked at the flagon.
Oh, if we draw a circle premature,
    Heedless of far gain,
Greedy for quick returns of profit, sure,
    Bad is our bargain!                                 100
Was it not great? did not he throw on God,
    (He loves the burthen)—
God's task to make the heavenly period
    Perfect the earthen?
Did not he magnify the mind, show clear        105
    Just what it all meant?
He would not discount life, as fools do here,
    Paid by instalment!
He ventured neck or nothing—Heaven's success
    Found, or earth's failure:                        110
"Wilt thou trust death or not?"  He answered "Yes!
    "Hence with life's pale lure!"
That low man seeks a little thing to do,
    Sees it and does it:
This high man, with a great thing to pursue,   115
    Dies ere he knows it.
That low man goes on adding one to one,
    His hundred's soon hit:
This high man, aiming at a million,
    Misses an unit.                                     120

That, has the world here—should he need the next,
    Let the world mind him!
This, throws himself on God, and unperplext
    Seeking shall find Him.
So, with the throttling hands of Death at strife,    125
    Ground he at grammar;
Still, thro' the rattle, parts of speech were rife:
    While he could stammer
He settled *Hoti's* business—let it be!—
    Properly based *Oun*—                              130
Gave us the doctrine of the enclitic *De*,
    Dead from the waist down.
Well, here's the platform, here's the proper place.
    Hail to your purlieus
All ye highfliers of the feathered race,             135
    Swallows and curlews!
Here's the top-peak! the multitude below
    Live, for they can, there.
This man decided not to Live but Know—
    Bury this man there?                               140
Here—here's his place, where meteors shoot, clouds
        form,
    Lightnings are loosened,
Stars come and go! let joy break with the storm,
    Peace let the dew send!
Lofty designs must close in like effects:            145
    Loftily lying,
Leave him—still loftier than the world suspects,
    Living and dying.

# XX. HOLY-CROSS DAY

## ON WHICH THE JEWS WERE FORCED TO ATTEND AN
## ANNUAL CHRISTIAN SERMON IN ROME

["Now was come about Holy-Cross Day, and now must my lord preach his first sermon to the Jews: as it was of old cared for in the merciful bowels of the Church, that, so to speak, a crumb at least from her conspicuous table here in Rome, should be, though but once yearly, cast to the famishing dogs, under-trampled and bespitten-upon beneath the feet of the guests. And a moving sight in truth, this, of so many of the besotted, blind, restive and ready-to-perish Hebrews! now maternally brought—nay, (for He saith, 'Compel them to come in') haled, as it were, by the head and hair, and against their obstinate hearts, to partake of the heavenly grace. What awakening, what striving with tears, what working of a yeasty conscience! Nor was my lord wanting to himself on so apt an occasion; witness the abundance of conversions which did incontinently reward him: though not to my lord be altogether the glory."—*Diary by the Bishop's Secretary*, 1600.]

Though what the Jews really said, on thus being driven to church, was rather to this effect :—

### I

Fee, faw, fum! bubble and squeak!
Blessedest Thursday's the fat of the week.
Rumble and tumble, sleek and rough,
Stinking and savoury, smug and gruff,
Take the church-road, for the bell's due chime          5
Gives us the summons—'tis sermon-time.

### II

Boh, here's Barnabas! Job, that's you?
Up stumps Solomon—bustling too?
Shame, man! greedy beyond your years
To handsel the bishop's shaving-shears?          10
Fair play's a jewel! leave friends in the lurch?
Stand on a line ere you start for the church.

### III

Higgledy piggledy, packed we lie,
Rats in a hamper, swine in a sty,
Wasps in a bottle, frogs in a sieve,                     15
Worms in a carcase, fleas in a sleeve.
Hist! square shoulders, settle your thumbs
And buzz for the bishop—here he comes.

### IV

Bow, wow, wow—a bone for the dog!
I liken his Grace to an acorned hog.                     20
What, a boy at his side, with the bloom of a lass,
To help and handle my lord's hour-glass!
Didst ever behold so lithe a chine?
His cheek hath laps like a fresh-singed swine.

### V

Aaron's asleep—shove hip to haunch,                      25
Or somebody deal him a dig in the paunch!
Look at the purse with the tassel and knob,
And the gown with the angel and thingumbob.
What's he at, quotha? reading his text!
Now you've his curtsey—and what comes next?             30

### VI

See to our converts—you doomed black dozen—
No stealing away—nor cog nor cozen!
You five that were thieves, deserve it fairly;
You seven that were beggars, will live less sparely;
You took your turn and dipped in the hat,               35
Got fortune—and fortune gets you; mind that!

### VII

Give your first groan—compunction's at work;
And soft! from a Jew you mount to a Turk.
Lo, Micah,—the self-same beard on chin
He was four times already converted in!          40
Here's a knife, clip quick—it's a sign of grace—
Or he ruins us all with his hanging-face.

### VIII

Whom now is the bishop a-leering at?
I know a point where his text falls pat.
I'll tell him to-morrow, a word just now          45
Went to my heart and made me vow
I meddle no more with the worst of trades—
Let somebody else pay his serenades.

### IX

Groan all together now, whee—hee—hee!
It's a-work, it's a-work, ah, woe is me!          50
It began, when a herd of us, picked and placed,
Were spurred through the Corso, stripped to the
    waist;
Jew-brutes, with sweat and blood well spent
To usher in worthily Christian Lent.

### X

It grew, when the hangman entered our bounds,    55
Yelled, pricked us out to his church like hounds.
It got to a pitch, when the hand indeed
Which gutted my purse, would throttle my creed.
And it overflows, when, to even the odd,
Men I helped to their sins, help me to their God.    60

### XI

But now, while the scapegoats leave our flock,
And the rest sit silent and count the clock,
Since forced to muse the appointed time
On these precious facts and truths sublime,—
Let us fitly employ it, under our breath,     65
In saying Ben Ezra's Song of Death.

### XII

For Rabbi Ben Ezra, the night he died,
Called sons and sons' sons to his side,
And spoke, "This world has been harsh and strange;
Something is wrong, there needeth a change.     70
But what, or where? at the last, or first?
In one point only we sinned, at worst.

### XIII

"The Lord will have mercy on Jacob yet,
And again in his border see Israel set.
When Judah beholds Jerusalem,     75
The stranger-seed shall be joined to them:
To Jacob's House shall the Gentiles cleave.
So the Prophet saith and his sons believe.

### XIV

"Ay, the children of the chosen race
Shall carry and bring them to their place:     80
In the land of the Lord shall lead the same,
Bondsmen and handmaids. Who shall blame,
When the slaves enslave, the oppressed ones o'er
The oppressor triumph for evermore?

### XV

"God spoke, and gave us the word to keep:     85
Bade never fold the hands nor sleep
'Mid a faithless world,—at watch and ward,
Till Christ at the end relieve our guard.
By His servant Moses the watch was set:
Though near upon cock-crow, we keep it yet.     90

### XVI

"Thou! if Thou wast He, who at mid-watch came,
By the starlight, naming a dubious Name!
And if, too heavy with sleep—too rash
With fear—O Thou, if that martyr-gash
Fell on Thee coming to take Thine own,     95
And we gave the Cross, when we owed the Throne—

### XVII

"Thou art the Judge. We are bruised thus.
But, the judgment over, join sides with us!
Thine too is the cause! and not more Thine
Than ours, is the work of these dogs and swine,    100
Whose life laughs through and spits at their creed,
Who maintain Thee in word, and defy Thee in deed!

### XVIII

"We withstood Christ then? be mindful how
At least we withstand Barabbas now!
Was our outrage sore? but the worst we spared,    105
To have called these—Christians, had we dared!
Let defiance to them, pay mistrust of Thee,
And Rome make amends for Calvary!

## XIX

"By the torture, prolonged from age to age,
By the infamy, Israel's heritage,                         110
By the Ghetto's plague, by the garb's disgrace,
By the badge of shame, by the felon's place,
By the branding-tool, the bloody whip,
And the summons to Christian fellowship,—

## XX

"We boast our proof that at least the Jew       115
Would wrest Christ's name from the Devil's crew.
Thy face took never so deep a shade
But we fought them in it, God our aid!
A trophy to bear, as we march, Thy band,
South, East, and on to the Pleasant Land!"      120

[*The present Pope abolished this bad business of the sermon.*—R.B.]

## XXI. THE STATUE AND THE BUST

There's a palace in Florence, the world knows well,
And a statue watches it from the square,
And this story of both do our townsmen tell.

Ages ago, a lady there,
At the farthest window facing the East           5
Asked, "Who rides by with the royal air?"

The brides-maids' prattle around her ceased;
She leaned forth, one on either hand;
They saw how the blush of the bride increased—

They felt by its beats her heart expand—　　10
As one at each ear and both in a breath
Whispered, "The Great-Duke Ferdinand."

That selfsame instant, underneath,
The Duke rode past in his idle way,
Empty and fine like a swordless sheath.　　15

Gay he rode, with a friend as gay,
Till he threw his head back—"Who is she?"
—"A Bride the Riccardi brings home to-day."

Hair in heaps lay heavily
Over a pale brow spirit-pure—　　20
Carved like the heart of the coal-black tree,

Crisped like a war-steed's encolure—
And vainly sought to dissemble her eyes
Of the blackest black our eyes endure.

And lo, a blade for a knight's emprise　　25
Filled the fine empty sheath of a man,—
The Duke grew straightway brave and wise.

He looked at her, as a lover can;
She looked at him, as one who awakes,—
The Past was a sleep, and her life began.　　30

Now, love so ordered for both their sakes,
A feast was held that selfsame night
In the pile which the mighty shadow makes.

(For Via Larga is three-parts light,
But the Palace overshadows one,　　35
Because of a crime which may God requite!

To Florence and God the wrong was done,
Through the first republic's murder there
By Cosimo and his cursed son.)

The Duke (with the statue's face in the square)   40
Turned in the midst of his multitude
At the bright approach of the bridal pair.

Face to face the lovers stood
A single minute and no more,
While the bridegroom bent as a man subdued—   45

Bowed till his bonnet brushed the floor—
For the Duke on the lady a kiss conferred,
As the courtly custom was of yore.

In a minute can lovers exchange a word?
If a word did pass, which I do not think,   50
Only one out of the thousand heard.

That was the bridegroom. At day's brink
He and his bride were alone at last
In a bed-chamber by a taper's blink.

Calmly he said that her lot was cast,   55
That the door she had passed was shut on her
Till the final catafalk repassed.

The world meanwhile, its noise and stir,
Through a certain window facing the East
She could watch like a convent's chronicler.   60

Since passing the door might lead to a feast,
And a feast might lead to so much beside,
He, of many evils, chose the least.

"Freely I choose too," said the bride—
"Your window and its world suffice,"        65
Replied the tongue, while the heart replied—

"If I spend the night with that devil twice,
May his window serve as my loop of hell
Whence a damned soul looks on Paradise!

"I fly to the Duke who loves me well,        70
Sit by his side and laugh at sorrow
Ere I count another ave-bell.

"'Tis only the coat of a page to borrow,
And tie my hair in a horse-boy's trim,
And I save my soul—but not to-morrow"—        75

(She checked herself and her eye grew dim)—
"My father tarries to bless my state:
I must keep it one day more for him.

"Is one day more so long to wait?
Moreover the Duke rides past, I know;        80
We shall see each other, sure as fate."

She turned on her side and slept. Just so!
So we resolve on a thing and sleep:
So did the lady, ages ago.

That night the Duke said, "Dear or cheap        85
As the cost of this cup of bliss may prove
To body or soul, I will drain it deep."

And on the morrow, bold with love,
He beckoned the bridegroom (close on call,
As his duty bade, by the Duke's alcove)        90

And smiled "'Twas a very funeral,
Your lady will think, this feast of ours,—
A shame to efface, whate'er befall!

"What if we break from the Arno bowers,
And try if Petraja, cool and green,          95
Cure last night's fault with this morning's flowers?"

The bridegroom, not a thought to be seen
On his steady brow and quiet mouth,
Said, "Too much favour for me so mean!

"But, alas! my lady leaves the South;          100
Each wind that comes from the Apennine
Is a menace to her tender youth:

"Nor a way exists, the wise opine,
If she quits her palace twice this year,
To avert the flower of life's decline."          105

Quoth the Duke, "A sage and a kindly fear.
Moreover Petraja is cold this spring:
Be our feast to-night as usual here!"

And then to himself—"Which night shall bring
Thy bride to her lover's embraces, fool—          110
Or I am the fool, and thou art the king!

"Yet my passion must wait a night, nor cool—
For to-night the Envoy arrives from France,
Whose heart I unlock with thyself, my tool.

"I need thee still and might miss perchance.          115
To-day is not wholly lost, beside,
With its hope of my lady's countenance:

"For I ride—what should I do but ride?
And passing her palace, if I list,
May glance at its window—well betide!"     120

So said, so done: nor the lady missed
One ray that broke from the ardent brow,
Nor a curl of the lips where the spirit kissed.

Be sure that each renewed the vow,
No morrow's sun should arise and set     125
And leave them then as it left them now.

But next day passed, and next day yet,
With still fresh cause to wait one day more
Ere each leaped over the parapet.

And still, as love's brief morning wore,     130
With a gentle start, half smile, half sigh,
They found love not as it seemed before.

They thought it would work infallibly,
But not in despite of heaven and earth—
The rose would blow when the storm passed by.     135

Meantime they could profit in winter's dearth
By winter's fruits that supplant the rose:
The world and its ways have a certain worth!

And to press a point while these oppose
Were a simple policy; better wait:     140
We lose no friends and we gain no foes.

Meantime, worse fates than a lover's fate,
Who daily may ride and pass and look
Where his lady watches behind the grate!

And she—she watched the square like a book  145
Holding one picture and only one,
Which daily to find she undertook:

When the picture was reached the book was done,
And she turned from the picture at night to scheme
Of tearing it out for herself next sun.  150

So weeks grew months, years—gleam by gleam
The glory dropped from their youth and love,
And both perceived they had dreamed a dream;

Which hovered as dreams do, still above,—
But who can take a dream for a truth?  155
Oh, hide our eyes from the next remove!

One day as the lady saw her youth
Depart, and the silver thread that streaked
Her hair, and, worn by the serpent's tooth,

The brow so puckered, the chin so peaked,—  160
And wondered who the woman was,
Hollow-eyed and haggard-cheeked,

Fronting her silent in the glass—
"Summon here," she suddenly said,
"Before the rest of my old self pass,  165

"Him, the Carver, a hand to aid,
Who fashions the clay no love will change,
And fixes a beauty never to fade.

"Let Robbia's craft so apt and strange
Arrest the remains of young and fair,  170
And rivet them while the seasons range.

"Make me a face on the window there
Waiting as ever, mute the while,
My love to pass below in the square!

"And let me think that it may beguile          175
Dreary days which the dead must spend
Down in their darkness under the aisle—

"To say, 'What matters it at the end?
I did no more while my heart was warm,
Than does that image, my pale-faced friend.'     180

"Where is the use of the lip's red charm,
The heaven of hair, the pride of the brow,
And the blood that blues the inside arm—

"Unless we turn, as the soul knows how,
The earthly gift to an end divine?          185
A lady of clay is as good, I trow."

But long ere Robbia's cornice, fine
With flowers and fruits which leaves enlace,
Was set where now is the empty shrine—

(And, leaning out of a bright blue space,      190
As a ghost might lean from a chink of sky,
The passionate pale lady's face—

Eyeing ever with earnest eye
And quick-turned neck at its breathless stretch,
Some one who ever is passing by—)          195

The Duke had sighed like the simplest wretch
In Florence, "Youth—my dream escapes!
Will its record stay?"  And he bade them fetch

Some subtle moulder of brazen shapes—
"Can the soul, the will, die out of a man          200
Ere his body find the grave that gapes?

"John of Douay shall effect my plan,
Set me on horseback here aloft,
Alive, as the crafty sculptor can,

"In the very square I have crossed so oft!          205
That men may admire, when future suns
Shall touch the eyes to a purpose soft,

"While the mouth and the brow stay brave in bronze—
Admire and say, 'When he was alive,
How he would take his pleasure once!'          210

"And it shall go hard but I contrive
To listen the while and laugh in my tomb
At idleness which aspires to strive."

---

So! while these wait the trump of doom,
How do their spirits pass, I wonder,          215
Nights and days in the narrow room?

Still, I suppose, they sit and ponder
What a gift life was, ages ago,
Six steps out of the chapel yonder.

Only they see not God, I know,          220
Nor all that chivalry of His,
The soldier-saints who, row on row,

Burn upward each to his point of bliss—
Since, the end of life being manifest,
He had burned his way thro' the world to this.          225

I hear you reproach "But delay was best,
For their end was a crime!"—Oh, a crime will do
As well, I reply, to serve for a test,

As a virtue golden through and through,
Sufficient to vindicate itself                    230
And prove its worth at a moment's view.

Must a game be played for the sake of pelf?
Where a button goes, 'twere an epigram
To offer the stamp of the very Guelph.

The true has no value beyond the sham:          235
As well the counter as coin, I submit,
When your table's a hat, and your prize, a dram.

Stake your counter as boldly every whit,
Venture as truly, use the same skill,
Do your best, whether winning or losing it,      240

If you choose to play!—is my principle.
Let a man contend to the uttermost
For his life's set prize, be it what it will!

The counter our lovers staked was lost
As surely as if it were lawful coin:            245
And the sin I impute to each frustrate ghost

Is, the unlit lamp and the ungirt loin,
Though the end in sight was a vice, I say.
You of the virtue, (we issue join)
How strive you? *De te, fabula!*                250

## XXII. "CHILDE ROLAND TO THE DARK TOWER CAME"

(See Edgar's Song in 'LEAR')

### I

My first thought was, he lied in every word,
  That hoary cripple, with malicious eye
  Askance to watch the working of his lie
On mine, and mouth scarce able to afford
Suppression of the glee that pursed and scored      5
  Its edge at one more victim gained thereby.

### II

What else should he be set for, with his staff?
  What, save to waylay with his lies, ensnare
  All travellers that might find him posted there,
And ask the road?  I guessed what skull-like laugh   10
Would break, what crutch 'gin write my epitaph
  For pastime in the dusty thoroughfare,

### III

If at his counsel I should turn aside
  Into that ominous tract which, all agree,
  Hides the Dark Tower.  Yet acquiescingly       15
I did turn as he pointed; neither pride
Nor hope rekindling at the end descried,
So much as gladness that some end might be.

### IV

For, what with my whole world-wide wandering,
  What with my search drawn out thro' years, my
        hope                                              20
  Dwindled into a ghost not fit to cope
With that obstreperous joy success would bring,—
I hardly tried now to rebuke the spring
  My heart made, finding failure in its scope.

### V

As when a sick man very near to death         25
  Seems dead indeed, and feels begin and end
  The tears and takes the farewell of each friend,
And hears one bid the other go, draw breath
Freelier outside, ("since all is o'er," he saith,
  "And the blow fallen no grieving can amend";)   30

### VI

While some discuss if near the other graves
  Be room enough for this, and when a day
  Suits best for carrying the corpse away,
With care about the banners, scarves and staves,—
And still the man hears all, and only craves     35
  He may not shame such tender love and stay.

### VII

Thus, I had so long suffered in this quest,
  Heard failure prophesied so oft, been writ
  So many times among "The Band"—to wit,
The knights who to the Dark Tower's search addressed 40
Their steps—that just to fail as they, seemed best,
  And all the doubt was now—should I be fit.

### VIII

So, quiet as despair, I turned from him,
  That hateful cripple, out of his highway
  Into the path he pointed. All the day          45
Had been a dreary one at best, and dim
Was settling to its close, yet shot one grim
  Red leer to see the plain catch its estray.

### IX

For mark! no sooner was I fairly found
  Pledged to the plain, after a pace or two,     50
  Than, pausing to throw backward a last view
To the safe road, 'twas gone; grey plain all round:
Nothing but plain to the horizon's bound.
  I might go on; nought else remained to do.

### X

So, on I went. I think I never saw              55
  Such starved ignoble nature; nothing throve:
  For flowers—as well expect a cedar grove!
But cockle, spurge, according to their law
Might propagate their kind, with none to awe,
  You'd think: a burr had been a treasure-trove.   60

### XI

No! penury, inertness and grimace,
  In some strange sort, were the land's portion. "See
  Or shut your eyes," said Nature peevishly,
"It nothing skills: I cannot help my case:
'Tis the Last Judgment's fire must cure this place, 65
  Calcine its clods and set my prisoners free."

## XII

If there pushed any ragged thistle-stalk
  Above its mates, the head was chopped—the bents
  Were jealous else. What made those holes and rents
In the dock's harsh swarth leaves—bruised as to
    baulk                             70
All hope of greenness? 'tis a brute must walk
  Pashing their life out, with a brute's intents.

## XIII

As for the grass, it grew as scant as hair
  In leprosy; thin dry blades pricked the mud
  Which underneath looked kneaded up with blood. 75
One stiff blind horse, his every bone a-stare,
Stood stupefied, however he came there:
  Thrust out past service from the devil's stud!

## XIV

Alive? he might be dead for aught I know,
  With that red, gaunt and colloped neck a-strain, 80
  And shut eyes underneath the rusty mane;
Seldom went such grotesqueness with such woe;
I never saw a brute I hated so;
  He must be wicked to deserve such pain.

## XV

I shut my eyes and turned them on my heart.    85
  As a man calls for wine before he fights,
  I asked one draught of earlier, happier sights,
Ere fitly I could hope to play my part.
Think first, fight afterwards—the soldier's art:
  One taste of the old time sets all to rights!    90

### XVI

Not it!  I fancied Cuthbert's reddening face
  Beneath its garniture of curly gold,
  Dear fellow, till I almost felt him fold
An arm in mine to fix me to the place,
That way he used.  Alas, one night's disgrace!  95
  Out went my heart's new fire and left it cold.

### XVII

Giles, then, the soul of honour—there he stands
  Frank as ten years ago when knighted first.
  What honest men should dare (he said) he durst.
Good—but the scene shifts—faugh! what hangman's
    hands  100
Pin to his breast a parchment? his own bands
  Read it.  Poor traitor, spit upon and curst!

### XVIII

Better this Present than a Past like that;
  Back therefore to my darkening path again.
  No sound, no sight as far as eye could strain.  105
Will the night send a howlet or a bat?
I asked: when something on the dismal flat
  Came to arrest my thoughts and change their train.

### XIX

A sudden little river crossed my path
  As unexpected as a serpent comes.  110
  No sluggish tide congenial to the glooms—
This, as it frothed by, might have been a bath
For the fiend's glowing hoof—to see the wrath
  Of its black eddy bespate with flakes and spumes.

### XX

So petty yet so spiteful! all along,                 115
  Low scrubby alders kneeled down over it;
  Drenched willows flung them headlong in a fit
Of mute despair, a suicidal throng:
The river which had done them all the wrong,
  Whate'er that was. rolled by, deterred no whit. 120

### XXI

Which, while I forded,—good saints, how I feared
  To set my foot upon a dead man's cheek,
  Each step, or feel the spear I thrust to seek
For hollows, tangled in his hair or beard!
—It may have been a water-rat I speared,         125
  But, ugh! it sounded like a baby's shriek.

### XXII

Glad was I when I reached the other bank.
  Now for a better country.  Vain presage!
  Who were the strugglers, what war did they wage
Whose savage trample thus could pad the dank   130
Soil to a plash? toads in a poisoned tank,
  Or wild cats in a red-hot iron cage—

### XXIII

The fight must so have seemed in that fell cirque.
  What penned them there, with all the plain to
      choose?
No foot-print leading to that horrid mews,         135
None out of it.  Mad brewage set to work
      brains, no doubt, like galley-slaves the Turk
  Pits for his pastime, Christians against Jews.

### XXIV

And more than that—a furlong on—why, there!
  What bad use was that engine for, that wheel, 140
  Or brake, not wheel—that harrow fit to reel
Men's bodies out like silk? with all the air
Of Tophet's tool, on earth left unaware,
  Or brought to sharpen its rusty teeth of steel.

### XXV

Then came a bit of stubbed ground, once a wood, 145
  Next a marsh, it would seem, and now mere earth
  Desperate and done with; (so a fool finds mirth,
Makes a thing and then mars it, till his mood
Changes and off he goes!) within a rood—
  Bog, clay and rubble, sand and stark black
    dearth. 150

### XXVI

Now blotches rankling, coloured gay and grim,
  Now patches where some leanness of the soil's
  Broke into moss or substances like boils;
Then came some palsied oak, a cleft in him
Like a distorted mouth that splits its rim 155
  Gaping at death, and dies while it recoils.

### XXVII

And just as far as ever from the end!
  Nought in the distance but the evening, nought
  To point my footstep further! At the thought,
A great black bird, Apollyon's bosom-friend, 160
Sailed past, nor beat his wide wing dragon-penned
  That brushed my cap—perchance the guide I sought.

## XXVIII

For, looking up, aware I somehow grew,
  'Spite of the dusk, the plain had given place
  All round to mountains—with such name to grace 165
Mere ugly heights and heaps now stolen in view.
How thus they had surprised me,—solve it, you!
  How to get from them was no clearer case.

## XXIX

Yet half I seemed to recognise some trick
  Of mischief happened to me, God knows when— 170
  In a bad dream perhaps. Here ended, then,
Progress this way. When, in the very nick
Of giving up, one time more, came a click
  As when a trap shuts—you're inside the den!

## XXX

Burningly it came on me all at once, 175
  This was the place! those two hills on the right
  Crouched like two bulls locked horn in horn in fight;
While to the left, a tall scalped mountain ... Dunce,
Fool, to be dozing at the very nonce,
  After a life spent training for the sight! 180

## XXXI

What in the midst lay but the Tower itself?
  The round squat turret, blind as the fool's heart,
  Built of brown stone, without a counterpart
In the whole world. The tempest's mocking elf
Points to the shipman thus the unseen shelf 185
  He strikes on, only when the timbers start.

### XXXII

Not see? because of night perhaps?—Why, day
  Came back again for that! before it left,
  The dying sunset kindled through a cleft:
The hills, like giants at a hunting, lay,     190
Chin upon hand, to see the game at bay,—
  "Now stab and end the creature—to the heft!"

### XXXIII

Not hear? when noise was everywhere! it tolled
  Increasing like a bell. Names in my ears,
  Of all the lost adventurers my peers,—     195
How such a one was strong, and such was bold,
And such was fortunate, yet each of old
  Lost, lost! one moment knelled the woe of years.

### XXXIV

There they stood, ranged along the hill-sides, met
  To view the last of me, a living frame     200
  For one more picture! in a sheet of flame
I saw them and I knew them all. And yet
Dauntless the slug-horn to my lips I set,
  And blew. "*Childe Roland to the Dark Tower came.*"

## XXIII. AN EPISTLE

### CONTAINING THE

##### STRANGE MEDICAL EXPERIENCE OF KARSHISH,

#### THE ARAB PHYSICIAN

Karshish, the picker-up of learning's crumbs,
The not-incurious in God's handiwork
(This man's-flesh He hath admirably made,
Blown like a bubble, kneaded like a paste,
To coop up and keep down on earth a space      5
That puff of vapour from His mouth, man's soul)
—To Abib, all-sagacious in our art,
Breeder in me of what poor skill I boast,
Like me inquisitive how pricks and cracks
Befall the flesh through too much stress and strain,  10
Whereby the wily vapour fain would slip
Back and rejoin its source before the term,—
And aptest in contrivance, under God,
To baffle it by deftly stopping such:—
The vagrant Scholar to his Sage at home      15
Sends greeting (health and knowledge, fame with
      peace)
Three samples of true snake-stone—rarer still,
One of the other sort, the melon-shaped,
(But fitter, pounded fine, for charms than drugs)
And writeth now the twenty-second time.      20

My journeyings were brought to Jericho:
Thus I resume. Who studious in our art
Shall count a little labour unrepaid?
I have shed sweat enough, left flesh and bone

On many a flinty furlong of this land.      25
Also, the country-side is all on fire
With rumours of a marching hitherward:
Some say Vespasian cometh, some, his son.
A black lynx snarled and pricked a tufted ear;
Lust of my blood inflamed his yellow balls:      30
I cried and threw my staff and he was gone.
Twice have the robbers stripped and beaten me,
And once a town declared me for a spy,
But at the end, I reach Jerusalem,
Since this poor covert where I pass the night,      35
This Bethany, lies scarce the distance thence
A man with plague-sores at the third degree
Runs till he drops down dead. Thou laughest here!
'Sooth, it elates me, thus reposed and safe,
To void the stuffing of my travel-scrip      40
And share with thee whatever Jewry yields.
A viscid choler is observable
In tertians, I was nearly bold to say,
And falling-sickness hath a happier cure
Than our school wots of: there's a spider here      45
Weaves no web, watches on the ledge of tombs,
Sprinkled with mottles on an ash-grey back;
Take five and drop them ... but who knows his mind,
The Syrian run-a-gate I trust this to?
His service payeth me a sublimate      50
Blown up his nose to help the ailing eye.
Best wait: I reach Jerusalem at morn,
There set in order my experiences,
Gather what most deserves, and give thee all—
Or I might add, Judæa's gum-tragacanth      55
Scales off in purer flakes, shines clearer-grained,

Cracks 'twixt the pestle and the porphyry,
In fine exceeds our produce.  Scalp-disease
Confounds me, crossing so with leprosy—
Thou hadst admired one sort I gained at Zoar—    60
But zeal outruns discretion.  Here I end.

Yet stay: my Syrian blinketh gratefully,
Protesteth his devotion is my price—
Suppose I write what harms not, though he steal?
I half resolve to tell thee, yet I blush,    65
What set me off a-writing first of all.
An itch I had, a sting to write, a tang!
For, be it this town's barrenness—or else
The Man had something in the look of him—
His case has struck me far more than 'tis worth.    70
So, pardon if—(lest presently I lose
In the great press of novelty at hand
The care and pains this somehow stole from me)
I bid thee take the thing while fresh in mind,
Almost in sight—for, wilt thou have the truth?    75
The very man is gone from me but now,
Whose ailment is the subject of discourse.
Thus then, and let thy better wit help all.

'Tis but a case of mania—subinduced
By epilepsy, at the turning point    80
Of trance prolonged unduly some three days,
When, by the exhibition of some drug
Or spell, exorcization, stroke of art
Unknown to me and which 'twere well to know,
The evil thing out-breaking all at once    85
Left the man whole and sound of body indeed,—
But, flinging, so to speak, life's gates too wide,

Making a clear house of it too suddenly,
The first conceit that entered might inscribe
Whatever it was minded on the wall          90
So plainly at that vantage, as it were,
(First come, first served) that nothing subsequent
Attaineth to erase those fancy-scrawls
The just-returned and new-established soul
Hath gotten now so thoroughly by heart          95
That henceforth she will read or these or none.
And first—the man's own firm conviction rests
That he was dead (in fact they buried him)
—That he was dead and then restored to life
By a Nazarene physician of his tribe:          100
—'Sayeth, the same bade "Rise," and he did rise.
"Such cases are diurnal," thou wilt cry.
Not so this figment!—not, that such a fume,
Instead of giving way to time and health,
Should eat itself into the life of life,          105
As saffron tingeth flesh, blood, bones and all!
For see, how he takes up the after-life.
The man—it is one Lazarus a Jew,
Sanguine, proportioned, fifty years of age,
The body's habit wholly laudable,          110
As much, indeed, beyond the common health
As he were made and put aside to show.
Think, could we penetrate by any drug
And bathe the wearied soul and worried flesh,
And bring it clear and fair, by three days' sleep! 115
Whence has the man the balm that brightens all?
This grown man eyes the world now like a child.
Some elders of his tribe, I should premise,
Led in their friend, obedient as a sheep,

To bear my inquisition. While they spoke,    120
Now sharply, now with sorrow,—told the case,—
He listened not except I spoke to him,
But folded his two hands and let them talk,
Watching the flies that buzzed: and yet no fool.
And that's a sample how his years must go.    125
Look if a beggar, in fixed middle-life,
Should find a treasure, can he use the same
With straitened habits and with tastes starved small,
And take at once to his impoverished brain
The sudden element that changes things,    130
That sets the undreamed-of rapture at his hand,
And puts the cheap old joy in the scorned dust?
Is he not such an one as moves to mirth—
Warily parsimonious, when no need,
Wasteful as drunkenness at undue times?    135
All prudent counsel as to what befits
The golden mean, is lost on such an one:
The man's fantastic will is the man's law.
So here—we'll call the treasure knowledge, say,
Increased beyond the fleshly faculty—    140
Heaven opened to a soul while yet on earth,
Earth forced on a soul's use while seeing Heaven.
The man is witless of the size, the sum,
The value in proportion of all things,
Or whether it be little or be much.    145
Discourse to him of prodigious armaments
Assembled to besiege his city now,
And of the passing of a mule with gourds—
'Tis one! Then take it on the other side,
Speak of some trifling fact—he will gaze rapt    150
With stupor at its very littleness,

(Far as I see)—as if in that indeed
He caught prodigious import, whole results;
And so will turn to us the bystanders
In ever the same stupor (note this point)      155
That we too see not with his opened eyes.
Wonder and doubt come wrongly into play,
Preposterously, at cross purposes.
Should his child sicken unto death,—why, look
For scarce abatement of his cheerfulness,      160
Or pretermission of his daily craft—
While a word, gesture, glance, from that same child
At play or in the school or laid asleep,
Will startle him to an agony of fear,
Exasperation, just as like! demand      165
The reason why—"'tis but a word," object—
"A gesture"—he regards thee as our lord
Who lived there in the pyramid alone,
Looked at us, dost thou mind?—when being young
We both would unadvisedly•recite      170
Some charm's beginning, from that book of his,
Able to bid the sun throb wide and burst
All into stars, as suns grown old are wont.
Thou and the child have each a veil alike
Thrown o'er your heads, from under which ye both  175
Stretch your blind hands and trifle with a match
Over a mine of Greek fire, did ye know!
He holds on firmly to some thread of life—
(It is the life to lead perforcedly)
Which runs across some vast distracting orb      180
Of glory on either side that meagre thread,
Which, conscious of, he must not enter yet—
The spiritual life around the earthly life!

The law of that is known to him as this—
His heart and brain move there, his feet stay here   185
So is the man perplext with impulses
Sudden to start off crosswise, not straight on,
Proclaiming what is Right and Wrong across,
And not along, this black thread through the blaze—
"It should be" baulked by "here it cannot be."   190
And oft the man's soul springs into his face
As if he saw again and heard again
His sage that bade him "Rise" and he did rise.
Something, a word, a tick of the blood within
Admonishes—then back he sinks at once   195
To ashes, that was very fire before,
In sedulous recurrence to his trade
Whereby he earneth him the daily bread;
And studiously the humbler for that pride,
Professedly the faultier that he knows   200
God's secret, while he holds the thread of life.
Indeed the especial marking of the man
Is prone submission to the Heavenly will—
Seeing it, what it is, and why it is.
'Sayeth, he will wait patient to the last   205
For that same death which must restore his being
To equilibrium, body loosening soul
Divorced even now by premature full growth:
He will live, nay, it pleaseth him to live
So long as God please, and just how God please.   210
He even seeketh not to please God more
(Which meaneth, otherwise) than as God please.
Hence I perceive not he affects to preach
The doctrine of his sect whate'er it be—
Make proselytes as madmen thirst to do:   215

How can he give his neighbour the real ground,
His own conviction? ardent as he is—
Call his great truth a lie, why, still the old
"Be it as God please" reassureth him.
I probed the sore as thy disciple should—    220
"How, beast," said I, "this stolid carelessness
Sufficeth thee, when Rome is on her march
To stamp out like a little spark thy town,
Thy tribe, thy crazy tale and thee at once?"
He merely looked with his large eyes on me.    225
The man is apathetic, you deduce?
Contrariwise he loves both old and young,
Able and weak—affects the very brutes
And birds—how say I? flowers of the field—
As a wise workman recognises tools    230
In a master's workshop, loving what they make.
Thus is the man as harmless as a lamb:
Only impatient, let him do his best,
At ignorance and carelessness and sin—
An indignation which is promptly curbed:    235
As when in certain travels I have feigned
To be an ignoramus in our art
According to some preconceived design,
And happed to hear the land's practitioners
Steeped in conceit sublimed by ignorance,    240
Prattle fantastically on disease,
Its cause and cure—and I must hold my peace!

Thou wilt object—why have I not ere this
Sought out the sage himself, the Nazarene
Who wrought this cure, enquiring at the source, 245
Conferring with the frankness that befits?

Alas! it grieveth me, the learned leech
Perished in a tumult many years ago,
Accused,—our learning's fate,—of wizardry,
Rebellion, to the setting up a rule          250
And creed prodigious as described to me.
His death which happened when the earthquake fell
(Prefiguring, as soon appeared, the loss
To occult learning in our lord the sage
That lived there in the pyramid alone)          255
Was wrought by the mad people—that's their wont—
On vain recourse, as I conjecture it,
To his tried virtue, for miraculous help—
How could he stop the earthquake? That's their
          way!
The other imputations must be lies:          260
But take one—though I loathe to give it thee,
In mere respect to any good man's fame!
(And after all our patient Lazarus
Is stark mad; should we count on what he says?
Perhaps not: though in writing to a leech          265
'Tis well to keep back nothing of a case.)
This man so cured regards the curer then,
As—God forgive me—who but God himself,
Creator and Sustainer of the world,
That came and dwelt in flesh on it awhile!          270
—'Sayeth that such an One was born and lived,
Taught, healed the sick, broke bread at his own
          house,
Then died, with Lazarus by, for aught I know,
And yet was...what I said nor choose repeat,
And must have so avouched himself, in fact,          275
In hearing of this very Lazarus

Who saith—but why all this of what he saith?
Why write of trivial matters, things of price
Calling at every moment for remark?
I noticed on the margin of a pool 280
Blue-flowering borage, the Aleppo sort,
Aboundeth, very nitrous. It is strange!

Thy pardon for this long and tedious case,
Which, now that I review it, needs must seem
Unduly dwelt on, prolixly set forth. 285
Nor I myself discern in what is writ
Good cause for the peculiar interest
And awe indeed this man has touched me with.
Perhaps the journey's end, the weariness
Had wrought upon me first. I met him thus— 290
I crossed a ridge of short sharp broken hills
Like an old lion's cheek-teeth. Out there came
A moon made like a face with certain spots
Multiform, manifold and menacing:
Then a wind rose behind me. So we met 295
In this old sleepy town at unaware,
The man and I. I send thee what is writ.
Regard it as a chance, a matter risked
To this ambiguous Syrian—he may lose,
Or steal, or give it thee with equal good. 300
Jerusalem's repose shall make amends
For time this letter wastes, thy time and mine;
Till when, once more thy pardon and farewell!

The very God! think, Abib; dost thou think?
So, the All-Great, were the All-Loving too— 305
So, through the thunder comes a human voice

Y. B. 8

Saying, "O heart I made, a heart beats here!
Face, My hands fashioned, see it in Myself.
Thou hast no power nor may'st conceive of Mine,
But love I gave thee, with Myself to love,    310
And thou must love Me who have died for thee!"
The madman saith He said so: it is strange.

## XXIV. FRA LIPPO LIPPI

I am poor brother Lippo, by your leave!
You need not clap your torches to my face.
Zooks, what's to blame? you think you see a monk!
What, it's past midnight, and you go the rounds,
And here you catch me at an alley's end    5
Where sportive ladies leave their doors ajar.
The Carmine's my cloister: hunt it up,
Do,—harry out, if you must show your zeal,
Whatever rat, there, haps on his wrong hole,
And nip each softling of a wee white mouse,    10
*Weke, weke,* that's crept to keep him company!
Aha, you know your betters? Then, you'll take
Your hand away that's fiddling on my throat,
And please to know me likewise. Who am I?
Why, one, sir, who is lodging with a friend    15
Three streets off—he's a certain...how d'ye call?
Master—a...Cosimo of the Medici,
In the house that caps the corner. Boh! you were
    best!
Remember and tell me, the day you're hanged,
How you affected such a gullet's-gripe!    20
But you, sir, it concerns you that your knaves
Pick up a manner nor discredit you.

Zooks, are we pilchards, that they sweep the streets
And count fair prize what comes into their net?
He's Judas to a tittle, that man is!                               25
Just such a face! why, sir, you make amends.
Lord, I'm not angry!  Bid your hangdogs go
Drink out this quarter-florin to the health
Of the munificent House that harbours me
(And many more beside, lads! more beside!)          30
And all's come square again.  I'd like his face—
His, elbowing on his comrade in the door
With the pike and lantern,—for the slave that holds
John Baptist's head a-dangle by the hair
With one hand ("look you, now," as who should
    say)                                                                    35
And his weapon in the other, yet unwiped!
It's not your chance to have a bit of chalk,
A wood-coal or the like? or you should see!
Yes, I'm the painter, since you style me so.
What, brother Lippo's doings, up and down,          40
You know them and they take you? like enough!
I saw the proper twinkle in your eye—
'Tell you, I liked your looks at very first.
Let's sit and set things straight now, hip to haunch.
Here's spring come, and the nights one makes up
    bands                                                                  45
To roam the town and sing out carnival,
And I've been three weeks shut within my mew,
A-painting for the great man, saints and saints
And saints again.  I could not paint all night—
Ouf!  I leaned out of window for fresh air.         50
There came a hurry of feet and little feet,
A sweep of lute-strings, laughs, and whiffs of song,—

*Flower o' the broom,*
*Take away love, and our earth is a tomb!*
*Flower o' the quince,*                                    55
*I let Lisa go, and what good's in life since?*
*Flower o' the thyme*—and so on.  Round they went.
Scarce had they turned the corner when a titter
Like the skipping of rabbits by moonlight,—three
      slim shapes—
And a face that looked up ... zooks, sir, flesh and
      blood,                                              60
That's all I'm made of!  Into shreds it went,
Curtain and counterpane and coverlet,
All the bed-furniture—a dozen knots,
There was a ladder!  down I let myself,
Hands and feet, scrambling somehow, and so dropped, 65
And after them.  I came up with the fun
Hard by Saint Laurence, hail fellow, well met,—
*Flower o' the rose,*
*If I've been merry, what matter who knows?*
And so as I was stealing back again                       70
To get to bed and have a bit of sleep
Ere I rise up to-morrow and go work
On Jerome knocking at his poor old breast
With his great round stone to subdue the flesh,
You snap me of the sudden.  Ah, I see!                    75
Though your eye twinkles still, you shake your head—
Mine's shaved,—a monk, you say—the sting's in that!
If Master Cosimo announced himself,
Mum's the word naturally; but a monk!
Come, what am I a beast for? tell us, now!                80
I was a baby when my mother died
And father died and left me in the street.

I starved there, God knows how, a year or two
On fig-skins, melon-parings, rinds and shucks,
Refuse and rubbish.  One fine frosty day        85
My stomach being empty as your hat,
The wind doubled me up and down I went.
Old Aunt Lapaccia trussed me with one hand,
(Its fellow was a stinger as I knew)
And so along the wall, over the bridge,         90
By the straight cut to the convent.  Six words, there,
While I stood munching my first bread that month:
"So, boy, you're minded," quoth the good fat father
Wiping his own mouth, 'twas refection-time,—
"To quit this very miserable world?             95
Will you renounce" . . . The mouthful of bread?
        thought I;
By no means!  Brief, they made a monk of me;
I did renounce the world, its pride and greed,
Palace, farm, villa, shop and banking-house,
Trash, such as these poor devils of Medici      100
Have given their hearts to—all at eight years old
Well, sir, I found in time, you may be sure,
'Twas not for nothing—the good bellyful,
The warm serge and the rope that goes all round,
And day-long blessed idleness beside!           105
"Let's see what the urchin's fit for"—that came next.
Not overmuch their way, I must confess.
Such a to-do! they tried me with their books.
Lord, they'd have taught me Latin in pure waste!
*Flower o' the clove,*                          110
*All the Latin I construe is, "amo" I love!*
But, mind you, when a boy starves in the streets
Eight years together, as my fortune was,

Watching folk's faces to know who will fling
The bit of half-stripped grape-bunch he desires,     115
And who will curse or kick him for his pains—
Which gentleman processional and fine,
Holding a candle to the Sacrament
Will wink and let him lift a plate and catch
The droppings of the wax to sell again,     120
Or holla for the Eight and have him whipped,—
How say I?—nay, which dog bites, which lets drop
His bone from the heap of offal in the street,—
Why, soul and sense of him grow sharp alike,
He learns the look of things, and none the less     125
For admonitions from the hunger-pinch.
I had a store of such remarks, be sure,
Which, after I found leisure, turned to use:
I drew men's faces on my copy-books,
Scrawled them within the antiphonary's marge,     130
Joined legs and arms to the long music-notes,
Found nose and eyes and chin for A.s and B.s,
And made a string of pictures of the world
Betwixt the ins and outs of verb and noun,
On the wall, the bench, the door. The monks looked
    black.     135
"Nay," quoth the Prior, "turn him out, d'ye say?
In no wise. Lose a crow and catch a lark.
What if at last we get our man of parts,
We Carmelites, like those Camaldolese
And Preaching Friars, to do our church up fine     140
And put the front on it that ought to be!"
And hereupon they bade me daub away.
Thank you! my head being crammed, their walls a
    blank,

Never was such prompt disemburdening.
First, every sort of monk, the black and white, 145
I drew them, fat and lean: then, folks at church,
From good old gossips waiting to confess
Their cribs of barrel-droppings, candle-ends,—
To the breathless fellow at the altar-foot,
Fresh from his murder, safe and sitting there 150
With the little children round him in a row
Of admiration, half for his beard and half
For that white anger of his victim's son
Shaking a fist at him with one fierce arm,
Signing himself with the other because of Christ 155
(Whose sad face on the cross sees only this
After the passion of a thousand years)
Till some poor girl, her apron o'er her head
Which the intense eyes looked through, came at eve
On tip-toe, said a word, dropped in a loaf, 160
Her pair of ear-rings and a bunch of flowers
The brute took growling, prayed, and then was
        gone.
I painted all, then cried "'tis ask and have—
Choose, for more's ready!"—laid the ladder flat,
And showed my covered bit of cloister-wall. 165
The monks closed in a circle and praised loud
Till checked,—taught what to see and not to see,
Being simple bodies,—"that's the very man!
Look at the boy who stoops to pat the dog!
That woman's like the Prior's niece who comes 170
To care about his asthma: it's the life!"
But there my triumph's straw-fire flared and funked—
Their betters took their turn to see and say:
The Prior and the learned pulled a face

And stopped all that in no time. "How? what's
    here?                                                    175
Quite from the mark of painting, bless us all!
Faces, arms, legs and bodies like the true
As much as pea and pea! it's devil's game!
Your business is not to catch men with show,
With homage to the perishable clay,                      180
But lift them over it, ignore it all,
Make them forget there's such a thing as flesh.
Your business is to paint the souls of men—
Man's soul, and it's a fire, smoke...no it's not...
It's vapour done up like a new-born babe—     185
(In that shape when you die it leaves your mouth)
It's...well, what matters talking, it's the soul!
Give us no more of body than shows soul!
Here's Giotto, with his Saint a-praising God!
That sets you praising,—why not stop with him?   190
Why put all thoughts of praise out of our heads
With wonder at lines, colours, and what not?
Paint the soul, never mind the legs and arms!
Rub all out, try at it a second time.
Oh, that white smallish female with the breasts, 195
She's just my niece...Herodias, I would say,—
Who went and danced and got men's heads cut off—
Have it all out!" Now, is this sense, I ask?
A fine way to paint soul, by painting body
So ill, the eye can't stop there, must go further 200
And can't fare worse! Thus, yellow does for white
When what you put for yellow's simply black,
And any sort of meaning looks intense
When all beside itself means and looks nought.
Why can't a painter lift each foot in turn,          205

Left foot and right foot, go a double step,
Make his flesh liker and his soul more like,
Both in their order?   Take the prettiest face,
The Prior's niece ... patron-saint—is it so pretty
You can't discover if it means hope, fear,          210
Sorrow or joy?  won't beauty go with these?
Suppose I've made her eyes all right and blue,
Can't I take breath and try to add life's flash,
And then add soul and heighten them threefold?
Or say there's beauty with no soul at all—          215
(I never saw it—put the case the same—)
If you get simple beauty and nought else,
You get about the best thing God invents,—
That's somewhat.   And you'll find the soul you have
          missed,
Within yourself when you return Him thanks.          220
"Rub all out!"  well, well, there's my life, in short,
And so the thing has gone on ever since.
I'm grown a man no doubt, I've broken bounds—
You should not take a fellow eight years old
And make him swear to never kiss the girls.          225
I'm my own master, paint now as I please—
Having a friend, you see, in the Corner-house!
Lord, it's fast holding by the rings in front—
Those great rings serve more purposes than just
To plant a flag in, or tie up a horse!          230
And yet the old schooling sticks, the old grave eyes
Are peeping o'er my shoulder as I work,
The heads shake still—"It's Art's decline, my son!
You're not of the true painters, great and old;
Brother Angelico's the man, you'll find:          235
Brother Lorenzo stands his single peer:

Fag on at flesh, you'll never make the third!"
*Flower o' the pine,*
*You keep your mistr ... manners, and I'll stick to mine!*
I'm not the third, then: bless us, they must know!  240
Don't you think they're the likeliest to know,
They, with their Latin? so I swallow my rage,
Clench my teeth, suck my lips in tight, and paint
To please them—sometimes do, and sometimes don't,
For, doing most, there's pretty sure to come          245
A turn, some warm eve finds me at my saints—
A laugh, a cry, the business of the world—
(*Flower o' the peach,*
*Death for us all, and his own life for each!*)
And my whole soul revolves, the cup runs over, 250
The world and life's too big to pass for a dream,
And I do these wild things in sheer despite,
And play the fooleries you catch me at,
In pure rage! the old mill-horse, out at grass
After hard years, throws up his stiff heels so,      255
Although the miller does not preach to him
The only good of grass is to make chaff.
What would men have?  Do they like grass or no—
May they or mayn't they? all I want's the thing
Settled for ever one way: as it is,                  260
You tell too many lies and hurt yourself.
You don't like what you only like too much,
You do like what, if given you at your word,
You find abundantly detestable.
For me, I think I speak as I was taught—             265
I always see the Garden and God there
A-making man's wife—and, my lesson learned,
The value and significance of flesh,

I can't unlearn ten minutes afterwards.
  You understand me: I'm a beast, I know.          270
But see, now—why, I see as certainly
As that the morning-star's about to shine,
What will hap some day. We've a youngster here
Comes to our convent, studies what I do,
Slouches and stares and lets no atom drop—          275
His name is Guidi—he'll not mind the monks—
They call him Hulking Tom, he lets them talk—
He picks my practice up—he'll paint apace,
I hope so—though I never live so long,
I know what's sure to follow. You be judge!          280
You speak no Latin more than I, belike—
However, you're my man, you've seen the world
—The beauty and the wonder and the power,
The shapes of things, their colours, lights and shades,
Changes, surprises,—and God made it all!          285
—For what? do you feel thankful, ay or no,
For this fair town's face, yonder river's line,
The mountain round it and the sky above,
Much more the figures of man, woman, child,
These are the frame to? What's it all about?          290
To be passed over, despised? or dwelt upon,
Wondered at? oh, this last of course, you say.
But why not do as well as say,—paint these
Just as they are, careless what comes of it?
God's works—paint anyone, and count it crime          295
To let a truth slip. Don't object, "His works
Are here already—nature is complete:
Suppose you reproduce her—(which you can't)
There's no advantage! you must beat her, then."
For, don't you mark, we're made so that we love          300

First when we see them painted, things we have
   passed
Perhaps a hundred times nor cared to see;
And so they are better, painted—better to us,
Which is the same thing. Art was given for that—
God uses us to help each other so,     305
Lending our minds out. Have you noticed, now,
Your cullion's hanging face? A bit of chalk,
And trust me but you should, though! How much
   more,
If I drew higher things with the same truth!
That were to take the Prior's pulpit-place,   310
Interpret God to all of you! oh, oh,
It makes me mad to see what men shall do
And we in our graves! This world's no blot for us,
Nor blank—it means intensely, and means good:
To find its meaning is my meat and drink.   315
"Ay, but you don't so instigate to prayer!"
Strikes in the Prior: "when your meaning's plain
It does not say to folks—remember matins,
Or, mind you fast next Friday." Why, for this
What need of art at all? A skull and bones,   320
Two bits of stick nailed cross-wise, or, what's best,
A bell to chime the hour with, does as well.
I painted a Saint Laurence six months since
At Prato, splashed the fresco in fine style:
"How looks my painting, now the scaffold's down?"  325
I ask a brother: "Hugely," he returns—
"Already not one phiz of your three slaves
That turn the Deacon off his toasted side,
But's scratched and prodded to our heart's content,
The pious people have so eased their own   330

When coming to say prayers there in a rage:
We get on fast to see the bricks beneath.
Expect another job this time next year,
For pity and religion grow i' the crowd—          334
Your painting serves its purpose!" Hang the fools!

—That is—you'll not mistake an idle word
Spoke in a huff by a poor monk, God wot,
Tasting the air this spicy night which turns
The unaccustomed head like Chianti wine!
Oh, the church knows! don't misreport me, now!          340
It's natural a poor monk out of bounds
Should have his apt word to excuse himself:
And hearken how I plot to make amends.
I have bethought me: I shall paint a piece          344
... There's for you! Give me six months, then go, see
Something in Sant' Ambrogio's! Bless the nuns!
They want a cast of my office. I shall paint
God in the midst, Madonna and her babe,
Ringed by a bowery, flowery angel-brood,
Lilies and vestments and white faces, sweet          350
As puff on puff of grated orris-root
When ladies crowd to church at midsummer.
And then in the front, of course a saint or two—
Saint John, because he saves the Florentines,
Saint Ambrose, who puts down in black and white          355
The convent's friends and gives them a long day,
And Job, I must have him there past mistake,
The man of Uz, (and Us without the z,
Painters who need his patience). Well, all these
Secured at their devotions, up shall come          360
Out of a corner when you least expect,

As one by a dark stair into a great light,
Music and talking, who but Lippo! I!—
Mazed, motionless and moon-struck—I'm the man!
Back I shrink—what is this I see and hear?        365
I, caught up with my monk's things by mistake,
My old serge gown and rope that goes all round,
I, in this presence, this pure company!
Where's a hole, where's a corner for escape?
Then steps a sweet angelic slip of a thing        370
Forward, puts out a soft palm—"Not so fast!"
—Addresses the celestial presence, "nay—
He made you and devised you, after all,
Though he's none of you!   Could Saint John there,
        draw—
His camel-hair make up a painting-brush?        375
We come to brother Lippo for all that,
*Iste perfecit opus!*"   So, all smile—
I shuffle sideways with my blushing face
Under the cover of a hundred wings
Thrown like a spread of kirtles when you're gay        380
And play hot cockles, all the doors being shut,
Till, wholly unexpected, in there pops
The hothead husband!   Thus I scuttle off
To some safe bench behind, not letting go
The palm of her, the little lily thing        385
That spoke the good word for me in the nick,
Like the Prior's niece ... Saint Lucy, I would say.
And so all's saved for me, and for the church
A pretty picture gained.   Go, six months hence!
Your hand, sir, and good-bye: no lights, no lights!        390
The street's hushed, and I know my own way back,
Don't fear me!   There's the grey beginning.   Zooks!

## XXV. ANDREA DEL SARTO

(CALLED "THE FAULTLESS PAINTER")

But do not let us quarrel any more,
No, my Lucrezia; bear with me for once:
Sit down and all shall happen as you wish.
You turn your face, but does it bring your heart?
I'll work then for your friend's friend, never fear, 5
Treat his own subject after his own way,
Fix his own time, accept too his own price,
And shut the money into this small hand
When next it takes mine. Will it? tenderly?
Oh, I'll content him,—but to-morrow, Love! 10
I often am much wearier than you think,
This evening more than usual, and it seems
As if—forgive now—should you let me sit
Here by the window with your hand in mine
And look a half hour forth on Fiesole, 15
Both of one mind, as married people use,
Quietly, quietly, the evening through,
I might get up to-morrow to my work
Cheerful and fresh as ever. Let us try.
To-morrow how you shall be glad for this! 20
Your soft hand is a woman of itself,
And mine the man's bared breast she curls inside.
Don't count the time lost, either; you must serve
For each of the five pictures we require—
It saves a model. So! keep looking so— 25
My serpentining beauty, rounds on rounds!
—How could you ever prick those perfect ears,

Even to put the pearl there! oh, so sweet—
My face, my moon, my everybody's moon,
Which everybody looks on and calls his,                30
And, I suppose, is looked on by in turn,
While she looks—no one's: very dear, no less!
You smile? why, there's my picture ready made.
There's what we painters call our harmony!
A common greyness silvers everything,—                35
All in a twilight, you and I alike
—You, at the point of your first pride in me
(That's gone you know),—but I, at every point;
My youth, my hope, my art, being all toned down
To yonder sober pleasant Fiesole.                     40
There's the bell clinking from the chapel-top;
That length of convent-wall across the way
Holds the trees safer, huddled more inside;
The last monk leaves the garden; days decrease
And autumn grows, autumn in everything.               45
Eh? the whole seems to fall into a shape
As if I saw alike my work and self
And all that I was born to be and do,
A twilight-piece.  Love, we are in God's hand.
How strange now, looks the life He makes us lead!     50
So free we seem, so fettered fast we are!
I feel He laid the fetter: let it lie!
This chamber for example—turn your head—
All that's behind us! you don't understand
Nor care to understand about my art,                  55
But you can hear at least when people speak;
And that cartoon, the second from the door
—It is the thing, Love! so such things should be—
Behold Madonna, I am bold to say.

I can do with my pencil what I know, 60
What I see, what at bottom of my heart
I wish for, if I ever wish so deep—
Do easily, too—when I say perfectly
I do not boast, perhaps: yourself are judge
Who listened to the Legate's talk last week, 65
And just as much they used to say in France.
At any rate 'tis easy, all of it,
No sketches first, no studies, that's long past—
I do what many dream of all their lives
—Dream? strive to do, and agonise to do, 70
And fail in doing. I could count twenty such
On twice your fingers, and not leave this town,
Who strive—you don't know how the others strive
To paint a little thing like that you smeared
Carelessly passing with your robes afloat,— 75
Yet do much less, so much less, Some one says,
(I know his name, no matter) so much less!
Well, less is more, Lucrezia! I am judged.
There burns a truer light of God in them,
In their vexed, beating, stuffed and stopped-up
      brain, 80
Heart, or whate'er else, than goes on to prompt
This low-pulsed forthright craftsman's hand of mine.
Their works drop groundward, but themselves, I know,
Reach many a time a heaven that's shut to me,
Enter and take their place there sure enough, 85
Though they come back and cannot tell the world.
My works are nearer heaven, but I sit here.
The sudden blood of these men! at a word—
Praise them, it boils, or blame them, it boils too.
I, painting from myself and to myself, 90

Y. B. 9

Know what I do, am unmoved by men's blame
Or their praise either.  Somebody remarks
Morello's outline there is wrongly traced,
His hue mistaken—what of that ? or else,
Rightly traced and well ordered—what of that ?    95
Speak as they please, what does the mountain care ?
Ah, but a man's reach should exceed his grasp,
Or what's a Heaven for ? all is silver-grey
Placid and perfect with my art—the worse !
I know both what I want and what might gain—
And yet how profitless to know, to sigh        101
"Had I been two, another and myself,
Our head would have o'erlooked the world !" No doubt.
Yonder's a work, now, of that famous youth
The Urbinate who died five years ago.        105
('Tis copied, George Vasari sent it me.)
Well, I can fancy how he did it all,
Pouring his soul, with kings and popes to see,
Reaching, that Heaven might so replenish him,
Above and through his art—for it gives way;    110
That arm is wrongly put—and there again—
A fault to pardon in the drawing's lines,
Its body, so to speak: its soul is right,
He means right—that, a child may understand.
Still, what an arm! and I could alter it.        115
But all the play, the insight and the stretch—
Out of me! out of me!  And wherefore out ?
Had you enjoined them on me, given me soul,
We might have risen to Rafael, I and you.
Nay, Love, you did give all I asked, I think—    120
More than I merit, yes, by many times.
But had you—oh, with the same perfect brow,

And perfect eyes, and more than perfect mouth,
And the low voice my soul hears, as a bird
The fowler's pipe, and follows to the snare—            125
Had you, with these the same, but brought a mind!
Some women do so.  Had the mouth there urged
"God and the glory! never care for gain.
The Present by the Future, what is that?
Live for fame, side by side with Angelo—            130
Rafael is waiting.  Up to God all three!"
I might have done it for you.  So it seems—
Perhaps not.  All is as God over-rules.
Beside, incentives come from the soul's self;
The rest avail not.  Why do I need you?            135
What wife had Rafael, or has Angelo?
In this world, who can do a thing, will not—
And who would do it, cannot, I perceive:
Yet the will's somewhat—somewhat, too, the power—
And thus we half-men struggle.  At the end,            140
God, I conclude, compensates, punishes.
'Tis safer for me, if the award be strict,
That I am something underrated here,
Poor this long while, despised, to speak the truth.
I dared not, do you know, leave home all day,            145
For fear of chancing on the Paris lords.
The best is when they pass and look aside;
But they speak sometimes; I must bear it all.
Well may they speak! That Francis, that first time,
And that long festal year at Fontainebleau!            150
I surely then could sometimes leave the ground,
Put on the glory, Rafael's daily wear,
In that humane great monarch's golden look,—
One finger in his beard or twisted curl

9—2

Over his mouth's good mark that made the smile,   155
One arm about my shoulder, round my neck,
The jingle of his gold chain in my ear,
I painting proudly with his breath on me,
All his court round him, seeing with his eyes,
Such frank French eyes, and such a fire of souls
Profuse, my hand kept plying by those hearts,—  161
And, best of all, this, this, this face beyond,
This in the background, waiting on my work,
To crown the issue with a last reward!
A good time, was it not, my kingly days?          165
And had you not grown restless—but I know—
'Tis done and past; 'twas right, my instinct said;
Too live the life grew, golden and not grey,
And I'm the weak-eyed bat no sun should tempt
Out  of  the  grange  whose  four  walls  make  his
        world.                                     170
How could it end in any other way?
You called me, and I came home to your heart.
The triumph was, to have ended there; then if
I reached it ere the triumph, what is lost?
Let my hands frame your face in your hair's gold,  175
You beautiful Lucrezia that are mine!
"Rafael did this, Andrea painted that—
The Roman's is the better when you pray,
But still the other's Virgin was his wife—"
Men will excuse me.  I am glad to judge          180
Both pictures in your  presence; clearer grows
My better fortune, I resolve to think.
For, do you know, Lucrezia, as God lives,
Said one day Angelo, his very self,
To Rafael...I have known it all these years...    185

(When    the    young    man    was    flaming    out    his
       thoughts
Upon a palace-wall for Rome to see,
Too lifted up in heart because of it)
"Friend, there's a certain sorry little scrub
Goes up and down our Florence, none cares how,    190
Who, were he set to plan and execute
As you are, pricked on by your popes and kings,
Would bring the sweat into that brow of yours!"
To Rafael's!—And indeed the arm is wrong.
I hardly dare—yet, only you to see,                       195
Give the chalk here—quick, thus the line should
       go !
Ay, but the soul! he's Rafael! rub it out!
Still, all I care for, if he spoke the truth,
(What he ? why, who but Michael Angelo ?
Do you forget already words like those?)           200
If really there was such a chance, so lost,—
Is, whether you're—not grateful—but more pleased.
Well, let me think so.  And you smile indeed!
This hour has been an hour!  Another smile?
If you would sit thus by me every night           205
I should work better, do you comprehend?
I mean that I should earn more, give you more.
See, it is settled dusk now; there's a star;
Morello's gone, the watch-lights show the wall,
The cue-owls speak the name we call them by.    210
Come from the window, Love,—come in, at last,
Inside the melancholy little house
We built to be so gay with.  God is just.
King Francis may forgive me.  Oft at nights
When I look up from painting, eyes tired out,    215

The walls become illumined, brick from brick
Distinct, instead of mortar, fierce bright gold,
That gold of his I did cement them with!
Let us but love each other. Must you go?
That Cousin here again? he waits outside?        220
Must see you—you, and not with me? Those loans!
More gaming debts to pay? you smiled for that?
Well, let smiles buy me! have you more to spend?
While hand and eye and something of a heart
Are left me, work's my ware, and what's it worth? 225
I'll pay my fancy. Only let me sit
The grey remainder of the evening out,
Idle, you call it, and muse perfectly
How I could paint, were I but back in France,
One picture, just one more—the Virgin's face,        230
Not yours this time! I want you at my side
To hear them—that is, Michael Angelo—
Judge all I do and tell you of its worth.
Will you? To-morrow, satisfy your friend.
I take the subjects for his corridor,        235
Finish the portrait out of hand—there, there,
And throw him in another thing or two
If he demurs; the whole should prove enough
To pay for this same Cousin's freak. Beside,
What's better and what's all I care about,        240
Get you the thirteen scudi for the ruff.
Love, does that please you? Ah, but what does he,
The Cousin! what does he to please you more?

I am grown peaceful as old age to-night.
I regret little, I would change still less.        245
Since there my past life lies, why alter it?

The very wrong to Francis!—it is true
I took his coin, was tempted and complied,
And built this house and sinned, and all is said.
My father and my mother died of want.    250
Well, had I riches of my own? you see
How one gets rich! Let each one bear his lot.
They were born poor, lived poor, and poor they died:
And I have laboured somewhat in my time
And not been paid profusely. Some good son    255
Paint my two hundred pictures—let him try!
No doubt, there's something strikes a balance. Yes,
You loved me quite enough, it seems to-night.
This must suffice me here. What would one have?
In Heaven, perhaps, new chances, one more chance—
Four great walls in the New Jerusalem    261
Meted on each side by the angel's reed,
For Leonard, Rafael, Angelo and me
To cover—the three first without a wife,
While I have mine! So—still they overcome    265
Because there's still Lucrezia,—as I choose.

Again the Cousin's whistle! Go, my Love.


## XXVI. THE BISHOP ORDERS HIS TOMB AT SAINT PRAXED'S CHURCH

[ROME, 15—]

Vanity, saith the preacher, vanity!
Draw round my bed: is Anselm keeping back?
Nephews—sons mine ... ah God, I know not! Well—
She, men would have to be your mother once,

Old Gandolf envied me, so fair she was!      5
What's done is done, and she is dead beside,
Dead long ago, and I am Bishop since,
And as she died so must we die ourselves,
And thence ye may perceive the world's a dream.
Life, how and what is it? As here I lie      10
In this state-chamber, dying by degrees,
Hours and long hours in the dead night, I ask
"Do I live, am I dead!" Peace, peace seems all.
Saint Praxed's ever was the church for peace;
And so, about this tomb of mine. I fought      15
With tooth and nail to save my niche, ye know:
—Old Gandolf cozened me, despite my care;
Shrewd was that snatch from out the corner South
He graced his carrion with, God curse the same!
Yet still my niche is not so cramped but thence      20
One sees the pulpit o' the epistle-side,
And somewhat of the choir, those silent seats,
And up into the aery dome where live
The angels, and a sunbeam's sure to lurk:
And I shall fill my slab of basalt there,      25
And 'neath my tabernacle take my rest,
With those nine columns round me, two and two,
The odd one at my feet where Anselm stands:
Peach-blossom marble all, the rare, the ripe
As fresh-poured red wine of a mighty pulse.      30
—Old Gandolf with his paltry onion-stone,
Put me where I may look at him! True peach,
Rosy and flawless: how I earned the prize!
Draw close: that conflagration of my church
—What then? So much was saved if aught were
      missed!      35

My sons, ye would not be my death? Go dig
The white-grape vineyard where the oil-press stood,
Drop water gently till the surface sinks,
And if ye find ... Ah God, I know not, I! ...
Bedded in store of rotten figleaves soft,                    40
And corded up in a tight olive-frail,
Some lump, ah God, of *lapis lazuli*,
Big as a Jew's head cut off at the nape,
Blue as a vein o'er the Madonna's breast ...
Sons, all have I bequeathed you, villas, all,               45
That brave Frascati villa with its bath,
So, let the blue lump poise between my knees,
Like God the Father's globe on both His hands
Ye worship in the Jesu Church so gay,
For Gandolf shall not choose but see and burst!   50
Swift as a weaver's shuttle fleet our years:
Man goeth to the grave, and where is he?
Did I say basalt for my slab, sons? Black—
'Twas ever antique-black I meant! How else
Shall ye contrast my frieze to come beneath?              55
The bas-relief in bronze ye promised me,
Those Pans and Nymphs ye wot of, and perchance
Some tripod, thyrsus, with a vase or so,
The Saviour at his sermon on the mount,
Saint Praxed in a glory, and one Pan                       60
Ready to twitch the Nymph's last garment off,
And Moses with the tables ... but I know
Ye mark me not! What do they whisper thee,
Child of my bowels, Anselm? Ah, ye hope
To revel down my villas while I gasp                       65
Bricked o'er with beggar's mouldy travertine
Which Gandolf from his tomb-top chuckles at!

Nay, boys, ye love me—all of jasper, then!
'Tis jasper ye stand pledged to, lest I grieve
My bath must needs be left behind, alas!                70
One block, pure green as a pistachio-nut,
There's plenty jasper somewhere in the world—
And have I not Saint Praxed's ear to pray
Horses for ye, and brown Greek manuscripts,
And mistresses with great smooth marbly limbs? 75
—That's if ye carve my epitaph aright,
Choice Latin, picked phrase, Tully's every word,
No gaudy ware like Gandolf's second line—
Tully, my masters? Ulpian serves his need!
And then how I shall lie through centuries,       80
And hear the blessed mutter of the mass,
And see God made and eaten all day long,
And feel the steady candle-flame, and taste
Good strong thick stupefying incense-smoke!
For as I lie here, hours of the dead night,       85
Dying in state and by such slow degrees,
I fold my arms as if they clasped a crook,
And stretch my feet forth straight as stone can point,
And let the bedclothes for a mortcloth drop
Into great laps and folds of sculptor's-work:     90
And as yon tapers dwindle, and strange thoughts
Grow, with a certain humming in my ears,
About the life before I lived this life,
And this life too, Popes, Cardinals and Priests,
Saint Praxed at his sermon on the mount,          95
Your tall pale mother with her talking eyes,
And new-found agate urns as fresh as day,
And marble's language, Latin pure, discreet,
—Aha, ELUCESCEBAT quoth our friend?

No Tully, said I, Ulpian at the best!                    100
Evil and brief hath been my pilgrimage.
All *lapis*, all, sons! Else I give the Pope
My villas: will ye ever eat my heart?
Ever your eyes were as a lizard's quick,
They glitter like your mother's for my soul,        105
Or ye would heighten my impoverished frieze,
Piece out its starved design, and fill my vase
With grapes, and add a vizor and a Term,
And to the tripod ye would tie a lynx
That in his struggle throws the thyrsus down,     110
To comfort me on my entablature
Whereon I am to lie till I must ask
"Do I live, am I dead?" There, leave me, there!
For ye have stabbed me with ingratitude
To death—ye wish it—God, ye wish it! Stone— 115
Gritstone, a-crumble! Clammy squares which sweat
As if the corpse they keep were oozing through—
And no more *lapis* to delight the world!
Well, go! I bless ye. Fewer tapers there,
But in a row: and, going, turn your backs          120
—Ay, like departing altar-ministrants,
And leave me in my church, the church for peace,
That I may watch at leisure if he leers—
Old Gandolf, at me, from his onion-stone,
As still he envied me, so fair she was!                125

## XXVII.  BISHOP BLOUGRAM'S APOLOGY

No more wine?  Then we'll push back chairs and
    talk.
A final glass for me, though: cool, i'faith!
We ought to have our Abbey back, you see.
It's different, preaching in basilicas,
And doing duty in some masterpiece        5
Like this of brother Pugin's, bless his heart!
I doubt if they're half baked, those chalk rosettes,
Ciphers and stucco-twiddlings everywhere;
It's just like breathing in a lime-kiln: eh?
These hot long ceremonies of our church     10
Cost us a little—oh, they pay the price,
You take me—amply pay it!  Now, we'll talk.

  So, you despise me, Mr Gigadibs.
No deprecation,—nay, I beg you, sir!
Beside 'tis our engagement: don't you know,    15
I promised, if you'd watch a dinner out,
We'd see truth dawn together?—truth that peeps
Over the glass's edge when dinner's done,
And body gets its sop and holds its noise
And leaves soul free a little.  Now's the time—  20
'Tis break of day!  You do despise me then.
And if I say, "despise me,"—never fear—
I know you do not in a certain sense—
Not in my arm-chair for example: here,
I well imagine you respect my place     25
(Status, *entourage*, worldly circumstance)
Quite to its value—very much indeed

—Are up to the protesting eyes of you
In pride at being seated here for once—
You'll turn it to such capital account!                    30
When somebody, through years and years to come,
Hints of the bishop,—names me—that's enough—
"Blougram? I knew him"—(into it you slide)
"Dined with him once, a Corpus Christi Day,
All alone, we two—he's a clever man—                        35
And after dinner,—why, the wine you know,—
Oh, there was wine, and good!—what with the
    wine ...
'Faith, we began upon all sorts of talk!
He's no bad fellow, Blougram—he had seen
Something of mine he relished—some review—                  40
He's quite above their humbug in his heart,
Half-said as much, indeed—the thing's his trade—
I warrant, Blougram's sceptical at times—
How otherwise? I liked him, I confess!"
*Che che*, my dear sir, as we say at Rome,                  45
Don't you protest now! It's fair give and take;
You have had your turn and spoken your home-
    truths—
The hand's mine now, and here you follow suit.


Thus much conceded, still the first fact stays—
You do despise me; your ideal of life                       50
Is not the bishop's—you would not be I—
You would like better to be Goethe, now,
Or Buonaparte—or, bless me, lower still,
Count D'Orsay,—so you did what you preferred,
Spoke as you thought, and, as you cannot help,             55
Believed or disbelieved, no matter what,

So long as on that point, whate'er it was,
You loosed your mind, were whole and sole yourself.
—That, my ideal never can include,
Upon that element of truth and worth          60
Never be based! for say they make me Pope
(They can't—suppose it for our argument)
Why, there I'm at my tether's end—I've reached
My height, and not a height which pleases you.
An unbelieving Pope won't do, you say.          65
It's like those eerie stories nurses tell,
Of how some actor played Death on a stage
With pasteboard crown, sham orb and tinselled dart,
And called himself the monarch of the world,
Then going in the tire-room afterward          70
Because the play was done, to shift himself,
Got touched upon the sleeve familiarly
The moment he had shut the closet door
By Death himself.  Thus God might touch a Pope
At unawares, ask what his baubles mean,          75
And whose part he presumed to play just now?
Best be yourself, imperial, plain and true!

So, drawing comfortable breath again,
You weigh and find whatever more or less
I boast of my ideal realized          80
Is nothing in the balance when opposed
To your ideal, your grand simple life,
Of which you will not realize one jot.
I am much, you are nothing; you would be all,
I would be merely much—you beat me there.          85

No, friend, you do not beat me,—hearken why.
The common problem, yours, mine, every one's,

Is not to fancy what were fair in life
Provided it could be,—but, finding first
What may be, then find how to make it fair    90
Up to our means—a very different thing!
No abstract intellectual plan of life
Quite irrespective of life's plainest laws,
But one, a man, who is man and nothing more,
May lead within a world which (by your leave)  95
Is Rome or London—not Fool's-paradise.
Embellish Rome, idealize away,
Make Paradise of London if you can,
You're welcome, nay, you're wise.

                        A simile!
We mortals cross the ocean of this world    100
Each in his average cabin of a life—
The best's not big, the worst yields elbow-room.
Now for our six months' voyage—how prepare?
You come on shipboard with a landsman's list
Of things he calls convenient—so they are!    105
An India screen is pretty furniture,
A piano-forte is a fine resource,
All Balzac's novels occupy one shelf,
The new edition fifty volumes long;
And little Greek books, with the funny type    110
They get up well at Leipsic, fill the next—
Go on! slabbed marble, what a bath it makes!
And Parma's pride, the Jerome, let us add!
'Twere pleasant could Correggio's fleeting glow
Hang full in face of one where'er one roams,    115
Since he more than the others brings with him
Italy's self,—the marvellous Modenese!

Yet 'twas not on your list before, perhaps.
—Alas! friend, here's the agent...is't the name?
The captain, or whoever's master here—          120
You see him screw his face up; what's his cry
Ere you set foot on shipboard? "Six feet square!"
If you won't understand what six feet mean,
Compute and purchase stores accordingly—
And if in pique because he overhauls          125
Your Jerome, piano and bath, you come on board
Bare—why, you cut a figure at the first
While sympathetic landsmen see you off;
Not afterwards, when, long ere half seas over,
You peep up from your utterly naked boards          130
Into some snug and well-appointed berth,
Like mine, for instance (try the cooler jug—
Put back the other, but don't jog the ice)
And mortified you mutter "Well and good—
He sits enjoying his sea-furniture—          135
'Tis stout and proper, and there's store of it,
Though I've the better notion, all agree,
Of fitting rooms up! hang the carpenter,
Neat ship-shape fixings and contrivances—
I would have brought my Jerome, frame and
    all!"          140
And meantime you bring nothing: never mind—
You've proved your artist-nature: what you don't,
You might bring, so despise me, as I say.

Now come, let's backward to the starting place.
See my way: we're two college friends, suppose—          145
Prepare together for our voyage, then,
Each note and check the other in his work,—

Here's mine, a bishop's outfit; criticize!
What's wrong? why won't you be a bishop too?

   Why, first, you don't believe, you don't and
    can't,                                                       150
(Not statedly, that is, and fixedly
And absolutely and exclusively)
In any revelation called divine.
No dogmas nail your faith—and what remains
But say so, like the honest man you are?      155
First, therefore, overhaul theology!
Nay, I too, not a fool, you please to think,
Must find believing every whit as hard,
And if I do not frankly say as much,
The ugly consequence is clear enough.         160

   Now, wait, my friend: well, I do not believe—
If you'll accept no faith that is not fixed,
Absolute and exclusive, as you say.
(You're wrong—I mean to prove it in due time.)
Meanwhile, I know where difficulties lie      165
I could not, cannot solve, nor ever shall,
So give up hope accordingly to solve—
(To you, and over the wine).  Our dogmas then
With both of us, though in unlike degree,
Missing full credence—overboard with them!    170
I mean to meet you on your own premise—
Good, there go mine in company with yours!

   And now what are we? unbelievers both,
Calm and complete, determinately fixed
To-day, to-morrow, and for ever, pray?        175
   Y. B.                                                      10

You'll guarantee me that? Not so, I think!
In no-wise! all we've gained is, that belief,
As unbelief before, shakes us by fits,
Confounds us like its predecessor. Where's
The gain? how can we guard our unbelief,　　180
Make it bear fruit to us?—the problem here.
Just when we are safest, there's a sunset-touch,
A fancy from a flower-bell, some one's death,
A chorus-ending from Euripides,—
And that's enough for fifty hopes and fears　　185
As old and new at once as Nature's self,
To rap and knock and enter in our soul,
Take hands and dance there, a fantastic ring,
Round the ancient idol, on his base again,—
The grand Perhaps! we look on helplessly,—　　190
There the old misgivings, crooked questions are—
This good God,—what He could do, if He would,
Would, if He could—then must have done long since:
If so, when, where, and how? some way must be,—
Once feel about, and soon or late you hit　　195
Some sense, in which it might be, after all.
Why not, "The Way, the Truth, the Life?"

　　　　　　　　　　　　　　　　　—That way
Over the mountain, which who stands upon
Is apt to doubt if it be indeed a road;
While if he views it from the waste itself,　　200
Up goes the line there, plain from base to brow,
Not vague, mistakeable! what's a break or two
Seen from the unbroken desert either side?
And then (to bring in fresh philosophy)
What if the breaks themselves should prove at last　205

The most consummate of contrivances
To train a man's eye, teach him what is faith,—
And so we stumble at truth's very test?
All we have gained then by our unbelief
Is a life of doubt diversified by faith,                    210
For one of faith diversified by doubt:
We called the chess-board white,—we call it black.

"Well," you rejoin, "the end's no worse, at least
We've reason for both colours on the board.
Why not confess, then, where I drop the faith   215
And you the doubt, that I'm as right as you?"

Because, friend, in the next place, this being so,
And both things even,—faith and unbelief
Left to a man's choice,—we'll proceed a step,
Returning to our image, which I like.                   220

A man's choice, yes—but a cabin-passenger's—
The man made for the special life of the world—
Do you forget him? I remember though!
Consult our ship's conditions and you find
One and but one choice suitable to all,                 225
The choice, that you unluckily prefer,
Turning things topsy-turvy—they or it
Going to the ground. Belief or unbelief
Bears upon life, determines its whole course,
Begins at its beginning. See the world                  230
Such as it is,—you made it not, nor I;
I mean to take it as it is,—and you
Not so you'll take it,—though you get nought else.
I know the special kind of life I like,
What suits the most my idiosyncrasy,                    235

10—2

Brings out the best of me and bears me fruit
In power, peace, pleasantness and length of days.
I find that positive belief does this
For me, and unbelief, no whit of this.
—For you, it does, however?—that we'll try!    240
'Tis clear, I cannot lead my life, at least,
Induce the world to let me peaceably,
Without declaring at the outset, "Friends,
I absolutely and peremptorily
Believe!"—I say faith is my waking life.    245
One sleeps, indeed, and dreams at intervals,
We know, but waking's the main point with us,
And my provision's for life's waking part.
Accordingly, I use heart, head and hands
All day, I build, scheme, study and make friends;    250
And when night overtakes me, down I lie,
Sleep, dream a little, and get done with it,
The sooner the better, to begin afresh.
What's midnight's doubt before the dayspring's faith?
You, the philosopher, that disbelieve,    255
That recognize the night, give dreams their weight—
To be consistent you should keep your bed,
Abstain from healthy acts that prove you a man,
For fear you drowse perhaps at unawares!
And certainly at night you'll sleep and dream,    260
Live through the day and bustle as you please.
And so you live to sleep as I to wake,
To unbelieve as I to still believe?
Well, and the common sense of the world calls you
Bed-ridden,—and its good things come to me.    265
Its estimation, which is half the fight,
That's the first cabin-comfort I secure—

The next... but you perceive with half an eye!
Come, come, it's best believing, if we may—
You can't but own that.

      Next, concede again— 270
If once we choose belief, on all accounts
We can't be too decisive in our faith,
Conclusive and exclusive in its terms,
To suit the world which gives us the good things.
In every man's career are certain points 275
Whereon he dares not be indifferent;
The world detects him clearly, if he dares,
As baffled at the game, and losing life.
He may care little or he may care much
For riches, honour, pleasure, work, repose, 280
Since various theories of life and life's
Success are extant which might easily
Comport with either estimate of these;
And whoso chooses wealth or poverty,
Labour or quiet, is not judged a fool 285
Because his fellows would choose otherwise:
We let him choose upon his own account
So long as he's consistent with his choice.
But certain points, left wholly to himself,
When once a man has arbitrated on, 290
We say he must succeed there or go hang.
Thus, he should wed the woman he loves most
Or needs most, whatsoe'er the love or need—
For he can't wed twice. Then, he must avouch
Or follow, at the least, sufficiently, 295
The form of faith his conscience holds the best,
Whate'er the process of conviction was:

For nothing can compensate his mistake
On such a point, the man himself being judge—
He cannot wed twice, nor twice lose his soul.     300

    Well now, there's one great form of Christian faith
I happened to be born in—which to teach
Was given me as I grew up, on all hands,
As best and readiest means of living by;
The same on examination being proved     305
The most pronounced moreover, fixed, precise
And absolute form of faith in the whole world—
Accordingly, most potent of all forms
For working on the world.  Observe, my friend,
Such as you know me, I am free to say,     310
In these hard latter days which hamper one,
Myself, by no immoderate exercise
Of intellect and learning, and the tact
To let external forces work for me,
—Bid the street's stones be bread and they are
      bread,     315
Bid Peter's creed, or, rather, Hildebrand's,
Exalt me o'er my fellows in the world
And make my life an ease and joy and pride,
It does so,—which for me's a great point gained,
Who have a soul and body that exact     320
A comfortable care in many ways.
There's power in me and will to dominate
Which I must exercise, they hurt me else:
In many ways I need mankind's respect,
Obedience, and the love that's born of fear:     325
While at the same time, there's a taste I have,
A toy of soul, a titillating thing,

Refuses to digest these dainties crude.
The naked life is gross till clothed upon:
I must take what men offer, with a grace        330
As though I would not, could I help it, take!
An uniform I wear though over-rich—
Something imposed on me, no choice of mine;
No fancy-dress worn for pure fancy's sake
And despicable therefore! now men kneel        335
And kiss my hand—of course the Church's hand.
Thus I am made, thus life is best for me,
And thus that it should be I have procured;
And thus it could not be another way,
I venture to imagine.

               You'll reply—        340
So far my choice, no doubt, is a success;
But were I made of better elements,
With nobler instincts, purer tastes, like you,
I hardly would account the thing success
Though it do all for me I say.

                      But, friend,        345
We speak of what is—not of what might be,
And how 'twere better if 'twere otherwise.
I am the man you see here plain enough—
Grant I'm a beast; why beasts must lead beasts' lives!
Suppose I own at once to tail and claws—        350
The tailless man exceeds me; but being tailed
I'll lash out lion-fashion, and leave apes
To dock their stump and dress their haunches up.
My business is not to remake myself,
But make the absolute best of what God made.        355

Or—our first simile—though you proved me doomed
To a viler berth still, to the steerage-hole,
The sheep-pen or the pig-stye, I should strive
To make what use of each were possible;
And as this cabin gets upholstery,                    360
That hutch should rustle with sufficient straw.


But, friend, I don't acknowledge quite so fast
I fail of all your manhood's lofty tastes
Enumerated so complacently,
On the mere ground that you forsooth can find    365
In this particular life I choose to lead
No fit provision for them.  Can you not?
Say you, my fault is I address myself
To grosser estimators than I need?
And that's no way of holding up the soul—         370
Which, nobler, needs men's praise perhaps, yet knows
One wise man's verdict outweighs all the fools',—
Would like the two, but, forced to choose, takes that?
I pine among my million imbeciles
(You think) aware some dozen men of sense         375
Eye me and know me, whether I believe
In the last winking Virgin, as I vow,
And am a fool, or disbelieve in her
And am a knave,—approve in neither case,
Withhold their voices though I look their way:   380
Like Verdi when, at his worst opera's end
(The thing they gave at Florence,—what's its name?)
While the mad houseful's plaudits near out-bang
His orchestra of salt-box, tongs and bones,
He looks through all the roaring and the wreaths   385
Where sits Rossini patient in his stall.

Nay, friend, I meet you with an answer here—
That even your prime men who appraise their kind
Are men still, catch a wheel within a wheel,
See more in a truth than the truth's simple self, 390
Confuse themselves. You see lads walk the street
Sixty the minute; what's to note in that?
You see one lad o'erstride a chimney-stack;
Him you must watch—he's sure to fall, yet stands!
Our interest's on the dangerous edge of things. 395
The honest thief, the tender murderer,
The superstitious atheist, demireps
That love and save their souls in new French books—
We watch while these in equilibrium keep
The giddy line midway: one step aside, 400
They're classed and done with. I, then, keep the line
Before your sages,—just the men to shrink
From the gross weights, coarse scales, and labels
        broad
You offer their refinement. Fool or knave?
Why needs a bishop be a fool or knave 405
When there's a thousand diamond weights between?
So I enlist them. Your picked Twelve, you'll find,
Profess themselves indignant, scandalized
At thus being held unable to explain
How a superior man who disbelieves 410
May not believe as well: that's Schelling's way!
It's through my coming in the tail of time,
Nicking the minute with a happy tact.
Had I been born three hundred years ago
They'd say, "What's strange? Blougram of course
        believes;" 415
And, seventy years since, "disbelieves of course."

But now, "He may believe; and yet, and yet
How can he?"—All eyes turn with interest.
Whereas, step off the line on either side—
You, for example, clever to a fault,                    420
The rough and ready man that write apace,
Read somewhat seldomer, think perhaps even less—
You disbelieve! Who wonders and who cares?
Lord So-and-So—his coat bedropt with wax,
All Peter's chains about his waist, his back          425
Brave with the needlework of Noodledom,
Believes! Again, who wonders and who cares?
But I, the man of sense and learning too,
The able to think yet act, the this, the that,
I, to believe at this late time of day!                430
Enough; you see, I need not fear contempt.

—Except it's yours! admire me as these may,
You don't. But whom at least do you admire?
Present your own perfections, your ideal,
Your pattern man for a minute—oh, make haste!   435
Is it Napoleon you would have us grow?
Concede the means; allow his head and hand,
(A large concession, clever as you are)
Good!—In our common primal element
Of unbelief (we can't believe, you know—           440
We're still at that admission, recollect)—
Where do you find—apart from, towering o'er
The secondary temporary aims
Which satisfy the gross tastes you despise—
Where do you find his star?—his crazy trust        445
God knows through what or in what? it's alive
And shines and leads him and that's all we want.

Have we aught in our sober night shall point
Such ends as his were, and direct the means
Of working out our purpose straight as his,      450
Nor bring a moment's trouble on success
With after-care to justify the same?
—Be a Napoleon and yet disbelieve!
Why, the man's mad, friend, take his light away.
What's the vague good of the world for which you'd
   dare      455
With comfort to yourself blow millions up?
We neither of us see it! we do see
The blown-up millions—spatter of their brains
And writhing of their bowels and so forth
In that bewildering entanglement      460
Of horrible eventualities
Past calculation to the end of time!
Can I mistake for some clear word of God
(Which were my ample warrant for it all)
His puff of hazy instincts, idle talk,      465
"The State, that's I," quack-nonsense about crowns,
And (when one beats the man to his last hold)
The vague idea of setting things to rights,
Policing people efficaciously,
More to their profit, most of all to his own;      470
The whole to end that dismallest of ends
By an Austrian marriage, cant to us the church,
And resurrection of the old *régime*.
Would I, who hope to live a dozen years,
Fight Austerlitz for reasons such and such?      475
No: for, concede me but the merest chance
Doubt may be wrong—there's judgment, life to come!
With just that chance, I dare not. Doubt proves right?

This present life is all?—you offer me
Its dozen noisy years without a chance          480
That wedding an Arch-Duchess, wearing lace,
And getting called by divers new-coined names,
Will drive off ugly thoughts and let me dine,
Sleep, read and chat in quiet as I like!
Therefore, I will not.

                Take another case;          485
Fit up the cabin yet another way.
What say you to the poets? shall we write
Hamlets, Othellos—make the world our own,
Without a risk to run of either sort?
I can't!—to put the strongest reason first.          490
"But try," you urge, "the trying shall suffice:
The aim, if reached or not, makes great the life.
Try to be Shakspeare, leave the rest to fate!"
Spare my self-knowledge—there's no fooling me!
If I prefer remaining my poor self,          495
I say so not in self-dispraise but praise.
If I'm a Shakspeare, let the well alone—
Why should I try to be what now I am?
If I'm no Shakspeare, as too probable,—
His power and consciousness and self-delight          500
And all we want in common, shall I find—
Trying for ever? while on points of taste
Wherewith, to speak it humbly, he and I
Are dowered alike—I'll ask you, I or he,
Which in our two lives realizes most?          505
Much, he imagined—somewhat, I possess.
He had the imagination; stick to that!
Let him say "In the face of my soul's works

Your world is worthless and I touch it not
Lest I should wrong them "—I'll withdraw my plea.  510
But does he say so? look upon his life!
Himself, who only can, gives judgment there.
He leaves his towers and gorgeous palaces
To build the trimmest house in Stratford town;
Saves money, spends it, owns the worth of things,  515
Giulio Romano's pictures, Dowland's lute;
Enjoys a show, respects the puppets, too,
And none more, had he seen its entry once,
Than "Pandulph, of fair Milan cardinal."
Why then should I who play that personage,  520
The very Pandulph Shakspeare's fancy made,
Be told that had the poet chanced to start
From where I stand now (some degree like mine
Being just the goal he ran his race to reach)
He would have run the whole race back, forsooth,  525
And left being Pandulph, to begin write plays?
Ah, the earth's best can be but the earth's best!
Did Shakspeare live, he could but sit at home
And get himself in dreams the Vatican,
Greek busts, Venetian paintings, Roman walls,  530
And English books, none equal to his own,
Which I read, bound in gold, (he never did).
—Terni and Naples' bay and Gothard's top—
Eh, friend? I could not fancy one of these—
But, as I pour this claret, there they are—  535
I've gained them—crossed St Gothard last July
With ten mules to the carriage and a bed
Slung inside; is my hap the worse for that?
We want the same things, Shakspeare and myself,
And what I want, I have: he, gifted more,  540

Could fancy he too had it when he liked,
But not so thoroughly that if fate allowed
He would not have it also in my sense.
We play one game.  I send the ball aloft
No less adroitly that of fifty strokes          545
Scarce five go o'er the wall so wide and high
Which sends them back to me: I wish and get.
He struck balls higher and with better skill,
But at a poor fence level with his head,
And hit—his Stratford house, a coat of arms,      550
Successful dealings in his grain and wool,—
While I receive heaven's incense in my nose
And style myself the cousin of Queen Bess.
Ask him, if this life's all, who wins the game?

   Believe—and our whole argument breaks up.      555
Enthusiasm's the best thing, I repeat;
Only, we can't command it; fire and life
Are all, dead matter's nothing, we agree:
And be it a mad dream or God's very breath,
The fact's the same,—belief's fire once in us,    560
Makes of all else mere stuff to show itself.
We penetrate our life with such a glow
As fire lends wood and iron—this turns steel,
That burns to ash—all's one, fire proves its power
For good or ill, since men call flare success.     565
But paint a fire, it will not therefore burn.
Light one in me, I'll find it food enough!
Why, to be Luther—that's a life to lead,
Incomparably better than my own.
He comes, reclaims God's earth for God, he says,    570
Sets up God's rule again by simple means,

Re-opens a shut book, and all is done.
He flared out in the flaring of mankind;
Such Luther's luck was—how shall such be mine?
If he succeeded, nothing's left to do:            575
And if he did not altogether—well,
Strauss is the next advance. All Strauss should be
I might be also. But to what result?
He looks upon no future: Luther did.
What can I gain on the denying side?              580
Ice makes no conflagration. State the facts,
Read the text right, emancipate the world—
The emancipated world enjoys itself
With scarce a thank-you—Blougram told it first
It could not owe a farthing,—not to him          585
More than St Paul! 'twould press its pay, you think?
Then add there's still that plaguy hundredth chance
Strauss may be wrong. And so a risk is run—
For what gain? not for Luther's, who secured
A real Heaven in his heart throughout his life,   590
Supposing death a little altered things!

" Ay, but since really you lack faith," you cry,
" You run the same risk really on all sides,
In cool indifference as bold unbelief.
As well be Strauss as swing 'twixt Paul and him.   595
It's not worth having, such imperfect faith,
Nor more available to do faith's work
Than unbelief like mine. Whole faith, or none!"

Softly, my friend! I must dispute that point.
Once own the use of faith, I'll find you faith.    600
We're back on Christian ground. You call for faith;
I show you doubt, to prove that faith exists.

The more of doubt, the stronger faith, I say,
If faith o'ercomes doubt. How I know it does?
By life and man's free will, God gave for that!   605
To mould life as we choose it, shows our choice:
That's our one act, the previous work's His own.
You criticize the soil? it reared this tree—
This broad life and whatever fruit it bears!
What matter though I doubt at every pore,   610
Head-doubts, heart-doubts, doubts at my fingers' ends,
Doubts in the trivial work of every day,
Doubts at the very bases of my soul ·
In the grand moments when she probes herself—
If finally I have a life to show,   615
The thing I did, brought out in evidence
Against the thing done to me underground
By Hell and all its brood, for aught I know?
I say, whence sprang this? shows it faith or doubt?
All's doubt in me; where's break of faith in this?   620
It is the idea, the feeling and the love
God means mankind should strive for and show forth,
Whatever be the process to that end,—
And not historic knowledge, logic sound,
And metaphysical acumen, sure!   625
"What think ye of Christ," friend? when all's done
      and said,
You like this Christianity or not?
It may be false, but will you wish it true?
Has it your vote to be so if it can?
Trust you an instinct silenced long ago   630
That will break silence and enjoin you love
What mortified philosophy is hoarse,
And all in vain, with bidding you despise?

If you desire faith—then you've faith enough:
What else seeks God—nay, what else seek our-
   selves?                                                    635
You form a notion of me, we'll suppose,
On hearsay; it's a favourable one:
"But still" (you add), "there was no such good man,
Because of contradictions in the facts.
One proves, for instance, he was born in Rome,   640
This Blougram—yet throughout the tales of him
I see he figures as an Englishman."
Well, the two things are reconcileable.
But would I rather you discovered that,
Subjoining—"Still, what matter though they be?  645
Blougram concerns me nought, born here or there."

Pure faith indeed—you know not what you ask!
Naked belief in God the Omnipotent,
Omniscient, Omnipresent, sears too much
The sense of conscious creatures to be borne.    650
It were the seeing Him, no flesh shall dare.
Some think, Creation's meant to show Him forth:
I say, it's meant to hide Him all it can,
And that's what all the blessed Evil's for.
Its use in Time is to environ us,               655
Our breath, our drop of dew, with shield enough
Against that sight till we can bear its stress.
Under a vertical sun, the exposed brain
And lidless eye and disemprisoned heart
Less certainly would wither up at once          660
Than mind, confronted with the truth of Him.
But time and earth case-harden us to live;
The feeblest sense is trusted most; the child

Feels God a moment, ichors o'er the place,
Plays on and grows to be a man like us.                665
With me, faith means perpetual unbelief
Kept quiet like the snake 'neath Michael's foot
Who stands calm just because he feels it writhe.
Or, if that's too ambitious,—here's my box—
I need the excitation of· a pinch                      670
Threatening the torpor of the inside-nose
Nigh on the imminent sneeze that never comes.
"Leave it in peace" advise the simple folk—
Make it aware of peace by itching-fits,
Say I—let doubt occasion still more faith !            675

 You'll say, once all believed, man, woman, child,
In that dear middle-age these noodles praise.
How you'd exult if I could put you back
Six hundred years, blot out cosmogony,
Geology, ethnology, what not,                          680
(Greek endings with the little passing-bell
That signifies some faith's about to die)
And set you square with Genesis again,—
When such a traveller told you his last news,
He saw the ark a-top of Ararat                         685
But did not climb there since 'twas getting dusk
And robber-bands infest the mountain's foot!
How should you feel, I ask, in such an age,
How act? As other people felt and did;
With soul more blank than this decanter's knob, 690
Believe—and yet lie, kill, rob, fornicate
Full in belief's face, like the beast you'd be!

 No, when the fight begins within himself,
A man's worth something.  God stoops o'er his head,

Satan looks up between his feet—both tug—    695
He's left, himself, in the middle: the soul wakes
And grows.  Prolong that battle through his life!
Never leave growing till the life to come!
Here, we've got callous to the Virgin's winks
That used to puzzle people wholesomely—    700
Men have outgrown the shame of being fools.
What are the laws of Nature, not to bend
If the Church bid them?—brother Newman asks.
Up with the Immaculate Conception, then—
On to the rack with faith!—is my advice.    705
Will not that hurry us upon our knees
Knocking our breasts, "It can't be—yet it shall!
Who am I, the worm, to argue with my Pope?
Low things confound the high things!" and so forth.
That's better than acquitting God with grace    710
As some folks do.  He's tried—no case is proved,
Philosophy is lenient—He may go!

    You'll say—the old system's not so obsolete
But men believe still: ay, but who and where?
King Bomba's lazzaroni foster yet    715
The sacred flame, so Antonelli writes;
But even of these, what ragamuffin-saint
Believes God watches him continually,
As he believes in fire that it will burn,
Or rain that it will drench him?  Break fire's law,    720
Sin against rain, although the penalty
Be just a singe or soaking?  No, he smiles;
Those laws are laws that can enforce themselves.

    The sum of all is—yes, my doubt is great,
My faith's still greater—then my faith's enough.    725

I have read much, thought much, experienced much,
Yet would die rather than avow my fear
The Naples' liquefaction may be false,
When set to happen by the palace-clock
According to the clouds or dinner-time.                    730
I hear you recommend, I might at least
Eliminate, decrassify my faith
Since I adopt it; keeping what I must
And leaving what I can—such points as this!
I won't—that is, I can't throw one away.                   735
Supposing there's no truth in what I said
About the need of trials to man's faith,
Still, when you bid me purify the same,
To such a process I discern no end,
Clearing off one excrescence to see two;                   740
There's ever a next in size, now grown as big,
That meets the knife—I cut and cut again!
First cut the Liquefaction, what comes last
But Fichte's clever cut at God himself?
Experimentalize on sacred things?                          745
I trust nor hand nor eye nor heart nor brain
To stop betimes: they all get drunk alike.
The first step, I am master not to take.


You'd find the cutting-process to your taste
As much as leaving growths of lies unpruned,               750
Nor see more danger in it, you retort.
Your taste's worth mine; but my taste proves more
    wise
When we consider that the steadfast hold
On the extreme end of the chain of faith
Gives all the advantage, makes the difference,             755

With the rough purblind mass we seek to rule.
We are their lords, or they are free of us
Just as we tighten or relax that hold.
So; other matters equal, we'll revert
To the first problem—which, if solved my way      760
And thrown into the balance, turns the scale—
How we may lead a comfortable life,
How suit our luggage to the cabin's size.

Of course you are remarking all this time
How narrowly and grossly I view life,      765
Respect the creature-comforts, care to rule
The masses, and regard complacently
"The cabin," in our old phrase!  Well, I do.
I act for, talk for, live for this world now,
As this world calls for action, life and talk—      770
No prejudice to what next world may prove,
Whose new laws and requirements, my best pledge
To observe then, is that I observe these now,
Shall do hereafter what I do meanwhile.
Let us concede (gratuitously though)      775
Next life relieves the soul of body, yields
Pure spiritual enjoyments: well, my friend,
Why lose this life in the meantime, since its use
May be to make the next life more intense?

Do you know, I have often had a dream      780
(Work it up in your next month's article)
Of man's poor spirit in its progress still
Losing true life for ever and a day
Through ever trying to be and ever being
In the evolution of successive spheres,      785

Before its actual sphere and place of life,
Halfway into the next, which having reached,
It shoots with corresponding foolery
Halfway into the next still, on and off!
As when a traveller, bound from North to South, 790
Scouts fur in Russia—what's its use in France?
In France spurns flannel—where's its need in Spain?
In Spain drops cloth—too cumbrous for Algiers!
Linen goes next, and last the skin itself,
A superfluity at Timbuctoo.                    795
When, through his journey, was the fool at ease?
I'm at ease now, friend—worldly in this world
I take and like its way of life; I think
My brothers who administer the means
Live better for my comfort—that's good too;   800
And God, if He pronounce upon it all,
Approves my service, which is better still.
If He keep silence,—why, for you or me
Or that brute-beast pulled-up in to-day's 'Times,'
What odds is't, save to ourselves, what life we
    lead?                                      805

You meet me at this issue—you declare,
All special pleading done with, truth is truth,
And justifies itself by undreamed ways.
You don't fear but it's better, if we doubt,
To say so, acting up to our truth perceived    810
However feebly. Do then,—act away!
'Tis there I'm on the watch for you! How one acts
Is, both of us agree, our chief concern:
And how you'll act is what I fain would see
If, like the candid person you appear,         815

You dare to make the most of your life's scheme
As I of mine, live up to its full law
Since there's no higher law that counterchecks.
Put natural religion to the test
You've just demolished the revealed with—quick, 820
Down to the root of all that checks your will,
All prohibition to lie, kill, and thieve
Or even to be an atheistic priest!
Suppose a pricking to incontinence—
Philosophers deduce you chastity                    825
Or shame, from just the fact that at the first
Whoso embraced a woman in the plain,
Threw club down, and forewent his brains beside,
So stood a ready victim in the reach
Of any brother-savage club in hand—                 830
Hence saw the use of going out of sight
In wood or cave to prosecute his loves—
I read this in a French book t'other day.
Does law so analyzed coerce you much?
Oh, men spin clouds of fuzz where matters end, 835
But you who reach where the first thread begins,
You'll soon cut that!—which means you can, but won't
Through certain instincts, blind, unreasoned-out,
You dare not set aside, you can't tell why,
But there they are, and so you let them rule.       840
Then, friend, you seem as much a slave as I,
A liar, conscious coward and hypocrite,
Without the good the slave expects to get,
Suppose he has a master after all!
You own your instincts—why, what else do I,        845
Who want, am made for, and must have a God
Ere I can be aught, do aught?—no mere name

Want, but the true thing with what proves its truth,
To wit, a relation from that thing to me,
Touching from head to foot—which touch I feel, 850
And with it take the rest, this life of ours!
I live my life here; yours you dare not live.

—Not as I state it, who (you please subjoin)
Disfigure such a life and call it names,
While, in your mind, remains another way          855
For simple men: knowledge and power have rights,
But ignorance and weakness have rights too.
There needs no crucial effort to find truth
If here or there or anywhere about—
We ought to turn each side, try hard and see,     860
And if we can't, be glad we've earned at least
The right, by one laborious proof the more,
To graze in peace earth's pleasant pasturage.
Men are not angels, neither are they brutes.
Something we may see, all we cannot see—          865
What need of lying? I say, I see all,
And swear to each detail the most minute
In what I think a Pan's face—you, mere cloud:
I swear I hear him speak and see him wink,
For fear, if once I drop the emphasis,            870
Mankind may doubt there's any cloud at all.
You take the simpler life—ready to see,
Willing to see—for no cloud's worth a face—
And leaving quiet what no strength can move,
And which, who bids you move? who has the
       right?                                     875
I bid you; but you are God's sheep, not mine—
"*Pastor est tui Dominus*." You find

In these the pleasant pastures of this life
Much you may eat without the least offence,
Much you don't eat because your maw objects,     880
Much you would eat but that your fellow-flock
Open great eyes at you and even butt,
And thereupon you like your mates so well
You cannot please yourself, offending them—
Though when they seem exorbitantly sheep,     885
You weigh your pleasure with their butts and bleats
And strike the balance.  Sometimes certain fears
Restrain you—real checks since you find them so—
Sometimes you please yourself and nothing checks;
And thus you graze through life with not one lie,     890
And like it best.

               But do you, in truth's name?
If so, you beat—which means, you are not I—
Who needs must make earth mine and feed my fill
Not simply unbutted at, unbickered with,
But motioned to the velvet of the sward     895
By those obsequious wethers' very selves.
Look at me, sir; my age is double yours:
At yours, I knew beforehand, so enjoyed,
What now I should be—as, permit the word,
I pretty well imagine your whole range     900
And stretch of tether twenty years to come.
We both have minds and bodies much alike.
In truth's name, don't you want my bishopric,
My daily bread, my influence and my state?
You're young, I'm old, you must be old one day;     905
Will you find then, as I do hour by hour,
Women their lovers kneel to, that cut curls

From your fat lap-dog's ears to grace a brooch—
Dukes, that petition just to kiss your ring—
With much beside you know or may conceive?   910
Suppose we die to-night: well, here am I,
Such were my gains, life bore this fruit to me,
While writing all the same my articles
On music, poetry, the fictile vase
Found at Albano, chess, or Anacreon's Greek.   915
But you—the highest honour in your life,
The thing you'll crown yourself with, all your days,
Is—dining here and drinking this last glass
I pour you out in sign of amity
Before we part for ever.  Of your power   920
And social influence, worldly worth in short,
Judge what's my estimation by the fact,
I do not condescend to enjoin, beseech,
Hint secrecy on one of all these words!   924
You're shrewd and know that should you publish one
The world would brand the lie—my enemies first,
Who'd sneer—"The bishop's an arch-hypocrite,
And knave perhaps, but not so frank a fool."
Whereas I should not dare for both my ears
Breathe one such syllable, smile one such smile,   930
Before my chaplain who reflects myself—
My shade's so much more potent than your flesh.
What's your reward, self-abnegating friend?
Stood you confessed of those exceptional
And privileged great natures that dwarf mine—   935
A zealot with a mad ideal in reach,
A poet just about to print his ode,
A statesman with a scheme to stop this war,
An artist whose religion is his art,

I should have nothing to object! such men 940
Carry the fire, all things grow warm to them,
Their drugget's worth my purple, they beat me.
But you,—you're just as little those as I—
You, Gigadibs, who, thirty years of age,
Write statedly for Blackwood's Magazine, 945
Believe you see two points in Hamlet's soul
Unseized by the Germans yet—which view you'll
    print—
Meantime the best you have to show being still
That lively lightsome article we took
Almost for the true Dickens,—what's its name? 950
"The Slum and Cellar—or Whitechapel life
Limned after dark!" it made me laugh, I know,
And pleased a month and brought you in ten pounds.
—Success I recognize and compliment, 954
And therefore give you, if you please, three words
(The card and pencil-scratch is quite enough)
Which whether here, in Dublin or New York,
Will get you, prompt as at my eyebrow's wink,
Such terms as never you aspired to get
In all our own reviews and some not ours. 960
Go write your lively sketches—be the first
"Blougram, or The Eccentric Confidence"—
Or better simply say, "The Outward-bound."
Why, men as soon would throw it in my teeth
As copy and quote the infamy chalked broad 965
About me on the church-door opposite.
You will not wait for that experience though,
I fancy, howsoever you decide,
To discontinue—not detesting, not
Defaming, but at least—despising me! 970

Over his wine so smiled and talked his hour
Sylvester Blougram, styled *in partibus*
*Episcopus, nec non*—(the deuce knows what
It's changed to by our novel hierarchy)
With Gigadibs the literary man,                          975
Who played with spoons, explored his plate's design,
And ranged the olive stones about its edge,
While the great bishop rolled him out his mind.


For Blougram, he believed, say, half he spoke.
The other portion, as he shaped it thus          980
For argumentatory purposes,
He felt his foe was foolish to dispute.
Some arbitrary accidental thoughts
That crossed his mind, amusing because new,
He chose to represent as fixtures there,          985
Invariable convictions (such they seemed
Beside his interlocutor's loose cards
Flung daily down, and not the same way twice)
While certain Hell-deep instincts, man's weak tongue
Is never bold to utter in their truth           990
Because styled Hell-deep ('tis an old mistake
To place Hell at the bottom of the earth)
He ignored these,—not having in readiness
Their nomenclature and philosophy:               994
He said true things, but called them by wrong names.
"On the whole," he thought, "I justify myself
On every point where cavillers like this
Oppugn my life: he tries one kind of fence—
I close—he's worsted, that's enough for him;     999
He's on the ground! if the ground should break away
I take my stand on, there's a firmer yet

Beneath it, both of us may sink and reach.
His ground was over mine and broke the first.
So let him sit with me this many a year!"

He did not sit five minutes.  Just a week    1005
Sufficed his sudden healthy vehemence.
(Something had struck him in the "Outward-bound"
Another way than Blougram's purpose was)
And having bought, not cabin-furniture
But settler's-implements (enough for three)    1010
And started for Australia—there, I hope,
By this time he has tested his first plough,
And studied his last chapter of St John.


## XXVIII. ONE WORD MORE

### TO E. B. B.

*London, September, 1855.*

#### I

There they are, my fifty men and women
Naming me the fifty poems finished!
Take them, Love, the book and me together:
Where the heart lies, let the brain lie also.

#### II

Rafael made a century of sonnets,    5
Made and wrote them in a certain volume
Dinted with the silver-pointed pencil
Else he only used to draw Madonnas:
These, the world might view—but One, the volume.
Who that one, you ask?  Your heart instructs you.    10

Did she live and love it all her life-time?
Did she drop, his lady of the sonnets,
Die, and let it drop beside her pillow
Where it lay in place of Rafael's glory,
Rafael's cheek so duteous and so loving—     15
Cheek, the world was wont to hail a painter's,
Rafael's cheek, her love had turned a poet's?

### III

You and I would rather read that volume,
(Taken to his beating bosom by it)
Lean and list the bosom-beats of Rafael,     20
Would we not? than wonder at Madonnas—
Her, San Sisto names, and Her, Foligno,
Her, that visits Florence in a vision,
Her, that's left with lilies in the Louvre—
Seen by us and all the world in circle.     25

### IV

You and I will never read that volume.
Guido Reni, like his own eye's apple
Guarded long the treasure-book and loved it.
Guido Reni dying, all Bologna
Cried, and the world cried too, "Ours—the treasure!"     30
Suddenly, as rare things will, it vanished.

### V

Dante once prepared to paint an angel:
Whom to please? You whisper "Beatrice."
While he mused and traced it and retraced it,
(Peradventure with a pen corroded     35
Still by drops of that hot ink he dipped for,

When, his left-hand i' the hair o' the wicked,
Back he held the brow and pricked its stigma,
Bit into the live man's flesh for parchment,
Loosed him, laughed to see the writing rankle,    40
Let the wretch go festering through Florence)—
Dante, who loved well because he hated,
Hated wickedness that hinders loving,
Dante standing, studying his angel,—
In there broke the folk of his Inferno.    45
Says he—"Certain people of importance"
(Such he gave his daily, dreadful line to)
"Entered and would seize, forsooth, the poet."
Says the poet—"Then I stopped my painting."

### VI

You and I would rather see that angel,    50
Painted by the tenderness of Dante,
Would we not?—than read a fresh Inferno.

### VII

You and I will never see that picture.
While he mused on love and Beatrice,
While he softened o'er his outlined angel,    55
In they broke, those "people of importance":
We and Bice bear the loss for ever.

### VIII

What of Rafael's sonnets, Dante's picture?

### IX

This: no artist lives and loves that longs not
Once, and only once, and for One only,    60
(Ah, the prize!) to find his love a language

Fit and fair and simple and sufficient—
Using nature that's an art to others,
Not, this one time, art that's turned his nature.
Ay, of all the artists living, loving,     65
None but would forego his proper dowry,—
Does he paint? he fain would write a poem,—
Does he write? he fain would paint a picture,
Put to proof art alien to the artist's,
Once, and only once, and for One only,     70
So to be the man and leave the artist,
Gain the man's joy, miss the artist's sorrow.


X

Wherefore? Heaven's gift takes earth's abatement!
He who smites the rock and spreads the water,
Bidding drink and live a crowd beneath him,     75
Even he, the minute makes immortal,
Proves, perchance, his mortal in the minute,
Desecrates, belike, the deed in doing.
While he smites, how can he but remember,
So he smote before, in such a peril,     80
When they stood and mocked—"Shall smiting help
    us?"
When they drank and sneered—"A stroke is easy!"
When they wiped their mouths and went their
    journey,
Throwing him for thanks—"But drought was pleasant."
Thus old memories mar the actual triumph;     85
Thus the doing savours of disrelish;
Thus achievement lacks a gracious somewhat;
O'er-importuned brows becloud the mandate,
Carelessness or consciousness, the gesture.

For he bears an ancient wrong about him, 90
Sees and knows again those phalanxed faces,
Hears, yet one time more, the 'customed prelude—
"How should'st thou, of all men, smite, and save us?"
Guesses what is like to prove the sequel—
"Egypt's flesh-pots—nay, the drought was better." 95

### XI

Oh, the crowd must have emphatic warrant!
Theirs, the Sinai-forehead's cloven brilliance,
Right-arm's rod-sweep, tongue's imperial fiat.
Never dares the man put off the prophet.

### XII

Did he love one face from out the thousands, 100
(Were she Jethro's daughter, white and wifely,
Were she but the Æthiopian bondslave,)
He would envy yon dumb patient camel,
Keeping a reserve of scanty water
Meant to save his own life in the desert; 105
Ready in the desert to deliver
(Kneeling down to let his breast be opened)
Hoard and life together for his mistress.

### XIII

I shall never, in the years remaining,
Paint you pictures, no, nor carve you statues, 110
Make you music that should all-express me;
So it seems: I stand on my attainment.
This of verse alone, one life allows me;
Verse and nothing else have I to give you.
Other heights in other lives, God willing— 115
All the gifts from all the heights, your own, Love!

Y. B. 12

### XIV

Yet a semblance of resource avails us—
Shade so finely touched, love's sense must seize it.
Take these lines, look lovingly and nearly,
Lines I write the first time and the last time.          120
He who works in fresco, steals a hair-brush,
Curbs the liberal hand, subservient proudly,
Cramps his spirit, crowds its all in little,
Makes a strange art of an art familiar,
Fills his lady's missal-marge with flowerets.          125
He who blows through bronze, may breathe through
          silver,
Fitly serenade a slumbrous princess.
He who writes, may write for once, as I do.

### XV

Love, you saw me gather men and women,
Live or dead or fashioned by my fancy,          130
Enter each and all, and use their service,
Speak from every mouth,—the speech, a poem.
Hardly shall I tell my joys and sorrows,
Hopes and fears, belief and disbelieving:
I am mine and yours—the rest be all men's,          135
Karshish, Cleon, Norbert and the fifty.
Let me speak this once in my true person,
Not as Lippo, Roland or Andrea,
Though the fruit of speech be just this sentence—
Pray you, look on these my men and women,          140
Take and keep my fifty poems finished;
Where my heart lies, let my brain lie also!
Poor the speech; be how I speak, for all things.

## XVI

Not but that you know me! Lo, the moon's self!
Here in London, yonder late in Florence,          145
Still we find her face, the thrice-transfigured.
Curving on a sky imbrued with colour,
Drifted over Fiesole by twilight,
Came she, our new crescent of a hair's-breadth.
Full she flared it, lamping Samminiato,          150
Rounder 'twixt the cypresses and rounder,
Perfect till the nightingales applauded.
Now, a piece of her old self, impoverished,
Hard to greet, she traverses the houseroofs,
Hurries with unhandsome thrift of silver,          155
Goes dispiritedly, glad to finish.

## XVII

What, there's nothing in the moon note-worthy?
Nay—for if that moon could love a mortal,
Use, to charm him (so to fit a fancy)
All her magic ('tis the old sweet mythos)          160
She would turn a new side to her mortal,
Side unseen of herdsman, huntsman, steersman—
Blank to Zoroaster on his terrace,
Blind to Galileo on his turret,
Dumb to Homer, dumb to Keats—him, even!          165
Think, the wonder of the moonstruck mortal—
When she turns round, comes again in heaven,
Opens out anew for worse or better!
Proves she like some portent of an iceberg
Swimming full upon the ship it founders,          170
Hungry with huge teeth of splintered crystals?

Proves she as the paved-work of a sapphire
Seen by Moses when he climbed the mountain?
Moses, Aaron, Nadab and Abihu
Climbed and saw the very God, the Highest,    175
Stand upon the paved-work of a sapphire.
Like the bodied heaven in his clearness
Shone the stone, the sapphire of that paved-work,
When they ate and drank and saw God also!

### XVIII

What were seen? None knows, none ever shall
    know.    180
Only this is sure—the sight were other,
Not the moon's same side, born late in Florence,
Dying now impoverished here in London.
God be thanked, the meanest of his creatures
Boasts two soul-sides, one to face the world with, 185
One to show a woman when he loves her.

### XIX

This I say of me, but think of you, Love!
This to you—yourself my moon of poets!
Ah, but that's the world's side—there's the wonder—
Thus they see you, praise you, think they know
    you.    190
There, in turn I stand with them and praise you,
Out of my own self, I dare to phrase it.
But the best is when I glide from out them,
Cross a step or two of dubious twilight,
Come out on the other side, the novel    195
Silent silver lights and darks undreamed of,
Where I hush and bless myself with silence.

XX

Oh, their Rafael of the dear Madonnas,
Oh, their Dante of the dread Inferno,
Wrote one song—and in my brain I sing it,        200
Drew one angel—borne, see, on my bosom!


XXIX. ABT VOGLER

(AFTER HE HAS BEEN EXTEMPORIZING UPON THE
MUSICAL INSTRUMENT OF HIS INVENTION)

I

Would that the structure brave, the manifold music
  I build,
  Bidding my organ obey, calling its keys to their
    work,
Claiming each slave of the sound, at a touch, as when
    Solomon willed
  Armies of angels that soar, legions of demons that
    lurk,
Man, brute, reptile, fly,—alien of end and of aim,  5
  Adverse, each from the other heaven-high, hell-deep
    removed,—
Should rush into sight at once as he named the
    ineffable Name,
  And pile him a palace straight, to pleasure the
    princess he loved!

II

Would it might tarry like his, the beautiful building
of mine,
This which my keys in a crowd pressed and im-
portuned to raise!                                    10
Ah, one and all, how they helped, would dispart now
and now combine,
Zealous to hasten the work, heighten their master
his praise!
And one would bury his brow with a blind plunge
down to hell,
Burrow awhile and build, broad on the roots of
things,
Then up again swim into sight, having based me my
palace well,                                          15
Founded it, fearless of flame, flat on the nether
springs.

III

And another would mount and march, like the ex-
cellent minion he was,
Ay, another and yet another, one crowd but with
many a crest,
Raising my rampired walls of gold as transparent as
glass,
Eager to do and die, yield each his place to the
rest:                                                 20
For higher still and higher (as a runner tips with fire,
When a great illumination surprises a festal night—
Outlining round and round Rome's dome from space
to spire)
Up, the pinnacled glory reached, and the pride of
my soul was in sight.

## IV

In sight? Not half! for it seemed, it was certain,
    to match man's birth, 25
Nature in turn conceived, obeying an impulse as I;
And the emulous heaven yearned down, made effort
    to reach the earth,
  As the earth had done her best, in my passion, to
    scale the sky:
Novel splendours burst forth, grew familiar and dwelt
    with mine,
  Not a point nor peak but found and fixed its wander-
    ing star; 30
Meteor-moons, balls of blaze: and they did not pale
    nor pine,
  For earth had attained to heaven, there was no
    more near nor far.

## V

Nay more; for there wanted not who walked in the
    glare and glow,
  Presences plain in the place; or, fresh from the
    Protoplast,
Furnished for ages to come, when a kindlier wind
    . should blow, 35
  Lured now to begin and live, in a house to their
    liking at last;
Or else the wonderful Dead who have passed through
    the body and gone,
  But were back once more to breathe in an old world
    worth their new;
What never had been, was now; what was, as it shall
    be anon;
  And what is,—shall I say, matched both? for I was
    made perfect too. 40

## VI

All through my keys that gave their sounds to a wish
of my soul,
 All through my soul that praised as its wish flowed
 visibly forth,
All through music and me! For think, had I painted
the whole,
 Why, there it had stood, to see, nor the process so
 wonder-worth:
Had I written the same, made verse—still, effect
proceeds from cause,                                    45
 Ye know why the forms are fair, ye hear how the
 tale is told;
It is all triumphant art, but art in obedience to laws,
 Painter and poet are proud in the artist-list en-
 rolled:—

## VII

But here is the finger of God, a flash of the will that
can,
 Existent behind all laws, that made them and, lo,
 they are!                                              50
And I know not if, save in this, such gift be allowed
to man,
 That out of three sounds he frame, not a fourth
 sound, but a star.
Consider it well: each tone of our scale in itself is
nought;
 It is everywhere in the world—loud, soft, and all is
 said:
Give it to me to use! I mix it with two in my
thought;                                                55
 And, there! Ye have heard and seen: consider and
 bow the head!

## VIII

Well, it is gone at last, the palace of music I reared;
   Gone! and the good tears start, the praises that
      come too slow;
For one is assured at first, one scarce can say that he
      feared,
   That he even gave it a thought, the gone thing was
      to go.                                          60
Never to be again! But many more of the kind
   As good, nay, better perchance: is this your comfort
      to me?
To me, who must be saved because I cling with my mind
   To the same, same self, same love, same God: ay,
      what was, shall be.

## IX

Therefore to whom turn I but to Thee, the ineffable
      Name?                                          65
   Builder and maker, Thou, of houses not made with
      hands!
What, have fear of change from Thee who art ever
      the same?
   Doubt that Thy power can fill the heart that Thy
      power expands?
There shall never be one lost good! What was, shall
      live as before;
   The evil is null, is nought, is silence implying
      sound;                                         70
What was good, shall be good, with, for evil, so much
      good more;
   On the earth the broken arcs; in the heaven, a
      perfect round.

## X

All we have willed or hoped or dreamed of good, shall
exist;
 Not its semblance, but itself; no beauty, nor good,
 nor power
Whose voice has gone forth, but each survives for the
melodist 75
 When eternity affirms the conception of an hour.
The high that proved too high, the heroic for earth too
hard,
 The passion that left the ground to lose itself in the
sky,
Are music sent up to God by the lover and the bard;
 Enough that He heard it once: we shall hear it
by-and-by. 80

## XI

And what is our failure here but a triumph's evidence
 For the fulness of the days? Have we withered or
agonized?
Why else was the pause prolonged but that singing
might issue thence?
 Why rushed the discords in, but that harmony should
be prized?
Sorrow is hard to bear, and doubt is slow to clear, 85
 Each sufferer says his say, his scheme of the weal
and woe:
But God has a few of us whom He whispers in the ear;
 The rest may reason and welcome: 't is we musicians
know.

XII

Well, it is earth with me; silence resumes her reign:
  I will be patient and proud, and soberly acquiesce. 90
Give me the keys. I feel for the common chord again,
  Sliding by semitones, till I sink to the minor,—yes,
And I blunt it into a ninth, and I stand on alien
    ground,
  Surveying awhile the heights I rolled from into the
    deep;
Which, hark, I have dared and done, for my resting-
    place is found,                                    95
  The C Major of this life: so, now I will try to sleep.


XXX.  RABBI BEN EZRA

I

Grow old along with me!
The best is yet to be,
The last of life, for which the first was made:
  Our times are in His hand
  Who saith "A whole I planned,                         5
"Youth shows but half; trust God: see all nor be
    afraid!"

II

Not that, amassing flowers,
Youth sighed "Which rose make ours,
"Which lily leave and then as best recall?"
  Not that, admiring stars,                            10
  It yearned "Nor Jove, nor Mars;
"Mine be some figured flame which blends, transcends
    them all!"

### III

Not for such hopes and fears
Annulling youth's brief years,
Do I remonstrate: folly wide the mark!                15
Rather I prize the doubt
Low kinds exist without,
Finished and finite clods, untroubled by a spark.

### IV

Poor vaunt of life indeed,
Were man but formed to feed                           20
On joy, to solely seek and find and feast:
Such feasting ended, then
As sure an end to men;
Irks care the crop-full bird? Frets doubt the maw-
      crammed beast?

### V

Rejoice we are allied                                 25
To That which doth provide
And not partake, effect and not receive!
A spark disturbs our clod;
Nearer we hold of God
Who gives, than of His tribes that take, I must
      believe.                                        30

### VI

Then, welcome each rebuff
That turns earth's smoothness rough,
Each sting that bids nor sit nor stand but go!

Be our joys three-parts pain!
Strive, and hold cheap the strain; 35
Learn, nor account the pang; dare, never grudge the
throe!

### VII

For thence,—a paradox
Which comforts while it mocks,—
Shall life succeed in that it seems to fail:
What I aspired to be, 40
And was not, comforts me:
A brute I might have been, but would not sink i' the
scale.

### VIII

What is he but a brute
Whose flesh hath soul to suit,
Whose spirit works lest arms and legs want play? 45
To man, propose this test—
Thy body at its best,
How far can that project thy soul on its lone way?

### IX

Yet gifts should prove their use:
I own the Past profuse 50
Of power each side, perfection every turn:
Eyes, ears took in their dole,
Brain treasured up the whole;
Should not the heart beat once "How good to live and
learn?"

### X

Not once beat "Praise be Thine!   55
   "I see the whole design,
"I, who saw Power, see now Love perfect too:
   "Perfect I call Thy plan:
   "Thanks that I was a man!
"Maker, remake, complete,—I trust what Thou shalt
      do!"   60

### XI

For pleasant is this flesh;
   Our soul, in its rose-mesh
Pulled ever to the earth, still yearns for rest:
   Would we some prize might hold
   To match those manifold   65
Possessions of the brute,—gain most, as we did best!

### XII

Let us not always say
   "Spite of this flesh to-day
"I strove, made head, gained ground upon the
      whole!"
   As the bird wings and sings,   70
   Let us cry "All good things
"Are ours, nor soul helps flesh more, now, than flesh
      helps soul!"

### XIII

Therefore I summon age
   To grant youth's heritage,
Life's struggle having so far reached its term:   75
   Thence shall I pass, approved
   A man, for aye removed
From the developed brute: a God though in the germ.

### XIV

And I shall thereupon
Take rest, ere I be gone 80
Once more on my adventure brave and new:
Fearless and unperplexed,
When I wage battle next,
What weapons to select, what armour to indue.

### XV

Youth ended, I shall try 85
My gain or loss thereby;
Be the fire ashes, what survives is gold:
And I shall weigh the same,
Give life its praise or blame:
Young, all lay in dispute; I shall know, being old. 90

### XVI

For note, when evening shuts,
A certain moment cuts
The deed off, calls the glory from the grey:
A whisper from the west
Shoots—"Add this to the rest, 95
"Take it and try its worth: here dies another day."

### XVII

So, still within this life,
Though lifted o'er its strife,
Let me discern, compare, pronounce at last,
"This rage was right i' the main, 100
"That acquiescence vain:
"The Future I may face now I have proved the Past."

### XVIII

For more is not reserved
To man, with soul just nerved
To act to-morrow what he learns to-day:          105
    Here, work enough to watch
    The Master work, and catch
Hints of the proper craft, tricks of the tool's true play.

### XIX

As it was better, youth
Should strive, through acts uncouth,          110
Toward making, than repose on aught found made:
    So, better, age, exempt
    From strife, should know, than tempt
Further.  Thou waitedst age; wait death nor be
        afraid!

### XX

Enough now, if the Right          115
    And Good and Infinite
Be named here, as thou callest thy hand thine own,
    With knowledge absolute,
    Subject to no dispute
From fools that crowded youth, nor let thee feel
        alone.          120

### XXI

Be there, for once and all,
Severed great minds from small,
Announced to each his station in the Past!
    Was I, the world arraigned,
    Were they, my soul disdained,          125
Right?  Let age speak the truth and give us peace
        at last!

XXII

Now, who shall arbitrate?
Ten men love what I hate,
Shun what I follow, slight what I receive;
    Ten, who in ears and eyes     130
    Match me: we all surmise,
They, this thing, and I, that: whom shall my soul
    believe?

XXIII

Not on the vulgar mass
Called "work," must sentence pass,
Things done, that took the eye and had the price;   135
    O'er which, from level stand,
    The low world laid its hand,
Found straightway to its mind, could value in a
    trice:

XXIV

But all, the world's coarse thumb
And finger failed to plumb,     140
So passed in making up the main account;
    All instincts immature,
    All purposes unsure,
That weighed not as his work, yet swelled the man's
    amount:

XXV

Thoughts hardly to be packed     145
Into a narrow act,
Fancies that broke through language and escaped;

All I could never be,
All, men ignored in me,
This, I was worth to God, whose wheel the pitcher
shaped. 150

### XXVI

Ay, note that Potter's wheel,
That metaphor! and feel
Why time spins fast, why passive lies our clay,—
Thou, to whom fools propound,
When the wine makes its round, 155
"Since life fleets, all is change; the Past gone, seize
to-day!"

### XXVII

Fool! All that is, at all,
Lasts ever, past recall;
Earth changes, but thy soul and God stand sure:
What entered into thee, 160
*That* was, is, and shall be:
Time's wheel runs back or stops: Potter and clay
endure.

### XXVIII

He fixed thee mid this dance
Of plastic circumstance,
This Present, thou, forsooth, wouldst fain arrest: 165
Machinery just meant
To give thy soul its bent,
Try thee and turn thee forth, sufficiently impressed

### XXIX

What though the earlier grooves
Which ran the laughing loves 170
Around thy base, no longer pause and press?
What though, about thy rim,
Scull-things in order grim
Grow out, in graver mood, obey the sterner stress?

### XXX

Look not thou down but up! 175
To uses of a cup,
The festal board, lamp's flash and trumpet's peal,
The new wine's foaming flow,
The Master's lips a-glow!
Thou, heaven's consummate cup, what need'st thou
with earth's wheel? 180

### XXXI

But I need, now as then,
Thee, God, who mouldest men;
And since, not even while the whirl was worst,
Did I,—to the wheel of life
With shapes and colours rife, 185
Bound dizzily,—mistake my end, to slake Thy thirst:

### XXXII

So, take and use Thy work:
Amend what flaws may lurk,
What strain o' the stuff, what warpings past the
aim!
My times be in Thy hand! 190
Perfect the cup as planned!
Let age approve of youth, and death complete the
same!

## XXXI. CALIBAN UPON SETEBOS; OR, NATURAL THEOLOGY IN THE ISLAND

"Thou thoughtest that I was altogether such a one as thyself."

['Will sprawl, now that the heat of day is best,
Flat on his belly in the pit's much mire,
With elbows wide, fists clenched to prop his chin;
And, while he kicks both feet in the cool slush,
And feels about his spine small eft-things course,          5
Run in and out each arm, and make him laugh;
And while above his head a pompion-plant,
Coating the cave-top as a brow its eye,
Creeps down to touch and tickle hair and beard,
And now a flower drops with a bee inside,          10
And now a fruit to snap at, catch and crunch:—
He looks out o'er yon sea which sunbeams cross
And recross till they weave a spider-web
(Meshes of fire, some great fish breaks at times)
And talks to his own self, howe'er he please,          15
Touching that other, whom his dam called God.
Because to talk about Him, vexes—ha,
Could He but know! and time to vex is now,
When talk is safer than in winter-time.
Moreover Prosper and Miranda sleep          20
In confidence he drudges at their task,
And it is good to cheat the pair, and gibe,
Letting the rank tongue blossom into speech.]

Setebos, Setebos, and Setebos!
'Thinketh, He dwelleth i' the cold o' the moon.          25

'Thinketh He made it, with the sun to match,
But not the stars; the stars came otherwise;
Only made clouds, winds, meteors, such as that:
Also this isle, what lives and grows thereon,
And snaky sea which rounds and ends the same. 30

'Thinketh, it came of being ill at ease:
He hated that He cannot change His cold,
Nor cure its ache. 'Hath spied an icy fish
That longed to 'scape the rock-stream where she
        lived,
And thaw herself within the lukewarm brine      35
O' the lazy sea her stream thrusts far amid,
A crystal spike 'twixt two warm walls of wave;
Only, she ever sickened, found repulse
At the other kind of water, not her life,
(Green-dense and dim-delicious, bred o' the sun)  40
Flounced back from bliss she was not born to
        breathe,
And in her old bounds buried her despair,
Hating and loving warmth alike: so He.

'Thinketh, He made thereat the sun, this isle,
Trees and the fowls here, beast and creeping thing. 45
Yon otter, sleek-wet, black, lithe as a leech;
Yon auk, one fire-eye in a ball of foam,
That floats and feeds; a certain badger brown
He hath watched hunt with that slant white-wedge
        eye
By moonlight; and the pie with the long tongue   50
That pricks deep into oakwarts for a worm,
And says a plain word when she finds her prize,
But will not eat the ants; the ants themselves

That build a wall of seeds and settled stalks
About their hole—He made all these and more,     55
Made all we see, and us, in spite: how else?
He could not, Himself, make a second self
To be His mate: as well have made Himself.
He would not make what he mislikes or slights,
An eyesore to Him, or not worth His pains:     60
But did, in envy, listlessness or sport,
Make what Himself would fain, in a manner, be—
Weaker in most points, stronger in a few,
Worthy, and yet mere playthings all the while,
Things He admires and mocks too,—that is it.     65
Because, so brave, so better though they be,
It nothing skills if He begin to plague.
Look now, I melt a gourd-fruit into mash,
Add honeycomb and pods, I have perceived,
Which bite like finches when they bill and kiss,—     70
Then, when froth rises bladdery, drink up all,
Quick, quick, till maggots scamper through my brain;
And throw me on my back i' the seeded thyme,
And wanton, wishing I were born a bird.
Put case, unable to be what I wish,     75
I yet could make a live bird out of clay:
Would not I take clay, pinch my Caliban
Able to fly?—for, there, see, he hath wings,
And great comb like the hoopoe's to admire,
And there, a sting to do his foes offence,     80
There, and I will that he begin to live,
Fly to yon rock-top, nip me off the horns
Of grigs high up that make the merry din,
Saucy through their veined wings, and mind me not.
In which feat, if his leg snapped, brittle clay,     85

And he lay stupid-like,—why, I should laugh;
And if he, spying me, should fall to weep,
Beseech me to be good, repair his wrong,
Bid his poor leg smart less or grow again,—
Well, as the chance were, this might take or else 90
Not take my fancy: I might hear his cry,
And give the manikin three legs for his one,
Or pluck the other off, leave him like an egg,
And lessoned he was mine and merely clay.
Were this no pleasure, lying in the thyme, 95
Drinking the mash, with brain become alive,
Making and marring clay at will? So He.

'Thinketh, such shows nor right nor wrong in Him,
Nor kind, nor cruel: He is strong and Lord.
'Am strong myself compared to yonder crabs 100
That march now from the mountain to the sea;
'Let twenty pass, and stone the twenty-first,
Loving not, hating not, just choosing so.
'Say, the first straggler that boasts purple spots
Shall join the file, one pincer twisted off; 105
'Say, this bruised fellow shall receive a worm,
And two worms he whose nippers end in red;
As it likes me each time, I do: so He.

Well then, 'supposeth He is good i' the main,
Placable if His mind and ways were guessed, 110
But rougher than His handiwork, be sure!
Oh, He hath made things worthier than Himself,
And envieth that, so helped, such things do more
Than He who made them! What consoles but this?
That they, unless through Him, do nought at all, 115

And must submit: what other use in things?
'Hath cut a pipe of pithless elder-joint
That, blown through, gives exact the scream o' the
      jay
When from her wing you twitch the feathers blue:
Sound this, and little birds that hate the jay     120
Flock within stone's throw, glad their foe is hurt:
Put case such pipe could prattle and boast forsooth
"I catch the birds, I am the crafty thing,
"I make the cry my maker cannot make
"With his great round mouth; he must blow through
      mine!"                                          125
Would not I smash it with my foot? So He.


But wherefore rough, why cold and ill at ease?
Aha, that is a question! Ask, for that,
What knows,—the something over Setebos
That made Him, or He, may be, found and fought,  130
Worsted, drove off and did to nothing, perchance.
There may be something quiet o'er His head,
Out of His reach, that feels nor joy nor grief,
Since both derive from weakness in some way.
I joy because the quails come; would not joy     135
Could I bring quails here when I have a mind:
This Quiet, all it hath a mind to, doth.
'Esteemeth stars the outposts of its couch,
But never spends much thought nor care that way.
It may look up, work up,—the worse for those     140
It works on! 'Careth but for Setebos
The many-handed as a cuttle-fish,
Who, making Himself feared through what He does,
Looks up, first, and perceives he cannot soar

To what is quiet and hath happy life; 145
Next looks down here, and out of very spite
Makes this a bauble-world to ape yon real,
These good things to match those as hips do grapes.
'T is solace making baubles, ay, and sport.
Himself peeped late, eyed Prosper at his books 150
Careless and lofty, lord now of the isle:
Vexed, 'stitched a book of broad leaves, arrow-shaped,
Wrote thereon, he knows what, prodigious words;
Has peeled a wand and called it by a name;
Weareth at whiles for an enchanter's robe 155
The eyed skin of a supple oncelot;
And hath an ounce sleeker than youngling mole,
A four-legged serpent he makes cower and couch,
Now snarl, now hold its breath and mind his eye,
And saith she is Miranda and my wife: 160
'Keeps for his Ariel a tall pouch-bill crane
He bids go wade for fish and straight disgorge;
Also a sea-beast, lumpish, which he snared,
Blinded the eyes of, and brought somewhat tame,
And split its toe-webs, and now pens the drudge 165
In a hole o' the rock and calls him Caliban;
A bitter heart, that bides its time and bites.
'Plays thus at being Prosper in a way,
Taketh his mirth with make-believes: so He.

His dam held that the Quiet made all things 170
Which Setebos vexed only: 'holds not so.
Who made them weak, meant weakness He might
    vex.
Had He meant other, while His hand was in,
Why not make horny eyes no thorn could prick,

Or plate my scalp with bone against the snow,     175
Or overscale my flesh 'neath joint and joint,
Like an orc's armour?  Ay,—so spoil His sport!
He is the One now: only He doth all.

'Saith, He may like, perchance, what profits Him.
Ay, himself loves what does him good; but why?     180
'Gets good no otherwise.  This blinded beast
Loves whoso places flesh-meat on his nose,
But, had he eyes, would want no help, but hate
Or love, just as it liked him: He hath eyes.
Also it pleaseth Setebos to work,     185
Use all His hands, and exercise much craft,
By no means for the love of what is worked.
'Tasteth, himself, no finer good i' the world
When all goes right, in this safe summer-time,
And he wants little, hungers, aches not much,     190
Than trying what to do with wit and strength.
'Falls to make something: 'piled yon pile of turfs,
And squared and stuck there squares of soft white
     chalk,
And, with a fish-tooth, scratched a moon on each,
And set up endwise certain spikes of tree,     195
And crowned the whole with a sloth's skull a-top,
Found dead i' the woods, too hard for one to kill.
No use at all i' the work, for work's sole sake;
'Shall some day knock it down again: so He.

'Saith He is terrible: watch His feats in proof!     200
One hurricane will spoil six good months' hope.
He hath a spite against me, that I know,
Just as He favours Prosper, who knows why?

So it is, all the same, as well I find.
'Wove wattles half the winter, fenced them firm 205
With stone and stake to stop she-tortoises
Crawling to lay their eggs here: well, one wave,
Feeling the foot of Him upon its neck,
Gaped as a snake does, lolled out its large tongue,
And licked the whole labour flat: so much for
    spite. 210
'Saw a ball flame down late (yonder it lies)
Where, half an hour before, I slept i' the shade:
Often they scatter sparkles: there is force!
'Dug up a newt He may have envied once
And turned to stone, shut up inside a stone. 215
Please Him and hinder this?—What Prosper does?
Aha, if He would tell me how! Not He!
There is the sport: discover how or die!
All need not die, for of the things o' the isle
Some flee afar, some dive, some run up trees; 220
Those at His mercy,—why, they please Him most
When ... when ... well, never try the same way
    twice!
Repeat what act has pleased, He may grow wroth.
You must not know His ways, and play Him off,
Sure of the issue. 'Doth the like himself: 225
'Spareth a squirrel that it nothing fears
But steals the nut from underneath my thumb,
And when I threat, bites stoutly in defence:
'Spareth an urchin that, contrariwise,
Curls up into a ball, pretending death 230
For fright at my approach: the two ways please.
But what would move my choler more than this,
That either creature counted on its life

To-morrow and next day and all days to come,
Saying forsooth in the inmost of its heart,          235
"Because he did so yesterday with me,
"And otherwise with such another brute,
"So must he do henceforth and always."—Ay?
'Would teach the reasoning couple what "must"
          means!
'Doth as he likes, or wherefore Lord? So He.    240

'Conceiveth all things will continue thus,
And we shall have to live in fear of Him
So long as He lives, keeps His strength: no change,
If He have done His best, make no new world
To please Him more, so leave off watching this,—    245
If He surprise not even the Quiet's self
Some strange day,—or, suppose, grow into it
As grubs grow butterflies: else, here are we,
And there is He, and nowhere help at all.

'Believeth with the life, the pain shall stop.          250
His dam held different, that after death
He both plagued enemies and feasted friends:
Idly! He doth His worst in this our life,
Giving just respite lest we die through pain,
Saving last pain for worst,—with which, an end. 255
Meanwhile, the best way to escape His ire
Is, not to seem too happy. 'Sees, himself,
Yonder two flies, with purple films and pink,
Bask on the pompion-bell above; kills both.
'Sees two black painful beetles roll their ball          260
On head and tail as if to save their lives:
Moves them the stick away they strive to clear.

Even so, 'would have Him misconceive, suppose
This Caliban strives hard and ails no less,
And always, above all else, envies Him.     265
Wherefore he mainly dances on dark nights,
Moans in the sun, gets under holes to laugh,
And never speaks his mind save housed as now:
Outside, 'groans, curses. If He caught me here,
O'erheard this speech, and asked "What chucklest
    at?"     270
'Would, to appease Him, cut a finger off,
Or of my three kid yearlings burn the best,
Or let the toothsome apples rot on tree,
Or push my tame beast for the orc to taste:
While myself lit a fire, and made a song     275
And sung it, "*What I hate, be consecrate*
"*To celebrate Thee and Thy state, no mate*
"*For Thee; what see for envy in poor me?*"
Hoping the while, since evils sometimes mend,
Warts rub away, and sores are cured with slime, 280
That some strange day, will either the Quiet catch
And conquer Setebos, or likelier He
Decrepit may doze, doze, as good as die.


[What, what? A curtain o'er the world at once!
Crickets stop hissing; not a bird—or, yes,     285
There scuds His raven that has told Him all!
It was fool's play, this prattling! Ha! The wind
Shoulders the pillared dust, death's house o' the
    move,
And fast invading fires begin! White blaze—
A tree's head snaps—and there, there, there, there,
    there,     290

His thunder follows! Fool to gibe at Him!
Lo! 'Lieth flat and loveth Setebos!
'Maketh his teeth meet through his upper lip,
Will let those quails fly, will not eat this month
One little mess of whelks, so he may 'scape!]    295

## XXXII. CONFESSIONS

### I

What is he buzzing in my ears?
  "Now that I come to die,
"Do I view the world as a vale of tears?"
  Ah, reverend sir, not I!

### II

What I viewed there once, what I view again,    5
  Where the physic bottles stand
On the table's edge,—is a suburb lane,
  With a wall to my bedside hand.

### III

That lane sloped, much as the bottles do,
  From a house you could descry        10
O'er the garden-wall: is the curtain blue
  Or green to a healthy eye?

### IV

To mine, it serves for the old June weather
  Blue above lane and wall;
And that farthest bottle labelled "Ether"    15
  Is the house o'ertopping all.

### V

At a terrace, somewhere near its stopper,
   There watched for me, one June,
A girl: I know, sir, it 's improper,
   My poor mind 's out of tune.        20

### VI

Only, there was a way ... you crept
   Close by the side, to dodge
Eyes in the house, two eyes except:
   They styled their house "The Lodge."

### VII

What right had a lounger up their lane ?    25
   But, by creeping very close,
With the good wall's help,—their eyes might strain
   And stretch themselves to Oes,

### VIII

Yet never catch her and me together,
   As she left the attic, there,       30
By the rim of the bottle labelled "Ether,"
   And stole from stair to stair,

### IX

And stood by the rose-wreathed gate. Alas,
   We loved, sir—used to meet:
How sad and bad and mad it was—    35
   But then, how it was sweet !

## XXXIII.　PROSPICE

Fear death?—to feel the fog in my throat,
　　The mist in my face,
When the snows begin, and the blasts denote
　　I am nearing the place,
The power of the night, the press of the storm,　　5
　　The post of the foe;
Where he stands, the Arch Fear in a visible form,
　　Yet the strong man must go:
For the journey is done and the summit attained,
　　And the barriers fall,　　　　　　　　　　10
Though a battle 's to fight ere the guerdon be gained,
　　The reward of it all.
I was ever a fighter, so—one fight more,
　　The best and the last!
I would hate that death bandaged my eyes, and
　　　forbore,　　　　　　　　　　　　　　15
　　And bade me creep past.
No! let me taste the whole of it, fare like my peers
　　The heroes of old,
Bear the brunt, in a minute pay glad life's arrears
　　Of pain, darkness and cold.　　　　　　　　20
For sudden the worst turns the best to the brave,
　　The black minute 's at end,
And the elements' rage, the fiend-voices that rave,
　　Shall dwindle, shall blend,
Shall change, shall become first a peace, then a joy, 25
　　Then a light, then thy breast,
O thou soul of my soul! I shall clasp thee again,
　　And with God be the rest!

## XXXIV. A FACE

If one could have that little head of hers
  Painted upon a background of pale gold,
Such as the Tuscan's early art prefers!
  No shade encroaching on the matchless mould
Of those two lips, which should be opening soft    5
  In pure profile; not as when she laughs,
For that spoils all: but rather as if aloft
  Yon hyacinth, she loves so, leaned its staff's
Burthen of honey-coloured buds to kiss
And capture 'twixt the lips apart for this.    10
Then her lithe neck, three fingers might surround,
How it should waver on the pale cold ground
Up to the fruit-shaped, perfect chin it lifts!
I know, Correggio loves to mass, in rifts
Of heaven, his angel faces, orb on orb    15
Breaking its outline, burning shades absorb:
But these are only massed there, I should think,
  Waiting to see some wonder momently
  Grow out, stand full, fade slow against the sky
  (That's the pale ground you'd see this sweet face
    by),    20
All heaven, meanwhile, condensed into one eye
Which fears to lose the wonder, should it wink.

## XXXV. THE RING AND THE BOOK.

### EPILOGUE TO BOOK I.

O lyric Love, half-angel and half-bird
And all a wonder and a wild desire—
Boldest of hearts that ever braved the sun,
Took sanctuary within the holier blue,
And sang a kindred soul out to his face,—          5
Yet human at the red-ripe of the heart—
When the first summons from the darkling earth
Reached thee amid thy chambers, blanched their blue,
And bared them of the glory—to drop down,
To toil for man, to suffer or to die,—          10
This is the same voice: can thy soul know change?
Hail then, and hearken from the realms of help!
Never may I commence my song, my due
To God who best taught song by gift of thee,
Except with bent head and beseeching hand—          15
That still, despite the distance and the dark,
What was, again may be; some interchange
Of grace, some splendour once thy very thought,
Some benediction anciently thy smile:
—Never conclude, but raising hand and head          20
Thither where eyes, that cannot reach, yet yearn
For all hope, all sustainment, all reward,
Their utmost up and on,—so blessing back
In those thy realms of help, that heaven thy home,
Some whiteness which, I judge, thy face makes
          proud,          25
Some wanness where, I think, thy foot may fall!

# NOTES

## I. From PARACELSUS

Published 1835.

Paracelsus is the mediaeval scholar and physician whose history Browning has told in a form which is something between drama and narrative. His ambitions and desires, boundless like those of Faustus, are concentrated upon the attainment of universal knowledge. This song records the passing of his earlier ideals.

> "Still, dreams
> They were, so let them vanish, yet in beauty
> If that may be. Stay: thus they pass in song!"

One might well imagine that Keats had written this song in which memories are distilled into perfumes.

1. **cassia.** A fragrant shrub or plant. This is partly a rhetorical use of the word from the Bible (Ps. xlv. 8), partly a reference to the cassia of Vergil and Ovid, explained by Lewis and Short as a fragrant plant, mezereon (N. E. D.).

2. **labdanum.** Or ladanum, a resinous exudation from certain plants growing in Mediterranean regions. The word has been taken over, as laudanum, to describe the drug prepared from opium. **aloe-balls.** No doubt the aloe-wood of the Bible, containing a dark fragrant resinous substance.

3. **nard.** Spikenard, an aromatic oil.

## II. From PIPPA PASSES

From *Bells and Pomegranates.* No. i. 1841.

Pippa is a poor child who passes singing through Asolo on her solitary holiday from the silk-mills. Her song falls upon the ears of four different groups of people, at critical moments in their lives. This lyric is heard by Ottima and her lover Sebald, who has murdered Ottima's husband.

14—2

# DRAMATIC LYRICS

## III. CAVALIER TUNES

From *Dramatic Lyrics. Bells and Pomegranates.* No. **III.** 1841.

These rousing songs, with their obvious cavalier sympathies, are probably the outcome of the poet's reading for the drama, *Strafford.*

MARCHING ALONG. 14. **Hazelrig, Fiennes, and young Harry.** Rigid parliamentarians all. Young Harry is Harry Vane, son of Sir Henry Vane the elder.

22. **to Nottingham.** This dates the incident at the commencement of the War.

BOOT AND SADDLE. 10. **Castle Brancepeth.** The castle lies a few miles south-west of Durham, and was anciently a seat of the Nevilles. None of the histories of the county record that it was in any way molested during the Civil War.

## IV. THE LOST LEADER

From *Dramatic Romances. Bells and Pomegranates.* No. **VII.** 1845.

This is a lament by the spokesman of a political party for the apostacy of a leader, whose greatness is still recognised and whose desertion is wistfully deplored. A letter from Browning to Grosart in 1875 shows the extent to which the parallel with the case of Wordsworth may be pressed. "I *did* in my hasty youth presume to use the great and venerable personality of Wordsworth as a sort of painter's model ; one from which this or the other particular feature may be selected and turned to account ; had I intended more, above all, such a boldness as portraying the entire man, I should not have talked about 'handfuls of silver and bits of ribbon.'" Wordsworth, Coleridge, and Southey had all recoiled from their extravagant early sympathies with the French Revolutionists. (Compare Coleridge's ode, *France*, and Wordsworth, *Prelude*, book xi.) Wordsworth's mind became strongly conservative. He was a sturdy opponent of the Reform Bill and of Catholic Emancipation. Browning was generally in sympathy with liberal sentiment. Professor Dowden suggests that possibly "some of the feeling attributed to Pym in relation to Strafford of the drama" may have crept into the poem.

13. **Shakespeare was of us.** The others may pass for democrats or republicans; it is not quite clear in what sense Browning supposes Shakespeare to share their sentiments.

20. **Still bidding crouch,** etc. His counsel will be for inaction, when other leaders command advance.


## V. "HOW THEY BROUGHT THE GOOD NEWS FROM GHENT TO AIX." (16—)

From *Dramatic Romances. Bells and Pomegranates.* No. vii. 1845.

If the good news is that of the pacification of Ghent (1578), by which its citizens gained a momentary advantage over the Spanish garrison, then Browning's date 16— must be interpreted with considerable freedom. There is no historical record of such a ride. The poet imagined it when he "had been long enough at sea to appreciate even the fancy of a gallop on the back of a certain good horse 'York' then in my stable at home." It has been suggested that the poet's journeyings through the Low Countries to Russia in 1834 familiarised him to some extent with the route and cities, though one may note that the names of the towns are given in four different languages. It would appear that the horse Roland, the hero of this "ballad of brave horses," covered some 120 miles in about 12 hours. This may well be named the "great pace." The metre, which is anapaestic with frequent substitutions of one accented syllable for two unaccented, is admirably suited to echo the clattering hoofs of the horses, and to reinforce the growing excitement of the narrative till it reaches its highest pitch in stanza ix.

Aix is Aix-la-Chapelle, called Aachen by the Germans, to whom it now belongs. It was founded by Charlemagne; until the sixteenth century the emperors were all crowned there.

10. **pique.** Probably the front point of the saddle. The New English Dictionary suggests that it is an erroneous form of peak.

81. **By Hasselt.** At this point they would have covered about 80 miles.

41. **Dalhem.** If this is the small town on the Prussian frontier, Browning's memory of position has failed him here; Aix is not in sight of Dalhem.

a **dome-spire.** A spire on the cathedral at Aix.

## VI.   GARDEN FANCIES

From *Dramatic Romances.   Bells and Pomegranates.* No. vii.   1845.

In these two poems, the delicate fancifulness of a lover, and the careless joviality of a bored student, frame themselves in appropriate though widely different garden settings.

SIBRANDUS SCHAFNABURGENSIS. The name of an imaginary botanical pedant. Browning discovered the name in Wanley's *Wonders of the Little World*, book vi. ch. vi. § 7. Schafnaburgensis means a dweller in Aschafnaburg.

7. **matin-prime.** The first hour after sunrise.

10. **arbute and laurustine.** Evergreen shrubs.

19. **pont-levis.** A draw-bridge. O. Fr. *leveis*, movable up and down.

80. **Chablis.** A white wine of Burgundy.

82. **Rabelais** (1490—1553). Priest, scholar and satirist of the corruption of his times in *La Vie de Gargantua et de Pantagruel.* Something of its inimitable humour and spirit is conveyed in the translation, eccentric as it is, by Sir Thomas Urquhart (1653).

38. *de profundis*, etc. Sing out of the depths with joyful accents.

50. **touse.** To pull about. M.E. *tūsen*, to tear.

52. **trover.** An action at law arising out of the finding of goods; here, the things found.

## VII. SOLILOQUY OF THE SPANISH CLOISTER

From *Dramatic Lyrics. Bells and Pomegranates*. No. III. 1842.
Originally with the *Incident of the French Camp*, under the title
*Camp and Cloister*.

Like *Sibrandus* and *Caliban* this is an exercise in the grotesque.
A monk, one of the discreditable products of asceticism, flames into
vituperative hatred against his inoffensive and saintly brother in
religion ; in petty spite he mangles his fruit and flowers, and specu-
lates on the means to rob him of salvation, till he is called to another
place, though not to another mood, by the Vesper bell.

10.  *Salve tibi !*  Hail to thee !

25—27.  **Dolores, Sanchicha.**  Spanish girls' names.  The monk
hints that there are sensual impulses in Brother Lawrence, if he
would but allow them sway.

37.  **the Trinity illustrate.**  The mean mind is here characterised
by a meticulous adherence to the forms of ritual.  He drinks in three
sips, remembering that there are three Persons in the Trinity.

39.  **the Arian.**  Arius propagated the belief in the fourth century
that Christ was not the eternal Son of God, but the chief and greatest
of created beings.

49.  **a great text in Galatians.**  Dr Berdoe conjectures this to be
Gal. iii. 10.  The twenty-nine (and more) curses are enumerated in
Deuteronomy xxviii.

56.  **a Manichee.**  A follower of Manes, a Persian, who sought to
combine Christianity with his own system, in which there are two
antagonistic principles, light and darkness.  The Manichees were held
to be heretics.

70.  *Hy, Zy, Hine....*  Imitating the Vesper bell.

71.  *Plena gratiâ Ave, Virgo !*  Hail ! Virgin full of grace.

## VIII. THE LOST MISTRESS

From *Dramatic Romances. Bells and Pomegranates*. No. VII. 1845.

The poem pictures the retreat, reluctant but manly, from love to
friendship.

## IX. EVELYN HOPE

From *Men and Women.* Vol. I. 1855.

The gentle and reticent passion of a man of middle age for a dying girl of sixteen is linked with a confidence that in some remote age or state his unspoken affection will find requital. The leaf is a simple token of his unshakeable faith that "God creates the love to reward the love."

## X. HOME THOUGHTS, FROM ABROAD

From *Dramatic Romances. Bells and Pomegranates.* No. VII. 1845.

## XI. HOME THOUGHTS, FROM THE SEA

From *Dramatic Romances. Bells and Pomegranates.* No. VII. 1845.

This was written about the same time and in the covers of the same Italian book as *How they brought the Good News.* This and the preceding poem are of a fine patriotic strain, the former inspired by a memory of the English countryside in spring; the second stirred by scenes of old-time English valour at Trafalgar and Gibraltar.

## XII. SAUL

From *Men and Women.* Vol. II. 1855. Stanzas i.—ix. had appeared
previously in *Bells and Pomegranates.* No. VII. 1845.

The foundation of the poem is the narrative in 1 Samuel xvi. 14—23. Possibly Browning's choice of the subject was a consequence of his lifelong admiration of Christopher Smart's *Song to David* (1763). In *Parleyings with Certain People* (1887), Browning claimed for Smart the power to

> "adjust
> Real vision to right language, till heaven's vault
> Pompous with sunset, storm-stirred sea's assault
> On the swilled rock-ridge, earth's embosomed brood
> Of tree and flower and weed, with all the life
> That flies or swims or crawls, in peace or strife,
> Above, below,—each had its note and name
> For Man to know by, ▄ "

The earlier sections of *Saul* define the themes of David's music; at first pastoral and idyllic; then a paean in praise of strength and valour and the power to command men; then a song of the prowess and statesmanship of Saul himself. All this Kenyon compared to "Homer's shield of Achilles thrown into lyrical whirl and life." But the king is scarcely stirred from his overwhelming lethargy. Then in section xvii., in a fashion a little reminiscent of Beethoven's Choral Symphony, David breaks into prophecy in place of song. His own tremulous love for Saul gathers force and broadens into a torrent of passionate reasoning in which he perceives the "Infinite care" and divines in a flash of vision the figure and purpose of the Christ. The thrill of the night and the awe of the dawn compose a marvellous epilogue in the closing Nocturne.

1. **Abner.** The captain of Saul's host.

9. **the Spirit.** The evil spirit from the Lord.

45. **the quick jerboa.** A small rodent quadruped. It is an Arabic word.

86. **not much—but the rest.** The little that was left unsaid.

101. **the cherubim-chariot.** See Ezekiel, ch. x. 8.

107. **leaves grasp of the sheet.** Relaxes its hold on the vast area of snow.

118. **all to traverse 'twixt hope and despair.** Saul was restored to consciousness, but it was not yet determined whether he should swing to hope or despair.

171. **Carouse in the Past.** There is rightful occasion for joy in the memories of youth; but it passes.

179. **First King.** Saul was the first king of the Israelites; they had previously been governed by prophets and judges. See 1 Samuel ix.

187. **The river's a-wave, etc.** The papyrus designed to record Saul's grandeur to posterity seems half conscious of its destiny.

199. **my voice to my heart.** Give me power to tell all my heart felt.

203. **Hebron.** A city of refuge south-west of the Jordan.

204. **Kidron.** A brook near Jerusalem.

244. **an abyss, where a dew-drop was asked.** He sought some trivial aspect of knowledge and stumbled upon the infinite.

253. **Man's nothing-perfect, etc.** Compare *Abt Vogler*, line 54; and *A Grammarian's Funeral*, line 103.

291. **Sabaoth.** Hosts. Hebrew *tseva'oth*, armies.

295. **'tis not what man Does, etc.** Compare *Rabbi Ben Ezra*, lines 133—150.

## XIII. BY THE FIRE-SIDE

From *Men and Women*. Vol. I. 1855.

There is much that is autobiographical in this poem, especially the sentiment of wedded intimacy and fidelity, on which theme the reader should compare *One Word More*, *Lyric Love*, and *Prospice*. But it must not be thought that this moment of revelation in the poet's own life occurred amid the scenes portrayed. These scenes are composed of memories partly of the chestnut woods about the Baths of Lucca in Tuscany, and partly of the Alps about the Lakes in Lombardy. The scene of Browning's courtship was No. 50, Wimpole Street, in London.

12. **deep in Greek.** At a later date Browning wrote *Balaustion's Adventure* (1871), including a transcript of the *Alcestis* of Euripides; *Aristophanes' Apology*, with a transcript of Euripides' *Herakles*; and the *Agamemnon of Aeschylus*.

18. **a branch-work.** So many allied interests which are to fill the remainder of life.

44. **How sharp the silver spear-heads charge, etc.** The poet has a liking for these images in which the background is cleft by some jagged and vivid outline. Compare the whole of section xv. of *Easter-Day*.

64. **freaked.** A coinage of Milton's, meaning streaked capriciously. "The pansy freak'd with jet." *Lycidas*, line 44.

73. **Cut hemp-stalks steep.** Hemp-stalks were put in a dyke till the soft part rotted away from the fibre.

74. **fret.** Eat into. O.E. *fretan* (*for-etan*), to devour entirely.

95. **'Five, six, nine.** Meaning of course 1569.

101. **Leonor.** Leonor is the wife-heroine of Beethoven's opera *Fidelio*; this may have suggested the name to Browning.

106—110. **A difficult stanza.** The following is a possible interpretation. The path grey-heads abhor is the period from old age to death, the crag's sheer edge. Those who die in youth find life flowery all the way. Those who grow older come upon two critical landmarks close together; first, the moment when youth falls into the gulf; second, a little inch farther on, death, which is what lies just beyond the hem of life.

113. **that great brow And the spirit-small hand propping it.** A favourite attitude of Mrs Browning.

116—120. **When, if I think**, etc. Their communion of thought is so intimate that it easily penetrates the flesh and has no need of spoken words.

155. **streaks and rings.** On the exposed breast of the hawk.

190. **Till the trouble grew**, etc. Nature reinforces destiny for this moment "one and infinite," then, having played its part, resumes its impassivity. "They relapsed to their ancient mood" (line 240). Compare stanza xx. Compare also the opening stanzas of Meredith's *Earth and Man*:

I.

"On her great venture, Man,
     Earth gazes while her fingers dint the breast
     Which is his well of strength, his home of rest,
And fair to scan.

II.

More aid than that embrace,
     That nourishment, she cannot give: his heart
     Involves his fate; she who urged the start
Abides the race."

230. **One near one is too far.** The poet will not be content with nearness; he demands identity. This line might be regarded as the theme of *Two in the Campagna*.

### XIV. THE GUARDIAN ANGEL:

A PICTURE AT FANO

From *Men and Women*. Vol. II. 1855.

Fano is a small coast-town, about thirty miles from Ancona. In the church of St Augustine is to be found the picture *L'Angelo Custode*, the composition of which can be realised from Browning's description. Guercino, the squinter, is the nickname of Barbieri (1590—1666). In the first few stanzas the poet describes the picture and the desire it stirs within him, to take the child's place and accept the child's serene trust and outlook. Then, as is more customary with him, he turns to speak of the artist, and to reclaim for him some measure of his former fame.

18. **Thou bird of God!** Borrowed from Dante, *Purgatorio*, IV. 129. "The bird of God who at the portal sits."

37. **Alfred.** Alfred Domett was a barrister friend whom Browning had already portrayed as Waring. He went to New Zealand and rose to the Premiership there, returning and resuming his friendship with Browning thirty years later.

46. **My angel.** The poet's wife.

55. **Wairoa.** A river in the northern island of New Zealand.

# DRAMATIC ROMANCES

## XV. INCIDENT OF THE FRENCH CAMP

From *Dramatic Lyrics*. *Camp and Cloister*. *Bells and Pomegranates*. No. III. 1842.

The story is true, but its actual hero was a man. (Mrs Orr.)

1. **Ratisbon.** A romantic city of Bavaria, on the right bank of the Danube. It was defended by the Austrians after their defeat at Eggmühl, when Napoleon stormed it in 1809.

11. **Lannes.** Afterwards the Duc de Montebello, a famous and trusted marshal of Napoleon. He was killed in the same year at the battle of Aspern.

## XVI. MY LAST DUCHESS

### FERRARA

From *Dramatic Lyrics*. *Bells and Pomegranates*. No. III. 1842. It then had the title "Italy."

This monologue is spoken in the presence of the ambassador of a foreign Count whose daughter is being sought in marriage by the widowed Duke. The basis of his character is the complacent egotism of the aristocrat whose name is centuries old, who regards his wife as a dependent, and her innocent gaiety and graciousness as presumptions to be summarily extinguished. His most salient idiosyncrasy is that connoisseurship and pride of mere possession of a masterpiece which Browning felt to be a phase of the decadent Renaissance. The Ferrarese duke shares it with the Bishop of St Praxed's. One may venture a suggestion that these pathetic stifled figures, the Last Duchess, and the Duchess of the *Flight*, owe something of their existence to the durance of Elizabeth Barrett in Wimpole Street.

Ferrara is a well-fortified city of Lower Lombardy. It was held by the Este family, sometimes under the suzerainty of the Pope, sometimes as independent lords, from the thirteenth to the sixteenth century. It was for long the home of Ariosto, and was the seat of one of the most cultured Italian courts of the Renaissance.

3. **Frà Pandolf.** An imaginary artist.

45. **I gave commands**, etc. A rare example of significant suggestion with economy in words.

56. **Claus of Innsbruck.** Another invented name.

## XVII.  THE LAST RIDE TOGETHER

From *Men and Women*. Vol. I. 1855.

A lover who has failed to win his lady's favour claims but the memory of his hope and one last ride together. The swift rush of the wind seems, as it were, to unfold his understanding. He contrasts his failure with that of the statesman, soldier, poet, musician, sculptor, who have given their talents, as he has given his youth, for no lasting reward. But they have none of the momentary glory of possession that he has in his last ride, in the intoxication of which he has some wild anticipation that the world may end that night and eternity break upon them as they ride side by side. In any case his spiritual exultation is enduring. The rhythmic beat of the verses is a fitting accompaniment to the movement, thought, and mood of the poem.

62. **Ten lines, a statesman's life in each!** So little is the world concerned with the memory of those who have reached high rank in the state, that a single line will sum up all it cares to record about them.

93. **Have a bliss to die with, dim-descried.** After all earthly success there still remains some greater attainment for the future. Browning never tires of probing apparent success. The stanza just hints how attainment may deaden nobler effort and desire.

## XVIII.  THE PIED PIPER OF HAMELIN;

### A Child's Story

*(written for, and inscribed to, W. M. the younger.)*

From *Dramatic Lyrics. Bells and Pomegranates.* No. III. 1842. The poem was not originally intended for publication, but was thrown in to fill a sheet in No. III. of *Bells and Pomegranates.*

W. M. the younger is William Macready, the son of the actor, through whose agency Browning's plays, *Strafford* (1837) and *A Blot on the Scutcheon* (1843) were presented. Browning's father had commenced a poem on the incident for the children of Mr Earles, a colleague at the Bank of England. A few lines are given which curiously illustrate the hereditary instinct for the fantastic and for ludicrous rhymes.

"There is a town at a moderate distance from Hanover—
    A town on the Weser of singular fame:
A place which the French and the rats often ran over—
    But though my tale varies
    Yet sage antiquaries
Are all in one story concerning its name—
'Tis Hammelin (but you had better perhaps
Turn over your atlas and look at the maps)—
    Which, without flattery,
    Seemed one vast rattery;
Where the rats came from no mortal could say—
    But for one put to flight
There were ten the next night;—
And for ten over night there were twenty next day."

Mr Browning gave up after 60 lines, on hearing that his son had made a version; though at a later date he completed the fragment. There can be no doubt, that whatever the remoter origin of the legend may be, the Brownings were brought to a knowledge of it in *The Wonders of the Little World*, by Nathaniel Wanley (1676); a strange collection of tales and miscellaneous information in the father's oddly assorted library. It is possible, since Wanley mentions Howell (author of the *Epistolae Ho-Elianae*, 1645), that some smaller suggestions come from this source. Browning must also have seen the story as told by Richard Verstegan in *The Restitution of Decayed Intelligence in Antiquities* (1605); Browning takes Verstegan's date, 1376, and like Verstegan he places Hamelin wrongly in Brunswick. The early history of the legend is treated in *Folklore*, vol. III.

**1. Hamelin.** Now an old-fashioned town 25 miles south-west of Hanover, situated at the confluence of the Weser and the Hamel.

**28. obese.** Occasionally the effect of the grotesque rhymes is enhanced by a cavalier disposal of the normal accent. Compare lines 35, 68, 138, 157 and 187.

**89. Cham.** An obsolete form of Khan, applied to the rulers of the Tartars.

**91. Nizam.** The title of the rulers of Hyderabad, of the dynasty of Asaf Jah (1713—1748).

**95. guilders.** A gold coin formerly current in the Netherlands; now the name of a Dutch coin worth about 1s. 8d.

**123. stout as Julius Caesar.** There is an apocryphal story that Caesar swam the harbour of Alexandria holding his commentaries above his head when he was besieged there by the Egyptians. Browning found the story in Wanley, book v. ch. xvi. "Of men notably practised in swimming."

**136. psaltery.** An old stringed instrument, like a dulcimer, but played by plucking the strings.

**139. nuncheon.** A light mid-day repast. O.E. *non-scenc*, noon-tide cup.

**182. stiver.** Dutch *stuiver*, a penny.

**220. Koppelberg Hill.** Wanley gives the name as Koppen. No hill of the name is now known. The hill nearest the town is called the Bassberg. The title has been claimed for other hills, but there is no established identification.

**246. fallow deer.** Fallow is the colour yellowish-brown.

**285. on the great Church-Window painted.** Neither column nor church-window now exists.

**290. in Transylvania there's a tribe.** This is from Verstegan. Transylvania is in the extreme east of Austria-Hungary. The inhabitants derive from very various sources, and many strange legends of their origins are current among them.

**296. trepanned.** Rightly trapanned, meaning trapped or caught. Compare French *attraper*.

## XIX.  A GRAMMARIAN'S FUNERAL

Shortly after the revival of learning in Europe.

From *Men and Women*.  Vol. II.  1855.

In *The Wonders of the Little World*, 1676, by Nathaniel Wanley, book III. ch. xli. is entitled: "Of the exceeding intentness of some men upon their Meditations and Studies." Here Aristotle and Aquinas rub shoulders with such forgotten worthies as Sir Francis Jeffreys and Schegkius. Of the fifteen martyrs the accounts of two are apropos to this poem. Paragraph 14 is as follows:

"Jacobus Milichius a German Physician, was so enflamed with a passionate desire of Learning, that he would not spare himself even then when ill in respect of his health, and when old age began to grow upon him, when some of his friends would reprehend this over-eagerness of his, and his too much attentiveness to his studies, his reply was that of Solon, γηράσκω δ'αἰὲν πολλὰ διδασκόμενος, i.e. *I grow old in learning many things*. He was so sparing and careful afterward of his time that no man could find him at his own house, but he was either reading or writing of some thing, or else (which was very rare with him) he was playing at Tables, a sport which he much delighted in after dinner. After supper and in the Night he was at his Studies and Lucubrations; which was the reason that he slept but little, and was also the cause of that disease which took away his life, for the over constant and the unseasonable intention of his mind in his studies, was doubtless the occasion of that affliction which he had in his Brain and in his Stomach, so that he died of an Apoplexy, Nov. 10th, 1559."

Wanley gives a side reference to Melchior Adam's *Lives of the German Physicians*. I referred to this book, to find that though it suggests that Milichius was a man of civil and humane as well as medical learning, there was nothing to show that Browning had made any use of the reference. Nevertheless there can be little doubt that Browning had in mind the German humanist of the Early Renaissance, rather than the Italian as has often been surmised. Whether the scene of the

poem does more closely resemble one of the castle-crowned hill-encir-
cling cities of Southern Germany, is matter for individual judgment.

Another paragraph, No. 2 in the same chapter, may have afforded
material for the poem:

"Dr *Reynolds* when the heads of the University of Oxford came to
visit him in his last sickness; which he had contracted merely by his
exceeding paines in his studies (whereby he brought his withered body
to be a very Sckeleton) they earnestly persuaded him that he would
not (*perdere substantiam propter accidentia*) *loose his life for learning,*
he with a smile answered out of the Poet,

> *Nec propter vitam vivendi perdere causas,*
> *Nor to save life lose that for which I live.*"

These passages are given from the edition of 1676; it is possible
that the edition which the poet found in his father's library was that
in two volumes published in 1806. The variations in any case are
very slight and do not affect these conclusions.

In this poem a life's accomplishment is measured by two different
standards; according as we take into account or ignore the life hereafter. The Grammarian, never doubting that "Man has Forever,"
has been content to forgo everything else in the painful pursuit of the
*minutiae* of Greek syntax. Born with the grace of Apollo, he has
become shrunken, leaden-eyed, subject to torturing disease and premature death. If a man's life, like that of "dogs and apes," has no
endurance beyond death, then it is clear that this has been a paltry
and grotesque existence. If on the other hand, the lofty belief which
he has inspired in these disciples is warranted, then this funeral
procession becomes a pageant of victory. The cortège winding its
way in the dawn steadily up the mountain-side until it achieves the
summit with its unlimited panorama, becomes a symbol of a life
spent in unrelaxing effort until it attains that infinite expansion of
the designs and talents of men, which the scholar anticipates with
such sublime faith. Are we then to suppose that Browning singles
out for special commendation a life devoted with almost ludicrous
heroism to the scientific detail of philology? No more than we are to
assume his approval of the crime contemplated in *The Statue and the
Bust.* Not the quality of the ambition, but the energy and sincerity
displayed in its pursuit is here as there the object of judgment.

**5. crofts.** Fields; in O. E. meant enclosed fields, those adjoining the homestead.

**thorpes.** Villages. O. E. *thorp*, hamlet; a Scandinavian word.

**8. Rimming the rock-row.** The suggestion is that the dawn comes earlier to these heights than to the sleeping shadowed plain. It is curious that this sublime poem should contain almost as many of Browning's most violent double rhymes as even the *Pied Piper*. Compare lines 72, 98, 110, 134, 142.

**26. 'Ware the beholders.** Remember that onlookers will note the nature of our tribute.

**34. Lyric Apollo.** In his youth the Grammarian had the splendid frame and signal beauty of Apollo who in Greece was the deity of many human activities, among them those of music, song and learning.

**37. the little touch.** The unobserved encroachment of disease.

**43. the signal.** The warning of disease; not that he should rest, but "leave play for work."

**57. Actual life comes next?** "Do you tell me to begin to live now? I find there is still much to learn; I must first satisfy my thirst for knowledge."

**68. Sooner, he spurned it.** He spurned the idea of commencing to live before (i.e. sooner than) he had gathered all books had to give.

**86.** *Calculus.* The stone, a painful disease of the bladder.

**88.** *Tussis.* A bronchial cough.

**95. soul-hydroptic.** Dropsical persons suffer from insatiable thirst.

**103. the heavenly period,** etc. Compare *Abt Vogler*, line 72, "On the earth the broken arcs; in the heaven a perfect round."

**108. Paid by instalment.** One suggestion implicit in this is that a man by receiving earthly rewards discounts what is due to him hereafter. Compare *The Patriot*, stanza vi. But there is more than this; for by earthly preoccupations we sacrifice the development of the greater capacities, which would have found exercise in another life. Compare the close of section xx. of *Easter-Day*,

> "Thou art shut
> Out of the heaven of spirit; glut
> Thy sense upon the world! 'tis thine
> For ever—take it!"

120. **Misses an unit.** These lines may be paraphrased thus. A man may set before himself some small aim and accomplish it; and this may be called success. Another man may set before himself some immensely greater aim, and may just fall below it; and this may be called failure. But there can be no question as to which is the nobler achievement.

129. *Hoti's* business, etc. He set out completely and finally all that was to be known about these Greek particles. ὅτι means "because" or "that"; οὖν is an adverb meaning "therefore"; the enclitic -δε is united to words so as to seem part of them, and gives them slightly varying significances. One commentator is rumoured to have thought that Hoti was a Chinese mandarin.

134. **purlieus.** Haunts.


## XX. HOLY-CROSS DAY

From *Men and Women*. Vol. ii. 1855.

Holy-Cross Day commemorates the miraculous appearance of the Cross in the sky to the Emperor Constantine; the festival falls on September 14th. It is not a historical fact that the Jews were compelled to attend an annual sermon on this day. Such things took place from time to time; in 1584 a papal bull was promulgated that the Jews should assemble in the church of St Angelo in Pescheria, which was near the Ghetto. At the same time the Jews had to provide the prizes for the horse-racing during the carnival. The extract from the Diary by the Bishop's Secretary is fictitious, but is in itself a piece of delicious satire. Gregory XVI., who abolished the sermon finally, was Pope from 1831 to 1846.

10. **handsel.** To be the first customer, with a view either to luck or to favours to follow. Compare Icelandic *hansal*, the conclusion of a bargain by shaking hands.

22. **hour-glass.** Doubtless to time his sermon.

52. **Were spurred through the Corso.** The Corso is the rather narrow main street of Rome. In imperial Rome it was called the *Via Flaminia*. It acquired its present name as being the scene of the carnival, the funds for which were extorted from the Jews.

66. **Ben Ezra's Song of Death.** A sudden ascent from the

ridiculous to the sublime. For Rabbi Ben Ezra see the note on
the poem with that title. This song of death is of Browning's
invention.

111. **Ghetto.** The quarter in an Italian city to which the Jews
were confined. The word is thought to be derived from Italian
*borghetto*, a little town.

## XXI. THE STATUE AND THE BUST

### From *Men and Women*. Vol. I. 1855.

The Florentine legend, which the poet here intersperses with
temperamental analysis and moral counsel, is thus given by Mrs Orr:
"In the piazza of the SS. Annunziata at Florence is an equestrian
statue of the Grand Duke Ferdinand the First, representing him as
riding away from the church, with his head turned in the direction of
the Riccardi Palace, which occupies one corner of the square. Tradi-
tion asserts that he loved a lady whom her husband's jealousy kept a
prisoner there; and that he avenged his love by placing himself in
effigy where his glance could always dwell upon her."

This is an instance in which Browning employs paradox to enforce
his principle, "Let a man contend to the uttermost for his life's set
prize." Two lovers allow their energy and resolution to be frittered
away through inaction, "like simpler and slighter Hamlets," and
thus they lose their life's prize: love dies through inanition. But to
gain it involves for one of them a violation of the marriage-vow.
The ordinary moralist, horror-struck, insists upon the criminal nature
of their enterprise. Browning insists that this was a supreme test
in their lives, and that in such instances it matters not at all whether
the end is great or small, good or bad. These lovers failed at their
test, and he condemns them, not for their purposed iniquity, but for
their pusillanimity and supineness.

The metre of the poem is *terza rima*, making use of short lines,
and having such a pause at the end of each stanza as there is generally
in Dante's *Divine Comedy*. "This law, though rarely neglected by
Dante, has seldom been observed by the few English poets who have
attempted the measure. Neither Byron in the *Prophecy of Dante*, nor

Shelley in *The Triumph of Life*, nor Mrs Browning in *Casa Guidi Windows*, has done so."—(Symons.)

1. **There's a palace, etc.** This palace must be the Palazzo Riccardi-Manelli, not the more famous Palazzo Riccardi, which is half a mile away˙from "the square," that is the Piazza della Annunziata. The failure to realise this has caused no little confusion. The statue is still in the square, facing this small palace. The bust is not there now; and though the poem speaks definitely of the "empty shrine," I am assured by residents in Florence that there is no shrine on the palace front; and the general belief is that no such bust ever actually existed.

12. **The Great-Duke Ferdinand.** Ferdinand I., one of the Medici, Grand Duke of Florence 1587—1609. He had previously been a cardinal. Actually he was a competent and popular ruler.

18. **the Riccardi.** A family of rank in Florence. The Riccardi later says that his bride is from the south.

22. **encolure.** Usually the neck of an animal; means here the mane.

33. **the pile which the mighty shadow makes.** The palace of the Medici towers above and darkens part of the Via Larga, now known as the Via Cavour. The poet draws a parallel between this and what he calls the murder, meaning the overthrow, of the first Florentine Republic, when Cosimo and afterwards Lorenzo the Magnificent (Cosimo's grandson, not his son) exalted themselves to the status of princes, though in outward show they preserved the forms of the Republic.

57. **catafalk.** Generally a stage or platform used at funerals; here evidently the bride's funeral car.

95. **Petraja.** The royal villa of Petraja is situated about three miles north of Florence. It was remodelled for Ferdinand whilst he was cardinal in 1575. Its gardens are still famous.

113. **the Envoy arrives from France.** Perhaps to discuss the marriage of Ferdinand's niece, Marie de' Medici, with the French King Henry IV.

140. **simple policy.** Foolish policy.

169. **Robbia's craft.** Luca della Robbia (1399—1482) first practised in Italy the art to which his name was attached, and which was pursued by many members of his family, down to the year 1566,

when the last of them died. It is clear therefore from the date that the lady must be speaking of some later artist of the school. This special art was the production of terra-cotta reliefs, covered with enamel. The secret of the process was to cover the clay with an enamel formed of the ordinary ingredients of glass, made an opaque white by oxide of tin.—(*Enc. Brit.*) By no means all Robbia's work is pure white in colour. The South Kensington Museum has the finest collection of this ware out of Italy.

186. **A lady of clay is as good, I trow.** The romance is dead; the Lady and the Duke (compare line 212) are both well aware that the statue and the bust are simply mockeries; symbols not of passion but of self-contempt.

202. **John of Douay.** Known also as Giovanni of Bologna (1524—1608), a sculptor, was born at Douay, but went early to Florence, where his *Mercury* and *Rape of the Sabines* still remain. They are characterised, as is the statue spoken of in the poem, by great spirit and elegance.

219. **Six steps out of the chapel.** The church of the Santissima Annunziata, on the north-east side of the square.

233. **an epigram.** The whole passage is difficult, and the crux of the difficulty is the word epigram. In response to an enquiry Professor Henry Bradley made the following suggestions:

Browning's use of *epigram* seems to be a pure individual licence, having no root in previous usage either in English or in any other language. Perhaps Browning's idea is something like this: An epigram is a condensed and pointed verbal expression of some thought, most commonly of something paradoxical or contemptuous. An action which does in another way what an epigram does by words may be called an epigram in a figurative sense. In *The Statue and the Bust* the meaning seems to be: If you insist on tendering coin where a button would pass, your action, if not mere folly, is an "epigrammatic" way of indicating your disdain for money, or your low valuation of the king's stamp. The application is that the elementary question whether cowardice and irresolution are unmanly does not depend on the question whether they happen to be exhibited in face of a moral decision or an immoral one. To invoke the moral law of the particular case to decide this question is to pay a coin instead of a button—which is not honouring the coin.

A rather different point of view is adopted in the note which follows for which I am indebted to my colleague, Miss Coning:

In this game of life, played out under shabbiest circumstance and for indifferent prizes or none (your table's a hat, etc.), the play's the thing. He who points out that you are playing Crime the counter, instead of Virtue the coin of the realm

> "golden through and through
> Sufficient to vindicate itself
> And prove its worth at a moment's view,"

is uttering a criticism that is irrelevant, obvious in the worst sense (i.e. keenly aware of *in*-essentials)—and has missed the point of the game.

He is a pedant, not a student of life—he] lives in epigrams—trite judgments whose value such as it is lies wholly in expression, face-value—and his objection is therefore not only irrelevant and obvious but quite literally *superficial* and of merely epigrammatic value.

234. **the stamp of the very Guelph.** A coin stamped with the image of the Queen, whose name was Guelph.

237. **When your table's a hat, etc.** The conditions under which the game is played and the reward at the end of it are not to be considered in any judgment on the player. The fact that the thing desired by the Duke and the Lady was iniquitous does not invalidate it as a test. In their test they failed for lack of initiative and resolve.

250. *De te, fabula.* The story applies to you.


## XXII. "CHILDE ROLAND TO THE DARK TOWER CAME"

### (See Edgar's Song in *Lear*)

A poem of romance, but having all the customary features of temper, substance, and treatment inverted. In place of the glowing ideal and eager adventurous spirit of chivalry, there is the worn, depressed constancy of the knight whose long years of errantry furnish him with none but derisive memories, and whose hope has dwindled almost to extinction. To replace the dreamy haze of beauty in

Spenserian landscape, there is pictured with gruesome realistic detail, the repulsive barrenness of the plain, the starved and penurious vegetation, the flat ugly mountain heaps, the squat grotesque Dark Tower. For the sensuous enchantment of *La Belle Dame sans Merci* is substituted the evil magic which shifts and lights up for a moment these loathsome and menacing scenes. The very hills laugh out a great contemptuous peal as he confronts his task at last. There is no necessity to seek for any allegorical interpretation ; the poem speaks for itself.

**Childe.** This simply means a youth of rank; it was afterwards applied to any knight. Compare *Child Maurice* and *Child Waters*. The final -e is a modern device to distinguish this usage.

**Edgar's Song.** *King Lear*, III. iv. 193. Professor Child's *English and Scottish Ballads* gives fragments of a ballad *Child Rowland and Burd Ellen*; but Browning's poem is simply a fantastic expansion of the single line "Child Rowland to the dark tower came."

**2. That hoary cripple.** Compare Chaucer's *Pardoner's Tale*, lines 710—765 (Globe edition).

**3. Askance.** Sidewise. One of a number of words, askew, askoyne, etc., of which the etymology is still undetermined. Skeat suggests that it is due to Italian *scansare*, to go a-slope. See N.E.D.

**16. neither pride Nor hope rekindling,** etc. The mood of battered indifferent resignation is just as remote from the true temper of heroic adventure as the scenery is from the conventional landscapes of romance in Malory, Spenser or Coleridge.

**24. finding failure in its scope.** The unaccustomed spring of joy was not due to the prospect of failure directly, but to the prospect of an end, which of course involved the possibility of failure.

**25. As when a sick man,** etc. It is possible that these two stanzas may have been suggested by the first verse of Donne's *Valediction*:

> As virtuous men pass mildly away,
> And whisper to their souls to go,
> Whilst some of their sad friends do say,
> "Now his breath goes," and some say, "Nay."

**48. estray.** Properly a stray animal.

**68. the bents.** The stiff flower-stalks of grasses.

72. **Pashing.** Treading violently upon watery ground.

76. **One stiff blind horse.** One of several vivid memories which Browning wove together in the poem. Mrs Orr (*Handbook*, p. 274) records them thus: "a tower which Mr Browning once saw in the Carrara Mountains, a painting which caught his eye years later in Paris; and the figure of a horse in the tapestry in his own drawing-room." Dr Furnivall describes it as "a red horse with a glaring eye, standing behind a dun one, on the right hand of a large tapestry."

80. **colloped.** In Wanley's description of the torture of Ravaillac, who murdered Henri IV. of France, "collops of flesh" were torn away with hot pincers. Browning probably formed his participle from this word.

85. **I shut my eyes, etc.** Compare *The Ancient Mariner*, part IV. stanzas v., vi., vii.

133. **cirque.** Any circular arena.

136. **brewage.** A decoction. Through French *breuvage*, a beverage.

141. **brake.** A rack, or frame of torture.

143. **Tophet's tool.** Some hellish instrument. Tophet was at first the name of part of the valley of Hinnom where the refuse of Jerusalem was burned; it later became synonymous with the place of the damned.

147. **so a fool finds mirth, etc.** Compare *Caliban*, lines 185—199.

160. **Apollyon's bosom-friend.** "So he went on and Apollyon met him. Now the monster was hideous to behold; he was clothed with scales like a fish, (and they were his pride,) he had wings like a dragon, feet like a bear, and out of his belly came fire and smoke, and his mouth was the mouth of a lion" (*Pilgrim's Progress*).

203. **slug-horn.** Skeat says of this word, "Ignorantly used by Chatterton and Browning to mean a sort of horn; but really Mid. Sc *slogorne*, a corruption of *slogan*, a war-cry."

# MEN AND WOMEN

## XXIII. AN EPISTLE

CONTAINING THE STRANGE MEDICAL EXPERIENCE OF
KARSHISH, THE ARAB PHYSICIAN

Here Browning sets forth, not as in *Blougram* and *Caliban* the
ambiguities of truth, but truth itself in an unfamiliar and arresting
light. It is mirrored in the mind of Karshish the Arab physician, by
whose two prepossessions it is for a moment amiably distorted. For,
first, he is an Arab, and therefore almost impervious to this conception of the Incarnation. (It should be noted however that the common
element of the Arabic and the Christian belief, the unity of God,
makes the transition at the close more credible and natural.) And,
secondly, being a physician, he diagnoses the case in familiar terms
and endeavours to range it finally under a well-known category; it is
"a case of mania subinduced by epilepsy." Through both these
obstacles the light breaks, though it is only a light reflected in the
resurrected features of a Jewish artisan; its glow irradiates the
traveller's mind so that he is driven to the almost involuntary confession of his postscript.

The broad historical background is a lawless Judea in perpetual
dread of the legions of Vespasian. The foreground is the village of
Bethany, beneath a rocky spur of Mount Olivet, the scene 35 years
earlier of the miracle recorded in St John, ch. xi., just preceding the
events in which the Nazarene leech "perished in a tumult." Here
the two are confronted; Karshish alert, observant, rather tolerant for
his time of novel ideas, noting the prevalence of Syrian diseases, the
fertility of the country in herbs useful to the pharmacist, and keenly
interested professionally in this case which only partially submits to
any known classification. On the other side is Lazarus, physically
refreshed, mentally an inhabitant of some other province of experience. In fact he has seen "the great ring of pure and endless
light," and is bewildered on his return by this confinement within

earthly and temporal restrictions. In no poem, even of Browning's, is the distribution of detail so cunning and so appropriate, nor the cumulative effect both of picture and of thought so rich and so convincing.

5. **To coop up**, etc. Compare *Rabbi Ben Ezra*, stanzas viii. and xi.

11. **the wily vapour.** That is the "puff of vapour," man's soul; Karshish believes in its pre-existence.

17. **true snake-stone.** A small rounded piece of stone popularly supposed to cure snake-bite. No stone having this power actually exists, and the physician seems to suggest, in line 19, that he is rather dubious of the medical efficacy of the specimens he sends.

28. **Vespasian.** Vespasian was in charge of the province of Judea from 67 to 69 A.D. In the latter year he became emperor, and left the conduct of the war against Jerusalem to his son Titus, who captured the town in the year 70. The poem refers therefore to a time nearly 40 years after the resurrection of Lazarus.

36. **This Bethany, lies scarce the distance,** etc. Bethany is actually about two miles from Jerusalem.

40. **void the stuffing**, etc. To set down all the experiences of my journeyings.

42. **choler.** Bile. The word has also the meaning "anger." Anger was thought to be due to excess of bile in the system. The word is connected with Greek χολή, bile.

43. **tertians.** Agues or fevers with paroxysms recurring every other day. M.F. *tertiane*, a tertian ague.

45. **a spider here**, etc. Dr Berdoe's note on this is as follows: "Dr H. McCook, a specialist in spider lore, has explained this passage in *Poet-Lore*, vol. I. p. 518. He says the spider referred to belongs to the Wandering group: they stalk their prey in the open field, or in divers lurking places, and are quite different in their habits from the webspinners. The spider sprinkled with mottles he thinks is the Zebra spider (*Epiblemum scenicum*). It belongs to the Saltigrade tribe."

49. **The Syrian run-a-gate.** Some native whom the physician has cured, in his own way, of the "ailing eye," and who has volunteered to convey the letter to some point whence its delivery may be counted upon. *Run-a-gate* is a corrupted form of M.E. *renegat*, an apostate

(from Latin *negare*, to deny). The corruption was due to a popular etymology from *runne a gate*, run on the road, hence, to be a vagabond.—(Skeat.)

50. **His service payeth me a sublimate.** "This service is what I get in return for the powder with which I healed him."

55. **gum-tragacanth.** Often known as gum-dragon; a white mucilage, much used in pharmacy, especially as a solvent.

57. **porphyry.** Here in the sense of a slab of stone used for grinding and triturating drugs upon. Chaucer already has the word in this sense: "Our grounden litarge eek on the porfurie" (*Can. Yeo. Tale* 222).

59. **crossing so with leprosy.** He means that he cannot diagnose the case when it is complicated by leprosy.

67. **a tang.** Literally, a strong taste or flavour.

79. **subinduced By epilepsy.** Brought on by epilepsy.

82. **exhibition.** The administration of a remedy.

91. **at that vantage.** Having that advantage of being the first remembered impression.

103. **a fume.** At first a vapour rising from the stomach to the brain; later an unsubstantial figment of the mind.

106. **saffron.** Once used as a cordial, being supposed to possess stimulant and anti-spasmodic properties.

107. **the after-life.** The remainder of his natural life, not the life after death.

109. **Sanguine.** Full-blooded, muscular and generally healthy. The four humours or habits of body in mediaeval medicine were the sanguine, the phlegmatic, the choleric and the melancholic.

117. **This grown man.** This resumes the sentence interrupted in line 108.

166. **object.** That is, 'if you object, "'tis but a word, a gesture."'

177. **Greek fire.** A combustible composition for setting fire to an enemy's ships, works, etc.; so called from being first used by the Greeks of Constantinople. Its invention is described in Wanley, book III. ch. xliii. § 6.

178. **some thread of life...Which runs across, etc.** Mortal life appears to him as no more than a black thread, almost lost sight of in the vast expanse of eternity, the vision of which has shattered his sense of proportion. Still he "holds firmly to it," that is, he carries

through its duties; but meanwhile he is perpetually distracted by the conflicting claims of the temporal and eternal worlds.

179. **the life to lead perforcedly.** He has no choice but to live thus.

200. **Professedly the faultier.** The more conscious of the evil within.

221. **"How, beast," said I, etc.** There is a robust medical vigour in the probing.

228. **affects the very brutes, etc.** This brings to mind the *Little Flowers of St Francis.* "Our sisters the birds are pleasing God," is his interpretation of the singing of birds. It is in consonance with all Browning's teaching that the one quality of which there is active expression in this man who has prematurely entered spiritual life, should be love.

253. **the loss To occult learning.** The physician transfers the significance of this portent in nature from the small Jewish tumult in which a leech perished to the worthier event of the decease of the sage who lived in the pyramid alone.

257. **On vain recourse, etc.** The report of the last scenes of the life of Christ which has come to the ears of Karshish is distorted. None of the Gospels say that the Jews had recourse, vain or otherwise, to Him for help against the earthquake. His "virtues" had been "tried" by previous miracles they had seen.

281. **Blue-flowering borage, etc.** A plant yielding a juice formerly much esteemed as a cordial. The ordinary British variety, as well as the Aleppo sort, has blue flowers and a nitrous stem.

304. **The very God.** The emotion to which this unexpected encounter and its accompanying revelation have given rise, has hitherto been suppressed; it breaks into fervid utterance in this postscript, pitched in a very different key from the rest of the poem.

## XXIV. FRA LIPPO LIPPI

From *Men and Women.* Vol. I. 1855.

Fra Filippo Lippi (1412—1469) being orphaned very early was taken by his aunt, Monna Lapaccia, to the Carmelite monastery in Florence, where he remained till 1432. From this date under the patronage of the Medici, he had many commissions, though their

prompt execution was interfered with by his love for dissipation
and good company. The frescoes at Prato and Spoleto and the
*Coronation of the Virgin*, the conception of which he describes at
the end of the poem, are among his chief works. Two delightful
lunettes in tempera, the *Seven Saints*, and the *Annunciation*, are
in the National Gallery. The latter bears the badge of the Medici,
three feathers held together by a ring.

The main outlines of the story are true and are drawn (as in the
case of the other Florentine artist, Andrea del Sarto) from Vasari's
*Lives of the Painters*. Even there, Brother Lippo Lippi figures as
what Chaucer would have called "a fish that is waterless."
Browning makes him an irrepressible jesting scape-grace—a tonsured
Falstaff—with an appetite for the delights of the palate and the
senses, and an artist with that inborn leaning towards realism, which
in such hearty natures turns to genial caricature. He is impatient
of the distorting pressure of piety upon art, and equally of any ideal
beauty beyond that sensible to the eye, being convinced that this
world, if we grasp it with both hands, "means intensely and means
good." In the poem he is, characteristically enough, pouring out
his beliefs, his escapades, and his ambitions, with a plentiful ad-
mixture of irreverence, to the captain of the watch who has
apprehended him upon his equivocal night expedition.

7. **The Carmine.** The monastery of the Carmelite Friars. In
the cloisters there are still frescoes by Masaccio, the "Hulking Tom"
of line 277.

17. **Cosimo of the Medici.** (1389—1464.) A Florentine who
returned from exile to make himself astutely master of the whole
state, which he ruled absolutely, though not nominally so, until
his death in 1464. He was a merchant, banker, statesman and a
generous patron of art and letters, and after his death was not
undeservedly called the Father of his country.

53. **Flower o' the broom.** These scattered flower-verses are in
the form of the Italian folk-songs called *stornelli*. They consist of
three lines. The first, five syllables long, contains the name of a
flower and sets the rhyme. Then the love theme is told in two lines
of eleven syllables each, rhyming or in assonance with the first. The
*stornelli* in the poem are plainly not completed.

67. **Saint Laurence.** One of the oldest churches in Italy.

Cosimo de' Medici is buried there, and in the New Sacristy near by are Michael Angelo's famous Tombs of the Medici.

73. **Jerome.** c. 340—420. The most learned of the fathers of the early church. His Latin translation of the Bible is the basis of the Vulgate. The last 35 years of his life were spent at Bethlehem in the practice of the strictest asceticism and in theological controversy.

84. **shucks.** Husks.

120. **The droppings of the wax.** The makers of ceremonial candles are always ready to buy them.

121. **the Eight.** The *Signoria*, a council of magistrates, holding office for two months at a time.

130. **antiphonary.** The service-book of the Roman Catholic Church, composed by Gregory the Great.

139. **Camaldolese.** A monkish order founded by Romuald in 1037, in the desolate waste of Campo Malduli in the Apennines. Their rule was that of St Benedict.

140. **Preaching Friars.** Dominicans founded by St Dominic and recognised under this name by Pope Innocent III. in 1216.

149. **To the breathless fellow,** etc. This word-picture, down to line 162, should be compared with those in lines 31—36, and 347—377.

172. **funked.** Stifled in smoke.

189. **Giotto.** 1276—1335. Angiolotto di Bondone, the friend of Dante, was the first of the great line of Florentine painters. With him the traditions of decadent classicism and Byzantine formalism are completely broken.

196. **She's just my niece...Herodias.** Fra Lippo's frescoes at Prato are on the subjects of John the Baptist and St Stephen. Among those on the Baptist is one representing the Feast of Herod, in which Salome offers the Saint's head to Herodias; there is a traditional belief that the Herodias of the picture is painted from Lucrezia Buti, the nun who escaped from the convent to marry the friar.

235. **Brother Angelico.** 1387—1455. His frescoes in San Marco in Florence establish his claim to be the "protagonist of pietistic painting." There is a *Christ in Glory* by him in the National Gallery.

236. **Brother Lorenzo.** 1870—1425. Usually called Monaco, the

Monk. He was a comparatively early Sienese painter, who entered the Camaldolese order in Florence. His fame spread and he executed commissions in Rome, and other parts of Italy.

276. **His name is Guidi.** Tommaso Guidi or Masaccio, 1401—1429, was supposed by Browning to be the pupil of Lippo. The relation was in fact exactly the reverse. His chief works are the frescoes still in the Brancacci Chapel, in the Carmine Monastery at Florence.

324. **Prato.** A small provincial town, 12 miles west of Florence, where Fra Lippo painted the frescoes which are accounted his masterpieces. See note, line 196.

328. **turn the Deacon off his toasted side.** The legend of St Laurence relates how being burned upon a gridiron, he asked to be turned, "being done on one side." The frescoes at Prato are not of St Laurence, but of St Stephen, the Baptist, and St Bernard.

339. **Chianti wine.** A famous red wine of Tuscany.

346. **in Sant' Ambrogio's.** Fra Lippo painted an altar-piece for the nuns of Sant' Ambrogio in 1441.

347. **I shall paint God in the midst, etc.** What follows as far as line 377 is a description of the *Coronation of the Virgin* as it may still be seen in the Accademia di Belli Arti in Florence.

354. **Saint John.** The Baptist. Children born in Florence are baptised in the church of St John.

355. **Saint Ambrose.** Archbishop of Milan, 340—397.

377. *Iste perfecit opus.* In the painting, Fra Lippo's picture of himself is at the lower right-hand corner. In his hand is a scroll on which is inscribed this Latin phrase, meaning, "It was he who did this work."

## XXV. ANDREA DEL SARTO

(CALLED " THE FAULTLESS PAINTER ")

From *Men and Women.* Vol. II. 1855.

The genesis of the poem is curious. Kenyon wrote to Browning for a copy of the painting, *Andrea del Sarto,* thought then, but not now, to be painted by the artist himself, which is in the Pitti Gallery in Florence. Being unable to procure the copy, Browning wrote the poem and sent it to him. The main outlines of the story are drawn from Vasari's *Lives of the Illustrious Painters,* etc. Andrea del Sarto (son of the tailor; he signed his pictures by the name d'Agnolo) was born in Florence, 1486. After apprenticeships to a goldsmith and a woodcarver he became a pupil of Piero di Cosimo. He was employed to decorate the church of the Annunziata, where he painted the *Madonna del Sacco*, his masterpiece. He fell in love with the wife of a Florentine tradesman—the Lucrezia of the poem—and married her on the decease of her husband in 1512. His work became known at the court of the king of France, and he was summoned to Fontainebleau, which he helped to decorate for his new patron, King Francis. The urgent appeals of his wife, however, brought him back to Florence, entrusted with moneys for the purchase of works of art for the king. The money was spent in erecting a house for his wife and in lavish hospitality. In spite of this disgrace his rare accomplishments gained for him many commissions, and he continued to paint till he died, deserted by his wife, in the plague which followed the siege of Florence in 1531.

The form of the dramatic monologue is nowhere more brilliantly utilised than here. The currents and eddies of speech, unchecked by any conventionalising audience, expose to view memories, aspirations, momentary impulses and actions, fears and desires, each reflecting some facet of underlying personality. With instinctive skill, too, the fresh and illuminating point of view is chosen; Andrea is the infatuated husband, but for the poem he is the unfortunate painter whose spiritless temperament is both cause and effect of his moral and artistic failures. Again, as the poet presents him, Andrea seeks no liberation from these fetters; the reader wishes it for him, against the painter's desire. The environment, too, the pallid beauty of twilight, and the sense of diminished vitality in the autumn evening in Florence, harmonise with the wistful fatalistic disposition of the man. His ineffective soul is revealed in the pictures which, technically flawless though they may be, yet are devoid of the fiery untamed spirit which in his contemporaries broke through the bond of rules, by the sheer force of inspiration. No passionate energy drives him to reach beyond the draughtsman's skill which has always been easily within his grasp. This same listlessness permits him to stoop to mean theft from his patron, to countenance his wife's open infidelities, and to proffer an insincere defence for filial delinquency. His moral and artistic debasement is completed by his voluntary enslavement to the shallow-minded wife, whose sole interest in his art is for its monetary gains, to whom his mere presence is irksome, and whose influence in his life has been uniformly disastrous. Nevertheless the situation appears pathetic rather than contemptible, and stirs sympathy rather than revulsion. Why? It is because we know that his life is a long purgatory of remorse. Those aspirations from which he shrinks, "Up to God, all three," are the measure of the anguish for which neither his apathy nor his infatuation is an effective opiate.

2. **Lucrezia.** Lucrezia del Fede was the wife of a hat-maker, named Recanati. Andrea fell in love with her, and when in 1512 she became a widow, married her. She was a woman of singular physical beauty, and so fascinated Andrea that the greater number of his saints and madonnas have her features and figure. In Browning's poem she is soulless and sensual. There is no definite historical warrant for this view. Vasari (at one time a pupil of Andrea) probably got into trouble with Lucrezia, whose temper was hasty. He catalogues her faults; she was overbearing and subtle, self-interested, harsh and mean to the apprentices: but it cannot be said that Vasari charges her directly with the infidelity which Browning has imputed to her.

5. **your friend's friend.** Some wealthy friend of his wife's lover has given a commission, for which Andrea has already pledged the payment to his wife. It is destined to pay the lover's gambling debts.

15. **Fiesole.** A small town about three miles north-west of Florence, situated on a hill-top which overhangs the Arno.

30. **Which everybody looks on,** etc. "Which" stands for the moon; Lucrezia resembles it in the sense that her beauty is visible to all, but she is cold to the individual admirer. "No one's" suggests the additional thought, "not even mine."

49. **we are in God's hand.** Here, the weakly fatalism of a drifting nature. Contrast *Rabbi Ben Ezra*.

65. **the Legate's talk.** Praise by some dignitary of the church or state, aesthetically inclined.

78. **less is more.** Achievements which fall short of completion because their aim is high are better than those completed when the aim is low.

88. **The sudden blood of these men.** Andrea feels keenly the

contrast in temperament between himself and his fellow-artists. He is passionless, unenthusiastic. Michael Angelo was the most irascible of painters.

93. **Morello's outline.** Morello is a spur of the Apennines, about seven miles distant from Florence, on the northern side.

97. **a man's reach,** etc. Browning's doctrines that man must never cease to strive, and that success which is thought to be final is in fact failure, are both embodied in these splendid lines. Compare *A Grammarian's Funeral*, and *Rabbi Ben Ezra*.

102. **Had I been two,** etc. There is throughout a pathetic consciousness of what the incompatibility of his wife has cost him in fame and endeavour.

105. **The Urbinate who died five years ago.** Rafael Santi (1483 —1520). It is impossible to assign supremacy to any one of the three Renaissance masters, da Vinci, Michael Angelo, and Rafael. The latter's greatest works are in the Vatican, where the *loggie* (galleries), the great tapestries, and the *Stanza della Segnatura*, containing the *School of Athens*, and the *Parnassus*, are his masterpieces. The cartoons for the tapestries are in the South Kensington Museum. Two famous Madonnas by him are in the National Gallery.

106. **George Vasari** (1512—1574). He was the author of *The Lives of the excellent Painters, Sculptors and Architects*, 1550. He studied under Michael Angelo and Andrea del Sarto. "With a few exceptions Vasari's judgments are acute and unbiassed."

110. **it gives way.** Craftsmanship is swept aside and inspiration seeks to find an immediate outlet in unregulated expression.

117. **Out of me.** I have lost these faculties.

129. **The Present by the Future.** The glory of future fame eclipses any present reward.

130. **Angelo.** Michael Angelo, or Michelagnuolo, 1475—1564. The most vigorous and forceful of these great Florentine artists. By nature he was a sculptor: in this art his genius found expression in his *David*, *Moses*, and the *Tombs of the Medici*. As a painter, the powerful frescoes on the ceiling and west wall of the Sistine Chapel in the Vatican, set him far beyond any rivalry in his own sculpture-like fashion of painting. He excelled too as poet, scholar, architect and, when Florence was besieged, as military engineer.

131. **Up to God all three.** Compare *Fra Lippo Lippi*, l. 237.

16—2

136. **What wife had Rafael**, etc. Rafael finally married his model La Fornarina. In the Barberini Palace in Rome there is a picture of her by Rafael, on the arm of which the painter has signed his name. Michael Angelo was never married, though in middle age (1535—1547) he cultivated a noble and inspiring friendship with Vittoria Colonna, the widow of the Marquis of Pescara.

146. **the Paris lords.** French nobles in Florence (there was constant communication, both diplomatic and artistic, between the two courts) who were aware of his action in the matter of King Francis' money.

150. **Fontainebleau.** The scene of King Francis' court. It is a sumptuous palace 40 miles south-east of Paris; Leonardo da Vinci, and Benvenuto Cellini were employed in its decoration as well as Andrea del Sarto.

173. **The triumph was**, etc. The ideal of triumph I had before me was to attain the topmost heights in my art, and then to gain your love. If I gained your love before I reached these heights, what is lost? For your love was to be the crown of my triumph. The text, but not the meaning, is changed in later editions.

178. **The Roman's.** That is, Rafael's Madonna has more glow of religious exaltation. Rafael was born at Urbino, but the bulk of his work was done in Rome.

187. **Upon a palace-wall**, etc. Doubtless the *stanze*, or apartments, in the Vatican, which Rafael decorated for Pope Julius II., with religious and allegorical frescoes. The story of this remark is not well authenticated; though it is supported to some extent by the enmity between Rafael and Michael Angelo, which was fostered by officious partisans.

199. **What he?** Lucrezia has not been heeding. She feigns a momentary interest, but it only reveals her complete indifference to the most cherished memories of her husband.

207. **I mean that I should earn more.** In a single line the life-long process of stifling ideals for this shallow woman is made pitiably plain.

210. **cue-owls.** An owl common on the shores of the Mediterranean. The Italian name *chiu* represents its cry—*ki-ou*.

220. **That Cousin.** Italian *cugino*, cousin, means here of course a lover.

**241. scudi.** Crowns. Italian *scudo* (Lat *scutum*, shield) is a piece about five shillings in value.

**261. Four great walls.** Revelation xxi. 15.

**263. Leonard.** Leonardo da Vinci, 1452—1519, was painter, sculptor, architect and critic. His magnificent power of design, his command of the technique of painting, of light and shade, perspective and the like, find their rarest exercise in his *Last Supper* in the Refectory at Maria delle Grazie, in Milan. His power of portraying the almost unfathomable subtleties of expression is shown in the haunting, mocking beauty of his *Monna Lisa* (until recently in the Louvre), the most glorious representation of the human face in any art. There is a Madonna by Leonardo in the Diploma Gallery in Burlington House, and in the National Gallery the more famous *Madonna of the Rocks.*

## XXVI. THE BISHOP ORDERS HIS TOMB AT SAINT PRAXED'S CHURCH

[ROME, 15—]

First printed in *Hood's Magazine*, March, 1845. Reprinted in
*Dramatic Romances*, 1845.

The church of Sta. Prassede, in Rome, has recently, as more than once formerly in the sixteenth century, suffered from injudicious modernisation. There is little in the poem which is derived directly from the existing structure; no Bishop Gandolf is buried here. There is a tomb, however, that of Cardinal Cetive, with his sleeping figure and the reliefs of St Peter and St Paul, and Sta. Prassede and Sta. Pudentiana, daughters of one of St Paul's first converts in Rome. Also there is a large granite slab on which the martyred sister Prassede is said to have slept.

**15—.** One may take the date to cover the pontificates of Alexander VI., 1492—1503 (a Borgia), Julius II., 1503—1513, and Leo X., 1513—1521 (a Medici), men whose indifference to the stricter vows of the Church, and lack of the spiritual earnestness requisite in their office, were only equalled by their participation in the Renaissance spirit. Ruskin thus defines this spirit in a generous criticism of this poem: " ...its worldliness, inconsistency, pride, hypocrisy, ignorance of itself, love of art, of luxury and of good Latin." (*Modern Painters*, v. xx. 34.)

The poem is a penetrating study of the emotions which welter in the Bishop's mind now that his natural forces are too enfeebled to restrain them. Two by their constant recurrence give the clue to his life and character; first, the life-long envy of his ancient rival Gandolf; second, his consuming desire for a monument, splendid in design and rich in ornament. Round these cluster the passions and thoughts excited by suspicion of the intentions of his sons, whom he vainly attempts to bribe with sensual and epicurean delights; by the tacit confession of broken vows; by the memories of thefts committed to adorn his tomb; by his gloating triumph over the slip-shod Latin of Gandolf's epitaph; by the soothing sense of the quiet incense-laden air of the "church for peace." All these diverse elements are composed into a consistent picture which reveals not simply the pagan humanistic Bishop, but at the same time the funda-mental characteristics of an epoch.

16. **my niche.** The recess which he had sought to reserve for his tomb. By some shrewd intrigue Gandolf has appropriated the envied space. Creighton, in *The Papacy during the Reformation*, vol. IV. p. 79, says: "Vanity suggested sepulchral monuments as a ready means of satisfying this desire for fame. Men vied with one another in elaborating great designs. Sculpture was encouraged in a way which at no other time has been possible, and the churches of Italy were filled with stately tombs which are still their chief monuments."

25. **basalt.** A hard grey or black marble of igneous origin.

26. **tabernacle.** The ornamental work over the statue; a decorated canopy.

29. **Peach-blossom marble.** A rare and exquisite marble in which the yellow ground is tinted with shades of rose.

31. **onion-stone.** This is the Italian *cipollino* (from *cipolla*, onion), a marble interfoliated with veins of talc, mica, quartz, etc., showing alternations of various colouring, especially white and green.

41. **olive-frail.** A frail is a basket made of rushes.

42. *lapis lazuli.* A mineral of a beautiful ultramarine colour, much used in ecclesiastical decoration.

**46. Frascati villa.** Frascati is a village about 15 miles south-west of Rome. In classical times Cicero had a villa near by; in the age of the Renaissance, Roman dignitaries built summer palaces there, some of which, like the Villa Aldobrandini, still remain.

**48. Like God the Father's globe.** The great church *Il Gesu*, in Rome, is the head church of the Jesuit order. The altar of St Ignatius Loyola is adorned with a group of the Trinity; in the hands of the Almighty is the globe of *lapis lazuli* to which the Bishop refers.

**54. antique-black.** More familiar in the untranslated form, *nero antico*, a black marble.

**57. Those Pans and Nymphs.** There is a curious blending of the pagan memories to which his taste leans, and of Christian scenes which long habit has made familiar.

**58. tripod, thyrsus.** The tripod was the seat on which the priestess of Apollo sat when she gave utterance from the oracular chasm at Delphi. The thyrsus was a wand wreathed with ivy and vine, carried by Dionysus and his attendants at their religious ceremonies.

**66. travertine.** A limestone formed by springs holding lime in solution. It appears to be durable rather than mouldy as the Bishop suggests. The external binding walls of the Coliseum are of tra-vertine or *lapis tiburtinus*, that is stone of Tibur (the ancient name of Tivoli).

**77. Tully's every word.** Marcus Tullius Cicero, the model of Latin prose for all writers of the Renaissance; the Bishop demands the most scholarly Latin for his epitaph.

**79. Ulpian.** A great Roman jurist and the chief adviser of the Emperor Alexander Severus, until murdered by soldiers in 228 A.D. He belongs to the silver age of Latin prose, using words and forms for which no warrant could be found in the writers of the Augustan period.

**87. I fold my arms, etc.** In his delirium words become a con-fused phantasmagoria; he imagines himself to be the effigy on the tomb he is designing for himself, that the bed-clothes are sculptured draperies, and that St Praxed is a man and the preacher of the Sermon on the Mount.

**99. "*elucescebat.*"** The verb found in Cicero is *eluceo*, and the form on the epitaph should have been *elucebat*, he shone forth. The inchoative form in the text belongs to a decadent age. It stirs the contemptuous mirth of the Bishop.

108. **a vizor.** One meaning of the word is " the sight of a helmet." M. F. *visiere*, from *vis*, countenance. It also means a mask, the more likely meaning here, since there is nothing else which belongs to the equipment of chivalry in the Bishop's design.

**a Term.** Images of Terminus, the Roman god of boundaries, were in the form of a square pillar surmounted by a bust.

111. **entablature.** He seems to mean simply the slab on which he is to lie in effigy. Generally the word describes all the design which rests on the columns.

## XXVII. BISHOP BLOUGRAM'S APOLOGY

From *Men and Women.* Vol. I. 1855.

There is no doubt that Browning based this character study upon Cardinal Wiseman, and he maintained, as Gavan Duffy reports, that his treatment of his model was generous. Though this cannot be easily admitted from any impartial standpoint, still we can see how the poet, with his zest for all forms of activity, would be attracted by a figure of so many and brilliant gifts, literary, social, controversial and administrative. (Wiseman re-established the Roman Catholic hierarchy in England in the teeth of much opposition in the year 1850.) The urbanity of the cardinal may be judged from the fact that he wrote a review (Jan. 1856, *The Rambler*) acknowledging the brilliance of the poem and deploring only the subversive influence it might be expected to exercise upon the Christian faith. An analysis of the poem is given in the succeeding notes; here it is only necessary to call attention to the confidential after-dinner atmosphere, the luxurious surroundings, the flavour of subtle talk which pervades the blank verse and invests its polemics with all the ease and lucidity of prose, and the astonishing mental agility of the poem. This may be best seen in the clear expression of the successive reflections and refractions of the truth. First, the Bishop is defending an untenable position (lines 1002—1004). Secondly, he is not actually in the position which he defends (lines 846—847). Thirdly, the case against him is so feebly and superficially put by Gigadibs that his reply is nothing but gymnastic trifling. Fourthly, there are moments of unquestioned sincerity in the discussion, not of unbelief, but of doubt. And lastly, while doubt is defended earnestly, the case for faith is put upon comparatively base and specious grounds. The threads of sophistry and truth are so subtly interwoven, that Mr Worldly Wiseman, Mr By-ends, Mr Facing-both-Ways, and Christian himself might each appropriate a section of this astounding Apology. The student might find another interest in determining how much of it is actually poetry.

4. **basilicas.** Originally a large oblong hall with double colonnades, and an apse, used as a place of public assembly. Later the word was used to describe churches generally; in Rome the seven churches founded by Constantine are distinctively called basilicas.

6. **brother Pugin's.** 1812—1852. Early became a Roman Catholic, and designed many Catholic churches in the Gothic style. Practically all the decorative design of the House of Commons is due to him.

45. *Che che.* A mere exclamation, meaning " What ! "

49—85. Gigadibs puts the case for the direct outspoken truth, the " grand simple life," he calls it.

52. **Goethe.** 1749—1832. The German scientist, philosopher, critic and poet; the greatest mind of his century.

54. **Count D'Orsay.** 1798—1852. " A celebrated leader of society in Paris and London, who added to the attractions of dandyism those of high intellectual and artistic gifts."

86—143. The Bishop's reply is on lines of common sense; we must conform to our present environment. If we have ideals that are unseaworthy they must be jettisoned.

108. **Balzac's novels.** 1799—1850. Balzac gathered his novels together in *La Comédie Humaine*, which was much admired by Browning. In the multitude and vitality of his creations of character he is surpassed only by Shakespeare.

113. **Parma's pride, the Jerome.** In the Pinacotheca at Parma is the *Virgin and Child with St Jerome*, painted by Correggio.

114. **Correggio.** He is the " marvellous Modenese," having been born at Modena in 1494. See *A Face*, lines 14—16 and note.

150—340. For the purpose of debate they agree upon abandoning dogma; then in three different lines of argument the Bishop shows the impossibility and the uselessness of this step. First (lines 173—212), entire unbelief is non-existent; emotions, intuitions and memories may at any moment fret the string we had resolved should never vibrate. Second (lines 221—270), we cannot put belief and unbelief upon an equal footing; for belief implies activity, which is the principle of waking life. Unbelief implies inactivity and sleep. The man without faith labels himself as bed-ridden. Third (lines 270—340), once we admit the superiority of belief it is important to emphasise it before the world. Hence he pronounces himself of the Roman Catholic faith, and in reward receives dignity, comfort and success.

160. **The ugly consequence.** That he is proved a hypocrite.

184. **Euripides.** Such for instance as this from the end of the *Bacchae* (Prof. Gilbert Murray's trans.):

> "There be many shapes of mystery
>   And many things God makes to be,
>       Past hope or fear.
>   And the end men looked for cometh not,
>   And a path is there where no man thought.
>       So hath it fallen here."

816—320. **Peter's creed, or, rather, Hildebrand's.** Hildebrand took the name of Pope Gregory VII. He was for long at enmity with the Emperor Henry IV., but his firmness of attitude and his skilful diplomacy largely increased the temporal power of the Papacy. He cleansed the Church of its besetting evils, simony and clerical incontinence; in fact he, to all intents, founded the mediaeval Papacy in theory and practice.

345—431. Here Blougram meets the accusation that the attainment of rank and dignity can only be called success because his motives and standards are low. His replies are either evasions or sophistries. First (lines 340—361), he says in effect, if he is a man of low standards then he will at least make the best of his case in the way of comfort. Secondly (lines 362—430), he shows how mistaken Gigadibs is in supposing that the dozen men of sense out of the million of the common herd are likely to pronounce him forthwith either fool or knave. Having refined and discriminating judgments, they will not pass these dogmatic sentences; they know there are a thousand alternative shades between fool and knave. Moreover his acknowledged learning and prominent office set him above all contempt in professing his belief. He becomes thereby one of those whose paradoxical characters exalt them to the "dangerous edge of things" where they challenge the notice of the universe.

377. **the last winking Virgin.** Used generally for the impositions which Gigadibs accuses the Roman Catholic Church of practising upon its simple adherents.

381. **Verdi.** 1813—1901. There was a time between 1844 and 1851 when all the operas Verdi composed proved failures. But after *Rigoletto* (1851), he entered upon a scarcely interrupted period of success.

386. **Rossini.** 1792—1868. He is best remembered by his operas, *Il Barbiere di Seviglia* (1816), and *Guillaume Tell* (1829).

395. **Our interest's on the dangerous edge of things.** This was a tendency in Browning which markedly increased in his later works. The *Ring and the Book, Fifine at the Fair, Red Cotton Night-Cap Country*, and *The Inn Album*, are all of them studies of crime and moral distortion.

407. **Your picked Twelve**, etc. These "prime men who appraise their kind" would have not a moment's difficulty in explaining how Blougram could at the same time believe and disbelieve.

411. **Schelling's way!** Schelling (1775—1854), in his doctrine of Identity, held that the real and the ideal, the physical and the spiritual are identical in the Absolute, of which they are but manifestations. On such a theory it is manifestly possible to do many feats of simultaneous belief and disbelief.

432—554. There is a subtle turn in the argument here by which Blougram begins to be the apologist, not for himself as an unbelieving bishop, but for the recognition of some kind of faith. He invites Gigadibs to exemplify his ideal of the great man without faith. Shall it be Napoleon? If Napoleon were in truth without any belief and aim beyond his immediate activities, how inhuman and how paltry his achievements were. Shall it be Shakespeare? True, he could imagine a universe, yet he sought not imaginary towers and palaces, but the possession of "the trimmest house in Stratford town." "If this life's all," then Blougram who keeps his semi-royal state clearly "wins the game."

466. "The State, that's I." The phrase "L'état c'est moi!"
was originally used by Louis Quatorze.

472. An Austrian marriage. Napoleon married Marie Louise,
daughter of the Emperor of Austria, soon after the battle of
Austerlitz.

475. Austerlitz. 1805. In this battle Napoleon defeated the
army of the Coalition of Austria, Russia and England.

513. his towers and gorgeous palaces. Compare *The Tempest*,
IV. i. 151:

> "And, like the baseless fabric of this vision,
> The cloud-capped towers, the gorgeous palaces,
> The solemn temples, the great globe itself,
> Yea, all which it inherit, shall dissolve
> And, like this insubstantial pageant faded,
> Leave not a rack behind."

514. the trimmest house in Stratford town. On May 4th, 1597,
Shakespeare purchased New Place, the largest house in Stratford, for
£60 (that is, nearly £500 in our money).

516. Giulio Romano's pictures. See *The Winter's Tale*, v. ii. 90:
"A piece" (the statue of Hermione) "many years in doing and now
newly performed by that rare Italian master, Julio Romano..." He
lived from 1492 to 1546.

Dowland's lute. In *The Passionate Pilgrim*, which was published
with Shakespeare's name on the title-page, is a sonnet on music and
poetry in which these lines occur:

> "Dowland to thee is dear, whose heavenly touch
> Upon the lute doth ravish human sense."

The sonnet is now known however to be not by Shakespeare, but by
his contemporary, Richard Barnfield. Dowland was a skilled lutanist
and composer, who after travelling in Italy published his *First Book
of Songs and Airs* in 1597.

519. "Pandulph, of fair Milan cardinal." The legate from
Pope Innocent to King John in Shakespeare's play. See *King John*,
III. i. 138.

533. Terni. Terni is about forty miles north of Rome; the
water-fall is of rare natural beauty. Byron describes it in *Childe
Harold*, canto IV. stanzas 69—71.

553. **the cousin of Queen Bess.** Blougram for an instant supposes both Shakespeare and himself to be living in the reign of Queen Elizabeth. Their rewards are then: Shakespeare to win his house at Stratford, Blougram to attain such office as to stand within the immediate circle of the monarch. "Coz" was a term of familiar address in Elizabeth's time.

555—591. Taking it for granted then that some form of faith is essential, the Bishop adds a corollary, that it must be enthusiastic. If we do not accept the enthusiasm of Luther with its dynamic power, we fall back upon the chill negations of Strauss, with the bare chance that they may be not only cold but wrong.

577. **Strauss.** 1808—1874. His rationalistic *Life of Jesus* was translated into English by George Eliot in 1846. In his last book, *The Old and the New Thought*, his conclusions were, briefly, that Christianity was practically dead, that there was no conscious or personal God, and that a new faith must be built up out of art and the scientific reading of nature.

585. **It could not owe a farthing.** Suppose I should release them from all claim upon their purses by the Church: is it to be thought of that they would insist upon paying still?

599—764. By another of the swift modulations which make the poem so actual, it develops into a sincere and eloquent defence of doubt. First (lines 599—646), he insists that faith with doubt is not only sufficient, but there is no other possible form of it. The mere wish that Christianity should be true avails to exalt a man from indifference to belief. Secondly (lines 647—675), an absolute faith is inconceivable; time and earth are designed by God to conceal Himself lest we should be struck blind with excess of light. Faith needs to be perpetually stimulated by the menace of unbelief. A parenthesis follows (lines 676—692), showing that even in the Middle Ages of unquestioning faith, belief in future punishment and reward was not sufficient to ensure correct moral conduct. Thirdly (lines 693—712), he resumes the apology for doubt, and demands impossibilities for faith to exercise itself upon. Fourthly (lines 724—764), he replies to Gigadibs' request to delete some of the grosser tenets in his profession. He will not abandon a single miracle, recognising that where one goes all must sooner or later follow.

617. **Against the thing done to me underground**, etc. It is

a matter of indifference who or what may have composed a man's soul; the question is, having that soul, what has he achieved?

644. **But would I rather, etc.** He would rather a man should be puzzled by contradictions than discover the truth and treat it as a thing of no importance. (Wiseman was actually born in Seville.)

654. **what all the blessed Evil's for.** Compare *Abt Vogler*, lines 83 and 84.

664. **ichors o'er the place.** The word is not given as a verb in the N.E.D. Pathologically ichor is a watery issue from a wound. Here it appears to convey some sense of healing as well.

667. **like the snake 'neath Michael's foot.** There is a picture by Rafael, in the Louvre, of St Michael slaying the dragon; and most Roman Catholic churches contain a painting on the subject.

703. **If the Church bid them.** To the Roman Catholic, the Church, the Pope being its voice, is the supreme authority not only in faith, but in every aspect of life.

**brother Newman.** 1801—1890. A leader of the Tractarian movement in the middle of the nineteenth century. After writing Tract xc. the Bishop of Oxford called upon him to cease the production of these pamphlets; Newman then passed over to the Roman Church in 1845. In a long debate with Kingsley, and in his *Apologia pro Vita Sua*, and in many other writings, especially his sermons, he proved himself one of the most powerful and subtle controversialists and one of the most gifted prose-writers in English.

704. **the Immaculate Conception.** The doctrine that the Virgin Mary was born free from the taint of original sin : in 1854 this was declared to be an article of faith of the Roman Catholic Church.

707. **It can't be, etc.** *Credo quia impossibile est*, I believe because it is impossible (Tertullian). Compare Sir Thomas Browne, *Religio Medici*: "I love to lose myself in a mystery, to pursue my Reason to an *O altitudo.*"

715. **King Bomba.** Ferdinand II., king of the two Sicilies, 1830—1859. The word means, "bragging liar." He got his name through his unjustifiable bombardment of Messina.

**lazzaroni.** Beggars in Naples, so called from Lazarus because they exhibit their deformities to excite public sympathy.

716. **Antonelli.** Cardinal Antonelli was the astute and diplomatic secretary of Pope Pius IX.

720. The ignorant beggar can see that to defy natural laws is to invoke an immediate penalty; but he has wit enough to see that moral laws may be broken without any immediate danger, in spite of all the Church may say.

728. **The Naples' liquefaction.** In the cathedral at Naples is preserved a small quantity of the blood of St Januarius, a martyr of the fourth century. On the feast-day of the Saint, September 19th, this blood is brought in a crystal vessel near to the head of the Saint, before the whole congregation, when it liquefies and flows to one side. As the liquefaction proceeds rapidly or tardily the people judge that it will go well or ill with their harvests in the succeeding season.

744. **Fichte's clever cut.** Fichte taught that each temporal limited self, such as we imagine ourselves to be, is a creative ego imposing limitations upon itself in order to transcend them. When all these limitations are overpassed we arrive at a universal self, in which we all partake, and this is God.

764—970. Here the apologist returns to his own case. In lines 781—806 he ridicules the premature preparation for the next world which sacrifices any of the amenities of the present. In lines 807—853 he attacks the inconsistency of Gigadibs. Since all revealed religion is a myth, why does he not take every satisfaction that life can give on that basis? It is because he is held in check by some instinct and intuition, and so it appears he is a slave and hypocrite, not daring any more than Blougram to follow reason unreservedly. To Gigadibs' reply that he refrains in consideration of his fellow-men, the Bishop responds (lines 854—970) with a pointed comparison of what each receives from his fellows; Gigadibs a gruff enmity, a bare tolerance : Blougram obsequious reverence and social estimation.

877. "*Pastor est tui Dominus.*" "God is your shepherd," with the implied suggestion that he acknowledges no priest in this office.

914. **On music, poetry, the fictile vase, etc.** Wiseman was an able and voluminous writer and lecturer on Art, Science and Religion. The poet names these as suggestive examples. Fictile means plastic, and hence is often used for earthenware. Albano is some five miles south of Rome. Anacreon was a Greek poet of the sixth century B.C. His convivial and erotic lyrics were frequently translated and imitated by English poets of the seventeenth century.

957. **in Dublin.** Wiseman with some others founded the *Dublin Review* in 1836.

972. *in partibus,* etc. Before 1850, when the Roman Catholic hierarchy was restored in England, a bishop exercised his functions here but drew his title from some consecrated see elsewhere. He was *Episcopus in partibus infidelium.* Wiseman, for instance, was consecrated bishop of Melipotamus in 1840.

## XXVIII. ONE WORD MORE

### TO E. B. B.

From *Men and Women.* Vol. II. 1855.

This poem, which formed the epilogue to *Men and Women,* was the response to Mrs Browning's *Sonnets from the Portuguese,* written in the months just preceding their marriage in 1846. In it, as in *By the Fireside,* we are admitted to the intimacies of devotion and affection which existed between the two. It is a splendid tribute based on Browning's fanciful interpretation of the minor artistic activities of Rafael and Dante. He imagines them employing these secondary talents in ingenious efforts to converse with their lovers in a language different from the emphatic speech in which they are wont to address their wider audience; for the coarser ear of the world demands these strident tones, and will not permit divergence from the *rôle* in which it most readily recognises its heroes. He, lacking that versatility which made Dante poet and painter, and Rafael painter and poet, adopts a graceful subterfuge. In place of a poem in dramatic guise, such as those in *Men and Women,* he writes one which glows with the undisguised warmth of personal emotion. Few poems express so much feeling with so much historical allusion and natural imagery. The fragrant memory of these "far-renowned brides of ancient song" mingles with the incense of the poet's worship, whilst he invokes the mysterious light of that unseen face of the moon to grace the secret ceremony.

1. **my fifty men and women.** The subjects of the poems in the two volumes of 1855. In later editions they have been distributed under various headings.

5. **Rafael made a** century of **sonnets.** This is a fiction on the

part of the poet; the four sonnets of Rafael now extant are all described as mediocre. He did leave a book containing a century of drawings, which disappeared in the manner related in stanza iv.

12. **his lady of the sonnets.** La Fornarina. See note to *Andrea del Sarto*, line 136.

22. **Her, San Sisto names, etc.** The *Madonna di San Sisto* is now in the Dresden Gallery. The *Madonna di Foligno* is in the Vatican.

23. **Her, that visits Florence, etc.** The *Madonna del Granduca* is in the Pitti Palace in Florence. In the picture she is appearing to a votary in a vision.

24. **Her, that's left, etc.** *La Belle Jardinière* in the Louvre; a group of three figures, the Mother, the Child and St John.

27. **Guido Reni.** 1575—1642. A prolific painter who maintained a great school in Bologna for twenty years. His most famous work is the *Aurora and the Hours*, in the Rospigliosi Palace in Rome.

32. **Dante once prepared to paint an angel.** Dante says in the *Vita Nuova* xxxv. that it was on the anniversary of the death of Beatrice that he drew an angel on a tablet. Browning adapts the incident.

33. **Beatrice.** The daughter of Folco Portinari, with whom, as we learn from the *Vita Nuova*, Dante fell in love at the age of nine. Afterwards he gave the name to the mystical figure whom he encounters at the end of the *Purgatory*, and who conducts him through *Paradise* in the *Divine Comedy*.

37. **his left-hand i' the hair o' the wicked.** *Inferno*, canto xxxii. line 97. Dante comes upon the Florentine traitor, Bocca degli Abati:

> "Then seizing on his hinder scalp I cried:
> 'Name thee, or not a hair shall tarry here.'"
> (Carey's trans.)

Browning speaks as though Dante had said the man were still living. Mr W. M. Rossetti, in the *Academy* for Jan. 10, 1891, shows that Browning must have confused Bocca with a traitor still living in Dante's time, Frate Alberigo, who was not however a Florentine, and could not rightly be spoken of as "festering through Florence."

57. **Bice.** Beatrice.

63. **nature that's an art to others.** Some different art in which he is not really skilled as others may be, but in which he speaks with the untrained directness of nature.

64. **art that's turned his nature.** The art which he has made his own.

73. **Heaven's gift takes earth's abatement.** What he does in his well-recognised capacity as artist is belittled and often slighted by his audience; further the infinite vision of his art is curbed by the finite forms in which it must find expression.

77. **his mortal in the minute.** A man and weak in temper as Moses proved.

88. **O'er-importuned brows.** Brows burdened with memories of the reception of his efforts in the past.

96. **the crowd must have emphatic warrant.** The crowd must always see a man in the full panoply of his profession, poet, prophet or whatever it may be.

97. **Sinai-forehead's cloven brilliance.** Exodus xxxiv. 29.

102. **the Æthiopian bondslave.** Numbers xii. 1.

117. **a semblance of resource avails us.** Not to work in another art, but in another aspect of his own, that is, not dramatically but in his proper person. This is the "shade so finely touched, love's sense must seize it."

121. **fresco.** A kind of painting executed in water-colour on a wall, ceiling, etc., of which the mortar or plaster is not quite dry, so that the colours sink in and become more durable.

145. **Here in London,** etc. The Brownings returned from Florence to London in 1855, Browning bringing with him *Men and Women*, and Mrs Browning *Aurora Leigh*, which was published in 1856.

150. **Samminiato.** The church of San Miniato in Florence.

160. **the old sweet mythos.** Of Endymion, the theme of Keats' longest though not his greatest poem.

163. **Zoroaster.** The Greek form of Zarathushtra, who in the *Zend-Avesta* set forth the doctrines still held by the Parsees of India. He was moreover a student of astronomy.

164. **Galileo.** The Italian mathematician who devised the concave lens for the telescope, and was arraigned for his belief that the earth moved round the sun.

165. **Dumb to Homer, dumb to Keats.** Homer wrote a *Hymn to Diana*, which Shelley translated. Keats' *Endymion* is a retelling of the "old sweet mythos" of the moon's love for a mortal.

169. **Proves she like some portent**, etc. Imagined pictures of the reverse side of the moon, never seen by mortals.

172. **the paved-work of a sapphire.** "And they saw the God of Israel: and there was under his feet as it were a paved work of a sapphire stone, and as it were the body of heaven in his clearness " (Exodus xxiv. 10).

187. **This I say of me, but think of you** It is true that he strives to show himself in some unique aspect to his wife; but it is much more true that she, whom the world knows only as a poetess, has in her spirit

"the novel

Silent silver lights and darks undreamed of,

Where I hush and bless myself with silence."

# DRAMATIS PERSONAE

## XXIX. ABT VOGLER

(AFTER HE HAS BEEN EXTEMPORIZING UPON THE MUSICAL
INSTRUMENT OF HIS INVENTION)

From *Dramatis Personae.* 1864.

The Abbé (or Abt) Vogler, unlike Master Hugues, was a historical person. A full account of him may be found by the very curious in the *Browning Society's Papers*, part III. He was born in 1749, educated for the Roman Catholic priesthood, founded schools of music at Mannheim and Stockholm (where he invented his Orchestrion, "a very compact organ, in which four keyboards of five octaves each, and a pedal board of thirty-six keys with swell complete, were packed into a cube of nine feet"). He founded a third school at Darmstadt, where Weber and Meyerbeer were his pupils and where he died in 1814. He travelled in most of the great European cities simplifying organs, and performing upon his portable Orchestrion. Of his extemporising Weber says "he drew from the organ angelic voices and words of thunder."

The thought and emotion of the poem move on three planes. The first is pictorially imaginative; here the form of the musical extemporisation is re-created in another art, architecture; just as the

**17—2**

sculptured figures of the *Grecian Urn* are, in the alembic of Keats'
imagination, distilled into poetry. The vastness of the palace increases
until it becomes immeasurable; deep calls unto deep; the infinite in
the human soul is unloosed and Heaven bows in communion. The
sundered worlds of Now and Hereafter are unified; the borders of
time and space being obliterated, the denizens of the Past, Present,
and Future people a common universe.

Secondly, there is a claim based partly on this lofty moment of
inspiration and partly on the magic of the chord, so different from
and so much more than mere consentaneity of sounds, that music is
not merely the sister of the arts of painting and poetry but a direct
mode of expression of the voice and will of God. Thirdly, there is the
human encouragement of his belief in the permanence of his creation,
since "there shall never be one lost good." Two characteristic notes
of optimism are struck, first in the generous interpretation of human
good which includes "all we have willed or hoped or dreamed"; and
second in the view that imperfection and evil are simply other names
for opportunity and the promise of fulfilment.

**8. when Solomon willed.** The legends of Solomon's powers as a
magician appear to be derived from a misinterpretation of 1 Kings iv.
33. They are considerably expanded in the Targums (commentaries
on the books of the Old Testament). Thence they passed into the
Koran, e.g. in ch. **xxvii.** "And his armies were gathered together unto
Solomon, consisting of genii and men and birds." He was said to
owe his control over these *jinns*, or spirits, to the possession of a talis-
man, a ring, sent to him from heaven on which was graven "the
most great name of God."

**7. the ineffable Name.** The true name of God was thought to be
known only to the prophets.

**8. the princess he loved.** Doubtless Pharaoh's daughter. See
1 Kings vii. 8 and Browning's poem *Popularity*.

**9. the beautiful building.** Compare the dome in Coleridge's
*Kubla Khan*.

**16. the nether springs.** "The roots of things."

**19. rampired.** Ramparted. O.Fr. *rempar*. Compare Shakespeare, *Timon*, v. iv. 47, "our rampired gates."

**21. as a runner tips with fire,** etc. In Rome in the eighteenth
century the façade of St Peter's was illuminated on festival occasions

by hundreds of lamps lit with extraordinary rapidity by "runners" with lighted torches, whilst the clock chimed the hour.

25. **to match man's birth.** To embody some element of the infinite, like the soul of man at his birth.

31. **Meteor-moons.** Meteors as large as moons.

32. **no more near nor far.** All sense of the limitations of space is annihilated. It is in music more than in any other human activity that we experience this sensation.

34—37. **or...or.** These stand for, either...or; the strong alternative conjunctions.

34. **the Protoplast.** The first made thing or being of its kind; hence the model from which all succeeding copies are derived. The "presences" are either those who were awaiting a period when conditions of existence should be appropriate to them, but have been induced to come forth into this palace; or else the "wonderful Dead."

38. **an old world worth their new.** The world created by Abt Vogler was a perfect one like that in which the Dead dwell.

39—40. Past, Present and Future are coincident.

44. **wonder-worth.** That is, there is nothing incomprehensible in the process of painting.

47. **art in obedience to laws.** He suggests that there is nothing which transcends human understanding in the arts of painting and poetry. We can formulate the conditions of their production; not so those of music.

49. **the will that can.** *Can* is used here as a main verb, meaning to have power.

52. **not a fourth sound, but a star.** A product utterly different in kind from and infinitely superior in worth to the elements of which it is compounded.

70. **The evil is null,** etc. Truth requires a medium of negation or falsehood, in contrast with which it may shine out and show itself to be the Truth.

72. **On the earth the broken arcs.** Compare *A Grammarian's Funeral*, lines 103 and 104.

77. **The high that proved too high.** Compare *Rabbi Ben Ezra*, lines 133—150.

91—96. **the common chord** (1)...**the minor** (2)...**a ninth** (3)...**the**

C major (4). I am indebted to a musical friend for the following explanation:

A common chord in music is a group of three notes wherein the interval between the highest and lowest is seven semitones and between the lowest and middle either four or three semitones. This is the fundamental position of the common chord, but either the middle or highest note, or even both, may be transposed one or more octaves higher, without altering the constitution of the chord. Thus

 transposed (1)   . Now this chord is a major

common chord (C major). If the top note (E) be lowered by a semi-

tone to E flat the resultant is a *minor* common chord (2) 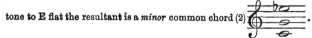 .

If this note be again lowered ("blunted" by) a semitone, i.e. to D, the highest note is at the interval of a *ninth* from the lowest note and the

result is a strong discord (3)  . If again this top note

be lowered by two semitones, the resulting chord is   , to

which if the middle note is again added as in (1) we have the chord of

C major once more   .

By "the C major" the poet means the level plain of ordinary existence.

## XXX. RABBI BEN EZRA

From *Dramatis Personae*. 1864.

The historical Ben Ezra was a famous Jewish scholar of the Middle Ages, born at Toledo about 1092. He travelled to Rome, Mantua, Rhodes and England and died about 1168. He was skilled in mathematics, grammar and astronomy, but his fame now rests chiefly upon his *Commentaries* on the books of the Old Testament.

An account of his writings may be found in Friedlander's *Essays on the writings of Abraham Ibn Ezra* (1877).

It has been suggested by Mr A. J. Campbell, in Berdoe's *Browning Cyclopædia*, that the poet incorporated some aspects of the historical Rabbi's teaching. But the similarities of expression in the poem and in the Rabbi's works are sufficiently accounted for by the close relations of each with the Scriptures. The truth is that the words put into the mouth of the scholar are an impassioned outpouring of Browning's own philosophy.

It is a survey of youth, age and the future from the vantage ground of age, "the last of life."

It asserts man's nobility; it applauds alike the passionate energy of youth and the tempered confidence of maturity. It interprets, with undeluded optimism, pain and care as discipline. It demands the uttermost from man, but is broadly tolerant of failure; and it points after the brave adventure of death to a life perfected for sublimer uses. The Scriptural phrasing and imagery are equally appropriate to the nationality of the speaker, and to the intense yet restrained optimism of the poem.

6. **Youth shows**, etc. Although this line is always given within the inverted commas, I cannot help thinking that it should be attributed to the Rabbi.

8. **Youth sighed**, etc. Youth hovers above some flower of desire, rejects it, and returns to it; or pursues some vast ambition beyond mortal conception, "some figured flame" or star more splendid than any known to experience. These are not signs of folly; they are marks of infinite range in the mind, whilst the beasts, which never doubt and never choose, are finite and mortal.

12. **figured flame.** Some imagined star, which combines the rarest qualities of all the others.

14. **Annulling youth's brief years.** Wasting its years and strength in diverse experiments.

24. **Irks care the crop-full bird?** A vigorous inversion. Does anxiety trouble the bird of prey when its appetite is satisfied? Irk is from M.E. *irken*, to weary.

29. **Nearer we hold of God**, etc. "To hold of" is "to derive title from." The meaning is, that we claim our rank from our relation with God, not from that with His creatures.

31. **Then, welcome each rebuff**, etc. Discipline is welcomed as the price to be paid for knowledge and progress.

39. **Shall life succeed**, etc. An inversion, "life shall succeed." This paradox, that the possibility of failure is the hall-mark of greatness, is frequently met in Browning. Compare *Abt Vogler*, stanza xi., and *A Grammarian's Funeral*, line 119.

45. **Whose spirit works**, etc. Who finds no occasions for activity of the spirit beyond those which end in physical satisfaction.

48. **How far can that project**, etc. Compare stanzas xi. and xii.

49—60. **Yet gifts should prove their use**, etc. That is, by gratitude. Youth (the Past) sees and enjoys wide-spread evidences of creative power. Age apprehends the complete design of presiding love. Each must show gratitude for its gift.

55. **Not once beat**, etc. Understand "Should it not once beat?"

61—72. In these stanzas two contrasted views of the body are set out. In stanza xi. the soul is regarded as in a pleasant languorous captivity to the body; accepting this view the speaker wishes there might be some reward for its struggle to rise, which would counterbalance the grosser pleasures the brute enjoys without pain or strife. In stanza xii. on the contrary the soul is neither subordinate nor hostile to the body, but in alliance with it; this is the case in the latter part of stanza viii. also.

62. **rose-mesh.** A net rose-scented, a pleasing captivity. Compare *Karshish*, lines 3—6.

73. **Therefore I summon age**, etc. Age is called upon to grant to youth, now stepping over the threshold into manhood, the wider outlook and capacities for which youth at this point has become fitted.

81. **my adventure brave and new.** This may mean "manhood," or "death."; I incline to think the latter.

86. **My gain or loss thereby.** That is, by the existence of the god-like germ when youth is ended; the little pure gold which is smelted out of the fire of years.

91. **when evening shuts**, etc. Sunset admonishes us that the day awaits judgment; so with age, the sunset of life.

103. **For more is not reserved**, etc. No more is reserved to us than to prepare for the future; youth to face age by ambitious striving; age by acquiring knowledge to face death.

115—132. The **argument** of these three stanzas may be briefly put thus. It is enough now if we learn to discriminate clearly the Good and the Infinite. Afterwards judgment with fuller knowledge will pass sentence between the individual and the world. In the press of life we have nothing but surmises, no one having more authority than another to confirm his conclusions.

118. **With knowledge absolute.** Take this adverbial clause with "Be named here."

124. Understand "whom" after "Was I."

133—150. Beneath the visible output of life, which is all the world's blunt understanding can appreciate, there are hidden motives striving for noble expression, purposes sincere but frustrated, dim intuitive fancies which stir goodness without finding a language; the sum of these constitutes a man's worth in the sight of God.

149. Understand "that" before "men."

151. **Potter's wheel.** A Scriptural metaphor. Compare Isaiah lxiv. and Jeremiah xviii. Here the wheel is Time which for a while impresses the immortal soul.

153. **passive lies our clay.** The poet does not suggest any determinist interpretation by the word "passive." He means simply, subjected to fashioning. The words "plastic circumstance" (line 164) show that the soul has power to shape circumstance and is not its victim.

154. **Thou, to whom fools propound, etc.** The doctrine of Omar Khayyam (stanza xxxvii.) :

> "Ah, fill the cup:—what boots it to repeat
> How Time is slipping underneath our Feet:
> Unborn To-morrow and dead Yesterday,
> Why fret about them if To-day be sweet!"

There are perishable elements in life, but they are simply to test and try the soul which is enduring.

170. **the laughing loves.** These like the "scull-things" are wrought by the carver's tools. They stand for the enjoyments of youth and the anxieties of age.

185. Shapes and colours are not produced by the wheel. The metaphor is impassioned rather than strictly representative.

189. **What strain o' the stuff, etc.** Defects in the material affecting its final shape.

## XXXI. CALIBAN UPON SETEBOS; OR, NATURAL THEOLOGY IN THE ISLAND.

" Thou thoughtest that I was altogether such a one as thyself."

From *Dramatis Personae*, 1864.

The Caliban of the poem, as far as origin, physical characteristics, and intimacy with the sights and sounds of the island go, is the Caliban of the *Tempest*. But unlike the Shakespearian creation he possesses a faculty of ingenious though misdirected speculation, which is exercised here in elaborating a conception of Setebos, the deity of his dam. On the assumption that this deity is altogether such a one as himself, he attributes to Setebos his own motives for action, namely, listlessness, envy and sport, and his own qualities, callousness, cruelty towards weaker creatures, and wanton caprice in the use of power, each of which he illustrates from some episode or memory of his own life. Moreover just as Caliban goes in craven fear that Setebos may notice and menace him, so Setebos in Caliban's supposition is in dread of some remoter inscrutable power, vaguely named "the Quiet." The poem therefore develops into a satire upon conjectures and beliefs about the Deity, framed upon man's reading of himself and his fellow-man. It is important to observe that Browning is ridiculing only these absurdities of anthropomorphism; there are many aspects of the conception of the Divine by the human mind, upon which the satire is silent. As often elsewhere the poet presents a partial view, grotesquely distorted, for the sake of the emphasis of surprise.

Thou thoughtest, etc. Psalm i. 21.

1. 'Will sprawl. I, Caliban, will sprawl. He speaks of himself for the most part in the third person, and generally omits the personal pronoun. This is puzzling till the appropriate subject is inserted. It has been suggested that the omission indicates the incomplete self-realisation of the monster. His stunted development is insisted on in the pleasure he derives from gross physical sensations (lines 1—4).

7. pompion-plant. In the sixteenth century the word was "pompon," which passed into the form "pompion," and in the nineteenth century to "pumpkin."

16. his dam. The foul witch Sycorax. *Tempest*, I. ii. 258.

**25. Thinketh, He dwelleth, etc.** Caliban conjectures that Setebos is uncomfortable in His dwelling "i' the cold o' the moon," but cannot by His nature exist elsewhere.

**27. But not the stars.** See line 138.

**43. so He.** That is, Setebos. Each section closing with these words defines some quality of the God by an analogy drawn either from Caliban's nature-lore, or from his own motives and actions.

**44—97.** Caliban supposes Setebos to have endowed the creatures of the universe with some few qualities superior to His own in order that they might provide the better sport for His capricious cruelty or favour.

**51. oakworts.** Oak-galls, excrescences on trees produced by insects.

**66. so better though they be.** Though they have these points of superiority.

**72. maggots scamper through my brain.** Figuratively describing intoxication.

**77. pinch my Caliban.** Force the clay into the shape and flight of a bird, which would then stand in relation to me, as I, Caliban, now stand to Setebos.

**79. hoopoe.** Formerly hoop; the *upupa epops*; a bird of gay plumage and high crest; a rare visitor to England.

**83. grigs.** Crickets or grasshoppers. The N.E.D. hesitates a little about the word; but Skeat points out that it occurs in five separate dialects.

**90. this might take or else Not take my fancy.** Emotions of pity and love have no existence for Caliban; so he cannot conceive them in his God. The incalculable whim of the moment is deemed to be the ground of action.

**103. Loving not, hating not, just choosing so.** A satirical perversion of the Calvinistic doctrines of election and reprobation. "God has predestinated some to eternal life, while the rest of mankind are predestinated to condemnation and eternal death" (Calvin's *Institutes*). It is easy to pervert the doctrines by imputing as motives for this choice the childish caprices of lines 104—107.

**109—126.** Caliban has a curious belief that Setebos is a Being of less refinement than His creatures; it is partly based on his observation that nature is often of finer grain than mankind, and that

inanimate creatures are often capable, by man's agency, of feats
beyond human skill. The conclusion in Caliban's mind is that the
Creator must be envious of these too capable subjects; and if they
should seem to boast, would stamp them under foot. This exercise
of tyranny is the Deity's only consolation where His creatures seem
to excel Him.

127—169. The staple pictorial stuff of the poem is a series of
analogies of which this is the most striking example. Caliban looks
up to Prosper and realises that he cannot attain such happiness and
serenity; therefore out of pure spite he creates a little world in
imitation of Prosper's (its most remarkable denizen is a tortured and
mangled sea-beast whom he calls Caliban) which he keeps in surly
subjection. Similarly, he thinks, Setebos, in despair of the serenity
of the supreme power of the Quiet (which "all it hath a mind to,
doth"), creates this universe to torment and vex, out of chagrin at
His subjection.

133. feels nor joy nor grief, Since both derive from weakness.
This is rather a lofty speculation for a Caliban, that consummate
strength involves immunity from all emotion.

142. The many-handed as a cuttle-fish. He endows his God
with fearsome physical attributes. It is the reference to characteristics so precisely primitive as this that caused Huxley to imply that
the poem is a scientific representation of religious ideas in primitive
man. Professor Herford rightly points out, however, that "primitive
religion is inseparable from the primitive tribe, and Caliban the
savage who has never known society was a conception as unhistorical
as it was exquisitely adapted to the individualist ways of Browning's
imagination."

156. oncelot. A young lynx.

170—179. Caliban firmly sets aside the belief of his dam that the
Quiet made all things well, but that Setebos had vexed them with
defects. He holds that since the Quiet might have made them strong,
but had on the contrary made them weak, there was proof that He
must have done this of set malicious intention.

177—184. It is admitted that there may exist a liking for those
who give benefits, but it is only on the ground of the benefits derived.
The moment these can be acquired without liking all affection is
at an end.

185—199.  Caliban in the warm grateful summer finds delight in the exercise of his wit and strength, not for any useful end, simply to satisfy an appetite for activity.  The product is so unnecessary that he will some day kick it over.  With equally little purpose he imagines the energies of Setebos to be employed.

200—240.  The one quality in Setebos which Caliban never doubts is unrelenting spite ; nature teems with evidences of it.  It is possible to propitiate the God however; Prosper had discovered the means. It is sport for Setebos to watch His creatures striving after this discovery.  If they fail their fate is death; if they succeed they are still not to imagine that the discovery ensures permanent safety. This would be to set bounds to His sovereign disposal of His creatures.

211.  a ball flame down late.  A meteor.

216.  Please Him and hinder this?  You suggest that I should learn how to please Him as Prosper does, and so turn aside His spite?  Yes.  But how ?

241—262.  Caliban sees no reason to anticipate change, unless perchance Setebos should make another universe, pleasing Him better and forget this; or should change His nature into that of the Quiet.  Neither has he any belief in a future life in which there is to be no more suffering.  He thinks Setebos has crowded all the suffering He can into this life with the worst pain, death, to close it; thereafter nothing.

263—282.  'would have Him misconceive.  A rare stroke of irony. Knowing that he himself dislikes ostentatious happiness, he takes steps to deceive Setebos ; reserves his dancing for dark nights ; in the daylight moans and curses; hides in corners to laugh, hoping mean· while, though without any too sanguine optimism, that Setebos may be annihilated by the Quiet, or possibly decay and die.

284.  A curtain o'er the world at once.  With dramatic sudden- ness a thunderstorm breaks.  To Caliban it is the signal that Setebos has overheard his unguarded prattling.  He grovels and seeks to propitiate the God's wrath with a lie, " 'loveth Setebos."

286.  His raven.  A new idea, that the birds are spies for Setebos.

## XXXII. CONFESSIONS

From *Dramatis Personae.* 1864.

A dying man's memory of the most vivid and treasured moment of his life sweeps aside the ministrations of the professional bearer of consolation; the very symbols of the sick-room, the medicine bottles and the drawn blind are fused into his unrepentant recollections.

## XXXIII. PROSPICE

From *Dramatis Personae.* 1864.

Like the Epilogue to *Asolando*, it is a poem of fearless self-assertion uttered under pressure of the thought of Death. Shrinking and cowardice are contemned through the twofold inspiration of the belief in immortality, and the hope of human love to be recovered.

*Prospice* means "look forward."

9. **the summit attained.** Life is one long ascent, yet there remains a last struggle even at the close of life. Compare the conception of death at the end of *Pilgrim's Progress.*

27. **soul of my soul.** His wife, who had died in 1861. Browning wrote this quotation from Dante in his wife's Testament after her death: "Thus I believe, thus I affirm, thus I am certain it is, that from this life I shall pass to another better, there, where that lady lives, of whom my soul was enamoured."

## XXXIV. A FACE

From *Dramatis Personae.* 1864.

One of the few poems of Browning inspired by no other motive than the pure expression of beauty; he describes just those features which would be recorded in an early Tuscan painting of the subject. The poem actually represents the profile of Emily Patmore, wife of the author of "The Angel in the House."

3. **the Tuscan's early art.** See such pictures in the National Gallery as those of Orcagna and Taddeo Gaddi. The gold ground is a relic of Byzantine traditions in painting.

14. **Correggio.** (1494—1534.) He excels in just such effects as the poet describes here, of marvellous *chiaroscuro*, and of massed cherubim. The frescoes in St Paul's, Parma, *The Virgin with St Sebastian* (Dresden) and *The Assumption* in the Cathedral at Parma, are examples. The *Ecce Homo* and *The Holy Family* in the National Gallery have only the former of these characteristics. See *Bishop Blougram's Apology*, lines 113—117.

## XXXV. From THE RING AND THE BOOK

### Epilogue to Book I

#### 1868.

Mr Arthur Symons (*Introduction to the Study of Browning*) says of this passage, "*The Ring and the Book* was the first important work which Browning wrote after the death of his wife, and her memory holds in it a double shrine: at the opening an invocation, at the close a dedication. I quote the invocation: the words are sacred, and nothing remains to be said of them except that they are worthy of the dead and of the living."

14. **To God who best taught song by gift of thee.** In Mrs Orr's *Life and Letters*, 1908, p. 235, Browning replies to Madame du Guaire on her expressing a preference for his poems over his wife's: " She has genius, I am only a painstaking fellow. Can't you imagine a clever sort of angel who plots and plans and tries to build up something—he wants to make you see it as he sees it—shows you one point of view, carries you off to another, hammering into your head the thing he wants you to understand; and, whilst this bother is going on, God Almighty turns you off a little star—that's the difference between us. The true creative power is hers, not mine."